WHY UNIVERSITIES MATTER

A conversation about values, means and directions

edited by

Tony Coady

ALLEN & UNWIN

First published in 2000 by
Allen & Unwin Pty Ltd
9 Atchison Street, St Leonards NSW 1590 Australia
Phone: (61 2) 8425 0100
Fax: (61 2) 9906 2218
E-mail: frontdesk@allen-unwin.com.au
Web: http://www.allen-unwin.com.au

National Library of Australia
Cataloguing-in-Publication entry:

Why universities matter: a conversation about values, means and directions.

Includes index.
ISBN 1 86508 038 1.

1. Education, Higher—Australia—Aims and objectives.
2. Universities and colleges—Australia. I. Coady, Tony.

378.94

Set in 11/13 pt Bembo by DOCUPRO, Sydney
Printed by South Wind Productions, Singapore

Contents

Contributors

Judith Brett is a Reader in Politics at La Trobe University, and is currently the visiting Professor of Australian History at University College Dublin. The author of *Robert Menzies' Forgotten People* and editor of *Political Lives*, Brett is currently writing a book about political imagination in Australia. She was editor of *Meanjin* from 1982–87 and is a frequent commentator on political issues for the media.

Tony Coady, Director of the Centre for Philosophy and Public Issues and Professorial Fellow, at the University of Melbourne, is currently an Australian Research Council Senior Research Fellow. He is the author of *Testimony: A Philosophical Study*, publishes widely in academic and popular journals and books, and is well known as a media commentator on the ethical dimension of public issues. He is chair of the ARC's Humanities Panel for Large Grants and is a Fellow of the Australian Academy of the Humanities.

Morag Fraser has been editor of *Eureka Street* journal since 1991. In 1998 she edited *Seams of Light: Best Antipodean Essays* and is currently working on a collection of Australian reportage.

She is vice-president of the Victorian Free Speech Committee, and a regular newspaper columnist and ABC radio and television commentator.

Raimond Gaita teaches at the Australian Catholic University and at King's College, University of London. He has contributed extensively to public discussion of issues such as Mabo, the 'Stolen Generation', the Demidenko controversy, the universities, and on the place of moral considerations in politics. His books include *Good and Evil: An Absolute Conception*, and *Romulus, My Father*.

Peter Karmel has had a long and distinguished career. He has been Vice-Chancellor of Flinders University and the Australian National University, and Chancellor of the University of Papua New Guinea; he was chair of the Australian Universities Commission and of the Commonwealth Tertiary Education Commission, and has presided over major inquiries into Australian education. He is currently chair of the Australian Council for Educational Research and of the board of the Institute of the Arts within the Australian National University.

Tony Klein held a Personal Chair in Physics at the University of Melbourne where he was head of the School of Physics and a member of the University Council. He continues as Professorial Fellow. Although originally trained as an electrical engineer, he has a distinguished record of research in experimental physics and is a Fellow of the Australian Academy of Science.

Bruce Langtry is Senior Lecturer in Philosophy, and Deputy Director of the Centre for Philosophy and Public Issues at the University of Melbourne. He is editor of the Centre's journal, *Res Publica*. He is also vice-president of the Australian Society for Professional and Applied Ethics. His work in applied ethics has resulted in a number of significant publications, including the edited collection, *All Connected: Universal Service in Telecommunications*.

Janet McCalman, the author of three award-winning social histories, *Struggletown*, *Journeyings* and *Sex and Suffering*, teaches history at the University of Melbourne's interdisciplinary Centre for the Study of Health and Society. She is a Fellow of the Australian Academy of the Humanities and a regular columnist in the *Age* newspaper. She was a member of the reference group for the Australian Research Council's strategic review of research in the humanities.

Stuart Macintyre, currently the Ernest Scott Professor of History at the University of Melbourne, chaired the Commonwealth government's Civics Expert Group from 1994 to 1996. He has a particular concern for the place of history in the country's schools and universities, and a broader concern for the humanities and social sciences. A prolific author, Macintyre's most recent book is *The Reds: The Communist Party of Australia from Origins to Illegality*.

Jane Marceau has taught and undertaken research at the universities of Cambridge, Essex, Nanterre (Paris X), Ecole des Hautes Etudes Commerciales, INSEAD, Liverpool (as Eleanor Rathbone Professor of Sociology) and the ANU (as founding Professor of Public Policy). She also has conducted research at the OECD and the Maison des Science de l'Homme with Pierre Bourdieu, and continues to work with a broad group of colleagues from different universities in Europe. Currently on secondment from the ANU as Pro-Vice-Chancellor (Research) at UWS Macarthur, she is director of the Australian Expert Group in Industry Studies (AEGIS). She has published widely on industry, technology and research policies.

Simon Marginson, a leading researcher on higher education and international education, is a Reader and Associate Dean (Research) in the Faculty of Education at Monash University. Marginson's many publications include *Educating Australia: Government, Economy and Citizen since 1960*, and *Markets in Education*. His current research includes a commissioned history of Monash University.

Seumas Miller is Professor of Social Philosophy, director of the Centre for Professional and Applied Ethics, and head of the School of Humanities and Social Sciences at Charles Sturt University. He is a Professorial Fellow in the Centre for Philosophy and Public Issues at the University of Melbourne. Miller's research interests include social and applied philosophy, and he has many publications in these areas, including the co-authored book *Police Ethics*.

John Molony, Emeritus Professor at the Australian National University, where he was Manning Clark Professor of Australian History, is currently Visiting Fellow at the Australian Dictionary of Biography. Molony is the author of ten books, including *The Penguin History of Australia*, *Eureka* and *I am Ned Kelly*, and has a long-standing interest in tertiary education policy issues.

Preface

This is a book in which a number of prominent Australian intellectuals, most of them academics, reflect on the dilemmas, new directions, follies, upheavals, and values of our universities. The book presents no united ideological front, but offers a kind of conversation among people who are here drawn together by their concern at the present state and future prospects of Australian universities. It is a book that Melbourne University Press did not want to publish. More accurately, the Board of Management of Melbourne University Press did not want to publish it.

The circumstances of that decision are controversial in a number of respects and this controversy is discussed in Morag Fraser's Afterword. I do not want to canvass the issues further here, but it should be said that the book was proposed to the Press by me, and enthusiastically supported by the Press's senior editor, as part of a series that I edit for MUP[1] on 'Ethics in Public Life'. There have been two books so far in the series and a third of a similar nature that preceded the formal introduction of the series. All were collections of integrated papers by separate authors arising from workshops conducted by the Centre for Philosophy and Public Issues at the University of

Melbourne. This book arose from the same process, though the initiative for the workshop originated with Professors Raimond Gaita and John Molony. I mention this not just for the purposes of record, but because one of the board's objections to the book was that it was a collection arising from a conference. In fact, a consequence of that rejection is that the book now contains three new chapters employing the skills of people who were not involved in the original workshop. These are contributions by Morag Fraser giving an overview of the controversy surrounding the decision of Melbourne University Press, one by Jane Marceau on the contestable future of Australian universities with particular reference to the future of research, and one by Stuart Macintyre and Simon Marginson on the university and its public. To those who participated in the original workshop but who did not write chapters for the book I offer my thanks for their significant contribution to the conversation. They were: Janna Thompson, Robert Young, Geoffrey Opat, Megan Laverty, Will Barrett and Richard Johnson. Thanks also to Will Barrett for his invaluable editorial assistance in the preparation of this book.

A book of this kind is important at the present time because of the high degree of alienation in Australian universities concerning the reigning values and associated policies and styles that have recently risen to prominence in our universities. In the United States, and to a far lesser degree in Australia, there has been much attention paid to the so-called culture wars in universities. These have been concerned with a variety of things but central to them have been the clashes between postmodernist thinkers and those opposed to them. In Australia, these 'wars' have produced much less drama. It is, I think, a tribute to our pragmatism and tolerance (others might say our anti-intellectualism and indifference) that they have here seldom gone beyond the odd skirmish and affray. Even so, they may to some degree have helped distract academics from giving concerted attention to the high levels of tension and hostility generated by the relations between the administration or, as it is now called, management, of universities and the majority of the academic staff. This has now reached the level of what might be termed a 'cool war', to distinguish it from the more serious Cold War, now of happy or unhappy memory depending upon one's political tastes. Like the Cold War, the cool war is undeclared, and indeed often unacknowledged, but it has involved a striking dissonance of values and language. It seldom issues in outright confrontations: it is marked rather by simmering resentments on the side of staff and the lofty complacencies of 'leadership' on the side of management. Strong in their conviction that they are riding the high tide of governance history, the vice-chancellors and their sundry deputies press on disdainful of the few dissident voices they hear and largely unaware of the widespread discontent. The strength of this discontent may be judged from the following personal anecdote which is only one of many that could have been cited. In the wake of MUP's rejection of the book and the attendant publicity it aroused, I was crossing a street near the university when I encountered a senior colleague from one of the professional faculties coming the other way. This man is no more than a casual acquaintance, so I was startled and a little apprehensive to see a scowl come over his face as he came nearer. Up close, he spat the words out: 'Keep giving the bastards hell!'

The context of this cool war is the transformation of the Australian higher education scene engendered by the Dawkins 'reforms' and their continuation by successive federal governments. In the midst of the turmoil consequent upon the initial implementation of Dawkinism, many academics found it hard to believe that the language and thinking of the federal government's green and white papers could be taken seriously by the administrative leadership of the universities. In this they were sadly mistaken, and there were two principal causes of this mistake. First, they underestimated the strength and implications of the financial control of universities made possible by the direct federal funding introduced in the Whitlam era and the later removal of checks upon the treatment of universities as branches of the public service. Second, they did not envisage the way that the changes would largely be internalised by university 'managers', who soon saw that the new framework meant a significant increase in their powers and status. These two factors support each other at certain points and are in tension at others, but their combined effect has been subordination of universities to political control to an alarming degree, and a related diminution of the autonomies and freedoms of departments and individual academics.

Some of these threats to freedoms are long-standing, some are very recent developments. Among the long-standing ones are the rights of teachers to determine standards and to grade students appropriately; among those more recently acquired are the democratic procedures of governance developed unevenly at different institutions in the 1970s. The latter, more political rights had long been regarded by university authorities with alarm and, with the increase in institutional complexity and size, there may indeed have been some reason to review them, but they have now been virtually extinguished. The rights of teachers have been subject to severe erosion as a result of the pressure to attract fee-paying students, and more generally the treating of students as customers; it is now notorious common knowledge within universities (though seldom admitted openly) that academically inadequate students, especially those who pay fees, are too often graded above their merits, and that those who fail such students will be subject to disapproval from above and below.

The cool war has had effects well beyond the confines of university campuses. Graduates of our universities and many influenced by them, as well as others who wish universities well, have begun to share the sense of alienation. They find it hard to see in all the strutting, boasting, inflating, aggrandising and expanding any semblance of the ethos they had thought characteristic of universities. Universities depend quite significantly upon the sympathy and goodwill of the wider community (and not just on politicians) so this alienation and confusion is likely to have long-term disadvantages even for the dominant commercial agenda of university management.

In the context of these changes, this book offers the opportunity for a value-guided and value-exploring assessment of the present situation in our universities. It seeks to provide timely articulations and defences of certain ideals of university life and work, fresh historical perspectives on the 'reforms' to university life and assessments of the opportunities that the changes in our academic and national circumstances provide for better development of policy directions. Compared with several recent publications in the area, it is distinctive in attempting an exploration in depth of the central values that universities should embody, whatever their changed circumstances, and in avoiding as much as possible the platitudes and formulae of managerial apologetics. The contributors are prominent academics (plus one outstanding cultural commentator) who are known for their input to public debate on a range of matters. Though united by a sense of concern at the challenge to core intellectual values in our universities at the end of the twentieth century, they do not share an ideology and those in the original group had many creative disagreements at the workshop from which this book emerged. Nor are their contributions mere exercises in nostalgia or self-interest, though these charges are commonly made against critics of the Dawkins 'revolution'. The contributions are perhaps best viewed as new and significant developments in a conversation about the direction of higher education which must continue and evolve if we are to avoid the twin disasters of mediocrity and trendy superficiality. Like all conversations, it contains disagreement, divergence, digression, engagement and progression. It is philosophical, it is historical, it is economic, it is at times polemical, it is educational.

The chapters in the book fall naturally into three parts. The first part (Coady, Gaita, Macintyre & Marginson, Molony, and Langtry) offers general accounts of the values at stake in the current ferment of change in Australian universities and seeks to provide, from different perspectives, normative assessments of the directions these changes are taking. The second part (Klein, Miller, McCalman, and Brett) looks more specifically at significant areas and values that are challenged and in some degree endangered by some of the changes. The third part (Karmel, Marginson, and Marceau) examines a number of concrete possibilities for future development. And finally, Morag Fraser provides an overview of the controversy surrounding the earlier non-publication of the book.

In chapter 1, I defend the possibility of giving a coherent account of 'an idea' of a university by treating it as a blueprint for providing certain norms or ideals of intellectual inquiry and development. I present, qualify and argue for a version of John Henry Newman's description of these norms, and I defend this enterprise against recent criticisms. I then survey current university developments in Australia in the light of these ideals.

Raimond Gaita, in chapter 2, probes the nature of a commitment to truth and argues that a concern for the intrinsic importance of truth is central to the vocation of a university and its members. The value of truth requires a certain adherence to truthfulness, but this is in jeopardy in the modern university, partly because there has been a loss of understanding of what truth means to the life of the mind and of how to express that meaning.

Instead of directly characterising the values and ideals that should animate a university (as several other contributors seek to do), Stuart Macintyre and Simon Marginson consider the historic role of the Australian university as a civic institution. They trace the complex history of our universities and show the ways in which the values of academic freedom and institutional autonomy slowly emerged as important to national culture, against a background of administrative caution and prohibition. They conclude that the relation of the university to the citizenry, and the range of functions for the public good associated with this, are challenged and cast in doubt by the shift from the old civic university to the new market-oriented semi-public enterprise.

In chapter 4, John Molony considers the major features of the changing university landscape and objects to the way that the understanding of ideals of academic community and academic accountability have been distorted by the 'managerial' revolution in our universities. He claims that a betrayal of trust is involved in the way that the principle that academics are accountable to their students and the scholarly community has been changed to make them primarily accountable to bureau-cracies and fund providers.

Bruce Langtry reviews the concerns expressed and problems posed in the preceding chapters and locates four problem areas for further discussion. He then assesses the tensions those four create for implementing the ideals of what he calls 'liberal education'. He argues for the importance of liberal education and suggests that its significance has been underestimated recently because of misapplications of economic theory to higher education.

In chapter 6, Tony Klein argues that present indications are that the future of pure scientific inquiry within Australian universities is bleak, and that the decline in speculative scientific thinking would represent a severe cultural and intellectual loss which cannot be compensated for by the survival of remnants of such thinking within applied scientific disciplines.

Seumas Miller in chapter 7 begins with an analysis of what he terms the 'hybridisation' of contemporary Australian univer-sities, and defends a traditional understanding of the university's role against the transformation of our universities by the use of innappropriate models of intellectual activity. In particular, he characterises cogent philosophical principles for the defence of rights to intellectual freedom and develops a definition of academic autonomy consistent with these.

Janet McCalman's chapter explores the research achieve-ments of Australian humanities scholars and demonstrates that these scholars are among the leaders of those responsible for Australia's high international academic repute. This has been achieved, she argues, because the conditions created for Aus-tralian universities in the past made for a climate of security and decency within which research creation could flourish. The contemporary university is in danger of undermining these research achievements because of teaching overloads, declining incentives for younger scholars and badly diminished library funding.

In chapter 9, Judith Brett challenges the hold that the ideology of competition has achieved over the management of contemporary Australian universities. She examines three areas

in which attachment to a competitive model has serious deleterious effects upon academic work. These are: the professional
collegial relations of academics, the psychological conditions
necessary for creative work, and the relationship embodied in
pupil–teacher exchanges.

Peter Karmel puts the economic problems facing Australian
universities in the context of their history and their central
animating values in chapter 10. He provides a comparative
assessment of the funding options available and assesses them
against criteria of equity, efficiency, and personal and institutional autonomy. He favours a national scholarship scheme
although he is also sympathetic to the system of post-school
education entitlements.

Simon Marginson argues in chapter 11 that the managerial
models of university research introduced recently have produced
numerous tensions and anomalies within the research community
and within the activities of researchers themselves. He argues for
the recognition and fostering of more independent research
cultures in the different disciplines and for more attention to the
'middle ground' between research and management. In particular,
he urges that funding emphasis be moved from research grants
to research fellowships.

In the final chapter, Jane Marceau concentrates her attention
upon the ways in which the generation of knowledge can best
be organised to reflect the realities of the contemporary shift to
a knowledge economy. She argues that the research enterprise
is ill-served by the current emphasis upon discipline, faculty and
university boundaries and the 'ownership' relations these are
thought to entail. She stresses the central organisational significance of national and international research networks linking
new and old disciplines and reaching beyond individual universities to other universities, businesses, professions, research units
and government bodies.

In her Afterword, Morag Fraser, editor of *Eureka Street*,
reflects on the circumstances surrounding Melbourne University
Press's rejection of the manuscript that became the basis of this
book, locating the rejection and the subsequent public controversy in the wider perspective of a general disquiet about the

state of Australia's universities today. She finds a disturbing lack of fit between the book's contents and the reasons given for its rejection. She argues that the way in which the book proposal was ultimately rejected by the Board of Melbourne University Press indicates that 'the tenacious operational management' described as a goal of 'the Melbourne agenda' on the university's web site is unlikely to promote the values appropriate to a university press.

TONY COADY
APRIL 1999

Note

1. I use MUP to abbreviate Melbourne University Press but the initials are now ambiguous and potentially confusing here since they may stand for the University of Melbourne's newly established private institution, Melbourne University Private; and Professor Barry Sheehan is both chairman of the Board of Management of Melbourne University Press which rejected the present book proposal, and Chief Executive Officer of Melbourne University Private.

PART I

VALUE PERSPECTIVES

· 1 ·

Universities and the ideals of inquiry

TONY COADY

It is now 147 years since John Henry Newman began the public lectures that resulted in his book *The Idea of a University*. Much has changed in that time and Newman would have been the first to acknowledge the positive and indeed vital role that change can have in human affairs. After all, he had also written extensively on the value of certain sorts of change, most notably in his *Development of Christian Doctrine*, where he said: 'In a higher world it is otherwise, but here below to live is to change, and to be perfect is to change often.' (Newman 1960a: 30)

This emphasis on the importance of change is worth initial attention, if only because anyone who follows Newman in exploring what ought to be the core animating values of universities is liable to be accused, especially in periods of dramatic change, of mere traditionalism, of a conservative abhorrence of alteration and adjustment. This is not my position, but nor do I believe in some primitive 'progressivism' whereby all change is 'reform' and all novelties improvements. So I want to test some of the changes that have affected our universities in the past dozen years or so against standards of value that have an appeal independent of fashion, and without resort to such criteria as 'what society wants'. This latter criterion is often invoked, but it suffers from the twin difficulty that it is commonly either vacuous or vicious; vacuous because the desires of a 'society' are frequently inscrutable, and vicious because the unqualified normative appeal to society's desires merely obscures the question as to whether those desires (where they can be coherently determined) are sensible, reasonable or good. If appeal is made to what the government wants, then this removes the problem of vacuity, but it reintroduces even more dramatically the need for an independent test of whether the government's desires are rationally and morally defensible. As for Newman, I do not want to revisit his discourse on the nature of universities in any detailed way, and I certainly do not want to agree with everything he wrote nor cling nostalgically to obsolete views. Rather, I want to look at certain features of our current thinking about higher education in the light of Newman's view that there is an 'idea' of such activity that it would serve us well to recall.

The first thing to remark, however, is that the intellectual times are not propitious to my proposal, even in such schematic form as it has so far assumed. To speak of the idea of a university is to risk contemptuous dismissal as 'essentialist' or 'logocentric', but fear of such abuse should deter no-one, since it is usually the result of rank but confident muddle rather than a serious thinking through of issues of definition, conceptual clarity or essential property. These issues do raise interesting and important problems, and some are addressed after a fashion within the modes of thought called 'post modernism', but, in my view, the level of engagement with them rarely reaches beyond that of slogan and cliché.

IDEAS AS IDEALS: NEWMAN'S OUTLOOK

In the present connection, we may in any case sidestep confrontation with the foes of 'essentialism' by recognising that what Newman meant by the word 'idea' is best understood ethically or normatively rather than semantically. His primary interest is not in trying to fix eternally the usage of the word 'university', but in seeking to provide an educational ideal. In this, of course, he was not to be alone, since others, like Ortega y Gasset, Thorstein Veblen, Karl Jaspers, and Jürgen Habermas (to name only a few among many) have followed his example in speculating on the value of university education and commenting on what they saw as distortions of it. In spite of varying, and even incompatible, emphases, such commentators have all aimed to characterise a certain type of valuable activity that should have a central place in some institutions of a good society. Another advantage of this interpretation of the task is that it does not involve any romanticism about the past. We need not think that there was a golden age of universities when the ideal was realised fully or nearly so: the history of such institutions, as of all institutions, abounds in corruption, unjustified privilege, mediocrity and venality. Indeed, Oxford in the period when Newman knew it best was slowly emerging from a phase that was far from the ideal. Nonetheless, Newman thought that the institution that best embodied this ideal should be called by the name 'university' and that this had some historical plausibility. But it would not matter much if he were wrong about the history, or if subsequently the word came to be used of quite different institutions—as the word 'academy', which had its original home in Plato's institution for the cultivation of the most abstract inquiries, has come in Australia to be used of a place where young cricketers are coached.

The strategy of treating 'idea' as roughly equivalent to 'ideal' is faithful to the word's philosophical origins since it ultimately derives from Plato's usage, of which Newman was certainly conscious, in which the ideas (or forms) partly serve a semantic function, but are primarily ideals or standards. The approach makes clear the error of commentators who simply declare universities to be rightly committed to whatever current or historic roles they have assumed or have been viewed as having. The strategy also has the merit of fending off some by-now routine, painful detours into amateur philosophy of language which seek to show that we are wrong to talk about 'the university' and its 'idea' since look! there are all sorts of things called universities here, there and everywhere. A recent manifestation of this tendency can be seen in Samuel Weber's address to the Power Institute of Fine Arts' symposium on the idea of a university (abbreviated version in the *Australian Higher Education Supplement*, 18 September 1996). Weber was writing as a professor of English and Comparative Literature at UCLA; he thinks that we are misled by language into thinking that 'the university is itself one and the same' and 'sufficiently self-identical to justify speaking of it in the singular'. This mistake he attributes mostly to our excessive interest in 'proper nouns' and their 'stability' as opposed to the fluidity of verbs, adjectives, conjunctions and the like. But the word 'university' is not a proper noun, so perhaps it is most charitable to interpret Weber as claiming that we tend wrongly to construe the semantics of common nouns on the model appropriate to proper nouns. On this topic, however, there is a huge and complex philosophical literature to which Weber makes no reference. It is a great advantage of my proposal about the use of 'idea' that we can avoid what are often fruitless forays into half comprehended philosophical intricacies.

Central to Newman's ideal is the thought that universities should be first and foremost centres of a certain type of learning. His picture of universities is one of communities of learning devoted to the pursuit of significant truth, as an end in itself, and, as such, fulfilling a central cultural and ethical role for society at large. Newman's concept of what he calls 'the gentleman' or, as we might say less misleadingly and offensively in a contemporary context, 'the educated person', invoked an ideal of intellectual cultivation and of knowledge (what he called 'the philosophical mind') that was, of course, seldom actualised fully but has been frequently honoured, at least rhetorically, as an aim of university educational processes and of its administrative structures.[1] The philosophical mind should not be construed as some outlook characteristically available only to a professional 'academic' philosopher, though one would hope that professional philosophers would share its features. Rather, it is an attitude towards the activities of intellect which presents as an ideal to be pursued a certain broad-ranging development of the intellectual powers. This goes beyond mere knowledge of items of fact, mere acquisition of information, or bare proficiency at such intellectual skills as the professions, for instance, may require (Newman 1960b: Discourses V and VI). Newman's emphasis is upon depth and integrated perspective, and such accompanying intellectual virtues as honesty, intellectual courtesy, indifference to mere fashion in ideas, and a dedication to the regulative ideal of truth.

Newman's 'idea' is also intensely personal and dialectical. He applauded the development of Mechanics' Institutes and the public lectures they sponsored, but he thought that the relatively passive reception of lectures from on high (including his own on universities) was no substitute for the interactive communication that characterised his ideal of higher education (Newman 1960b: 367–8).

MISUNDERSTANDINGS AND CLARIFICATIONS

Of course, the picture and the rhetoric had the power to mislead as well as inspire. Ideals are essential guides to action, but they can sometimes distract our attention from the messy reality of the contexts in which action must take place. Universities have always had a professional and vocational training role, they have always had to be financed either by patronage, fees or taxation; they have always been distributors of a certain amount of power and privilege. These realities can be obscured by too-narrowly focussed contemplation of the lofty ideals presented by Newman, though even here, three things should be remembered by critics.

The first is that Newman never meant his talk of the philosophical mind and ideal of truth as an end in itself and the accompanying need to develop the intellectual virtues as excluding utility altogether. He was opposed to the merely utilitarian outlook on education that he detected in John Locke, but Newman, like Aristotle before him, realised that something, such as health or knowledge or pleasure, could be valuable in itself and also valuable for its effects. These effects are worth aiming at as long as such attention does not divert us from the intrinsic values that should mediate them (Newman 1960b: Discourse VII, especially 124–6). It is good that individuals learn skills that will help them earn a living and contribute to the wellbeing of the society in a variety of ways. If properly educated people make better employees or better teachers or better lawyers, and we as a community need such 'products', then there can be no objection to the community funding such education, either privately or through government. Nor can universities object if the community is concerned with the quality of the teachers, lawyers, doctors or technologists that emerge from universities. If a course in social work does not help its graduates to alleviate the misery of disadvantaged people, it has failed a crucial test; if a course in engineering does not help its graduates build satisfactory structures, it is a failure. This much the Newman perspective can (and does) certainly allow. What it cautions against, however, is the danger of the tail wagging the dog, as happens when debased and superficial ideas of what university graduates should be like are used to determine how university teaching, research and life should be fashioned.

The second is that professional and vocational courses should themselves be motivated by the ideal of truth and its associated virtues—such as honesty and objectivity—as much as courses less geared to work in the non-university world. Personally, I have always been impressed by the dedication to significant truth and related values displayed by some of the engineers, architects, lawyers, chemists and doctors among whom I work and with whom I was educated. Such people do not want their activities reduced to the level of mere training (important as training is as an element in all education), nor do they see them solely in terms of their contribution to personal advancement. They also value the play of intellect that their discipline can make possible, and the significant contribution that it makes to a deeper understanding of the human condition and to its amelioration. They also know that they need to locate their professional learning in a wider intellectual context.

The third is that individuals and groups who have power, privilege and advantage conferred on them by higher education may well use such assets for the wider benefit of the community and, moreover, may be more likely to do so if the context in which they became so advantaged approximates to Newman's ideal. Newman was indeed insistent that education was not identical with religion or morality, and that people could achieve intellectual virtues without attaining anything like holiness. Nonetheless, it is arguable that at least the grosser forms of selfishness and greed are in tension with the intellectual virtues, and that the philosophical perspective to which Newman adverts has valuable implications for the powerless and disadvantaged. The very existence of intellectual cultivation of the kind that the ideal envisages can be significant for the wider community, whether directly through the willing commitments of the educated, or more indirectly in the ways that ideas inevitably spread through a culture. If theory without application is open to the charge of irrelevance, activism without insight is positively dangerous.

I do not mean to suggest that the powers and privileges implicit in higher education automatically confer wider benefits, because a countervailing tendency of any form of power is a certain exclusivity and a disposition to reject any change in the conditions that have made it possible. Attempts to widen the franchise for access to university education, for instance, have met with resistance over the years, most notably in the denial of access to women who were, for instance, only admitted to Oxford with full status in 1920 and to Cambridge in 1946. Similar things could be said of various groups which have been disadvantaged because of class or race. There are indeed problems posed by the widening of the opportunities for university education, especially to groups who have, through no fault of their own, been ill-prepared for it but these problems are there to be solved. As I shall discuss later, one of the main difficulties faced by our universities today is that the funding required to meet such challenges is not available.

The Newmanite rhetoric can also be misleading in another way. It can be widely shared as rhetoric, given extensive lip-service, but play no significant part in people's engagement with the actual institutions they work in. Broad acceptance of the language and slogans of the ideal can leave those who genuinely believe in it and base their lives on it unprepared for the undermining onslaughts of those who are mere lip-servers.

So people within universities, especially (though by no means exclusively) in the humanities, initially failed to recognise the threats posed by the managerialist 'reformers' who held sway in the federal Labor government in the late 1980s, and whose clones continue to dominate government policy today.

THE TRIUMPH OF THE MYOPICS

These so-called reformers and their allies I shall refer to, with studied neutrality, as myopics. The myopics see universities and other crucial social institutions, such as hospitals, as no more than corporate operations aimed at generating products. These corporations have CEOs, boards, workers and managers of different sorts, products, markets and customers (or, in a softer version, clients), forced redundancies, quality assurance and a plethora of accountability procedures. The task of 'tertiary training' is to grind out 'graduates' at a certain rate for *the consumption by society*. It is fairly clear (though somewhat puzzling) from the statements and documents emanating from both government and bureaucratic sources that not only do the myopics misunderstand or ignore Newman's ideal, but they hold it and the university sector in considerable contempt and hostility. These attitudes are reflected in the irritable public rebukes to universities delivered by the former federal Minister for Higher Education, Senator Vanstone. Some of the misunderstanding, and perhaps the hostility, spring from a narrowing of vision that seems these days endemic to many people with a background in the study of economics or commerce, or people influenced by those with such a background, though such blinkering effects would have astonished the likes of Adam Smith or John Maynard Keynes. Fixated on bottom lines, the myopics have a natural tendency to flatten the variety and multiform values of human life and its social institutions into the one dimension. For individuals, it is a peculiarly narrow version of self-interest; for institutions a peculiarly narrow version of efficiency.

Nonetheless, it remains puzzling that the myopics seem to have missed altogether in their own progress through university something many others experience in one way or another. That 'something' is what Newman was really on about. It is the element of expansion of understanding, of being among people for whom learning, ideas, clarity, criticism and exploration of significant, difficult thinking really matter. It involves being inducted into a dialogue with the great thinkers of the past and the impressive thinkers of the present day.

One's own part in this dialogue is humble enough, but it is real. I often encounter former students of my own discipline who look back with immense pleasure upon their studies, who talk of the way philosophy 'opened their eyes', and who record the enjoyment and insight they got from their reading, discussions and writing.[2] These people have seldom parlayed their education into a fortune, but they are often making significant contributions to the wider culture. I can recall the same sort of intellectual awakening from my initial years at Sydney University. The chance to read and discuss great books and challenging articles, to listen to the lecturers expounding and criticising, to argue and debate anything and everything with my contemporaries, who included such now well-known names as Clive James, Peter Wilenski, Ed Campion, Robert Hughes, Genevieve Lloyd, Richard Hall, Les Murray, and a host of others. To study philosophy under John Anderson, certainly the most original philosopher Australia has produced, and to have my Christian faith challenged and refined by his atheistic pluralism was an exemplary university experience.

This sort of experience and the activities that evoke and surround it are crucial to the existence and value of real universities, and they are not only intrinsically important for individuals but also for the societies those individuals constitute.

THE POLITICAL BACKGROUND AND ITS COSTS

Blindness to these matters is particularly dangerous in the present political circumstances, since a primary motive for the myopic attack was to erode the Australian tradition of strong public support for universities. The effectiveness of this attack can be gauged from the fact that the proportion of revenue universities receive from the Commonwealth declined from 77.1 per cent in 1989 to 53.8 per cent in 1997 (Australian Vice-Chancellors Committee figures reported in the *Weekend Australian* 19–20 June 1999, p. 4, under the heading 'Fees Replace Funding: Uni Finance Going Private'). Politicians have become convinced that the Australian polity can no longer afford to fulfil many of its public responsibilities, including higher education; we are living beyond our means and have to face economic facts. A major cause of this belief can be traced to the effects of a globalised economy upon Australia and the need to become a less commodity-dependent country. Competition and export orientation are increasingly stressed as goals for business. This has driven a clutch of so-called social and political 'reforms' in the past decade in both federal and state politics which have involved the retreat of governments from traditional involvements in health care, banking, transport and basic services such as electricity, water, gas and communications. This motivation co-exists with another belief: that all these activities should always have been the concern of private enterprise, since they are businesses and are either more efficiently run for private gain or more 'rightfully' so run since 'minimal' government is economically and morally desirable. This second motivation is comforting, because it helps us believe that a high standard of services can be maintained by pushing the costs onto private providers. In some cases, the comfort may be realistic, but there is good reason to think that, for many areas, it is mere dogma based, if it is based on anything, upon the idea that all social goods are economic goods and that the market must produce a proper distribution and flourishing of them. Of course, few economists harbour this belief in its pure form or, if they do, they give a special, broad sense to key terms like 'cost', 'price' or 'product' and they talk about what must be done for instances of 'market failure'. But the value many of the major goods in life is distorted by being treated either narrowly or broadly as economic, and this is especially true of the value of knowledge.

Of course, economic facts need to be considered, and perhaps the economic realities dictate that we must abandon accessible, quality education, health care, and so on, but we should not be blind to the losses involved. These losses are likely to be particularly severe in Australia where much of the institutional fabric of our society has been the conscious creation of community concern rather than a by-product of individualistic enterprise. This struck nineteenth-century visitors, such as the Harvard philosopher Josiah Royce who thought Australia would become the first great 'socialist' experiment. It impresses many newcomers today just as forcibly: I was amused to be told recently by a visiting Chinese academic that Australia was far more socialist ('in the best sense') than mainland China. The word 'socialist' is a red rag to the economic mystics who nowadays control our destinies, so I will not unduly excite them by endorsing these usages. When he praised our public transport services and our national parks, my Chinese friend was not really talking about socialism, nor was Royce when he praised the recently built Melbourne Public Library; they were both admiring a suitable government and community involvement in providing quality community services. It is this proud Australian tradition that our current leaders (of both major parties) seek to dismantle in the name of managerial and economic efficiency.

Politicians and other 'leaders', like the rest of us, find this prospect of loss in quality of public life very hard to face. Hence, as remarked above, the comforting thought emerges that retreating from the public support of major social institutions will not only save money but improve the institutions. Whether this is true or not is a matter for empirical discovery, but it is common now to treat it as a matter of faith. In the case of universities, the faith is bolstered by the pretense that universities are merely business corporations, and so it was made to seem natural that universities should aim to become predominantly (and perhaps eventually, totally) self-funding. It helped to further this agenda to believe that universities were inefficient and somehow defective in quality. Hence the cry for output statistics, 'accountability' and 'quality measures' and 'sound management'. Under pressure, the universities have moved further and further in this direction although this has produced serious distortions in what they do and should aspire to do.

I should make it clear that I do not regard the private

funding of universities as inherently objectionable. Some great universities overseas, such as Oxford, Cambridge, Harvard and Princeton, operate with a mix of public and very substantial private funding, but context and tradition are all-important, and Australian circumstances are not friendly to this experiment. Countries like the United States maintain a significant number of private universities by resort to high fees and large private benefactions. But Australians are not psychologically prepared for such fees and there are reasons to see them as socially regressive. In addition, we do not have the healthy supply of benefactors with the wealth and traditions of magnanimity towards education that America can boast. Where there are reasonable benefactions available here, they seldom go to subjects and disciplines that have no immediate utility, such as classical studies, pure mathematics or philosophy. Overwhelmingly, the support goes to business and management schools, applied medical research and technology. Consequently, our universities get what they can from such sources and then hunt for fee-paying students wherever they can be found. This has led to much dubious competition for recruitment in Asia, fee-paying courses wherever possible, weighting academic appointments in favour of candidates who can attract outside money, factoring outside money into the formulae whereby the university funds departments, pressure for upfront fees for all students, and a general culture of 'the main chance' that has depressingly little to do with the search for truth and its accompanying reflective attitudes.

The commercialisation of Australian universities has similarities with the sordid and comical antics of 'Russian privatisation', though it fortunately lacks the violence associated with that phenomenon.[3] Much of this has indeed arisen from conditions that have been forced upon university administrators and those within universities responsible for their financial viability, and one can have sympathy with their problems. What is dispiriting, however, is the enthusiasm with which so many university authorities have embraced the new culture and the power it has given them.

THE MYTHS OF MANAGEMENT

At this stage, I must venture a word about management. No one can doubt that inefficient forms of administration and managing within universities (as within any institution) can be, and have been, harmful to their members and to outsiders affected by the decisions taken. But the search for good management in universities has begun to endanger the fundamental values that university education should embody, and without which it is a worthless shell. In spite of what some pictures of management science might suggest, it needs to be stressed that good management cannot be an end in itself but takes what value it has from the non-management purposes it serves. This is true in all institutions, but its truth is particularly pertinent to university life. The idea that management is an entirely topic-neutral thing that could be mastered in and of itself and then applied to any subject matter is essentially absurd, but it has proved immensely seductive. I do not mean to deny that there are some overlapping, even some perfectly general, principles of management, such as 'Don't waste money', 'Pay attention to the feelings of colleagues and employees', but even they are schematic and their precise import needs a concrete sense of what the activity in question is all about in order to be relevant and applicable. Some expenditures that appear to an outsider to involve 'waste' will be no such thing when seen from the inside. Expenditure on conference leave will seem like waste to someone who does not understand the importance of face-to-face discussion and personal contact among intellectuals.

When the central values of universities are submerged by a torrent of 'managerese' it is not just language which suffers, though it suffers very severely, as anyone who has to read many of the products of university and government bureaucracies knows only too well, but the actual decisions and policies that the academy adopts. The insistent pressure on people within universities to write, respond and think in management clichés has been depressingly successful in shaping attitudes and responses among those whose vocational activities should make them hostile to cliché, jargon and fashionable babble. Although much sneered at in private, the largely meaningless terminology of 'benchmarks', 'world's best practice', 'excellence' and the rest has become the currency of public discourse in universities. This leads to the subordination of intellectual value to the imperatives of 'management'. There is an interesting example from another field that is worth citing in this connection, and I take this version of it from an article by an American philosopher writing about engineering ethics. Michael Davis uses the Challenger disaster to illustrate the way in which professional ethics arise from the practices within which certain characteristic values of an activity are embedded, and how the values involved can be subverted by the intrusion of outlooks and values inimical to those of the practice. Davis rehearses the way in which the engineers with responsibility for the efficiency and safety of the launch recommended against proceeding with it because of the risks involved to certain key mechanisms in the very cold conditions prevailing. The O-rings on the rocket had not been tested in conditions as cold as those prevailing and there was some reason to be concerned about whether they would hold. Against the engineers' caution stood the need for NASA to have a success after numerous disappointments, and, more specifically, the need for President Reagan to have some good, patriotic news to announce in his forthcoming state-of-the-union television address. Senior administrators in the organisation prevailed upon the engineers to think again. Their crucial piece of advice: 'Think like a manager, not like an engineer'. Unfortunately, it was taken, with the awful results that eventuated (Davis 1991: 150–6). What is so chilling about the advice, and what contributed so much to the dreadful outcome, is the stark opposition between managing and engineering, an opposition that treats management as a practice independent of what is being managed.

SURVEYING SOME OF THE DAMAGE

The cult of management has led to some absurd and damaging 'reforms' and processes (if nothing quite as dramatic as the Challenger disaster) that are familiar to all academics, but too seldom mentioned aloud. I shall list just a few, and, for reasons of space and since they are discussed elsewhere in this book by

Janet McCalman, will ignore the major problems created by 'reforms' to the funding of research.

(1) There has been a vast increase within the daily academic round in the burdens of bureaucracy. A certain amount of this is essential to the workings of any large institution, but the increased emphases on 'accountability', central surveillance (even where partially decentralised), compilation of reports and response to reviews, 'data' gathering, not only adds to the intensifying pressures of more teaching and productivity research demands, but also produces a certain trivialisation of academic focus. This effect is compounded by the fact that many such tasks (though not all) have very little serious utility. The increased bureaucratisation of the working academic's life runs parallel to the striking increases in the ratio of administrative to academic staff in recent years, which seems to have been particularly acute in the newer universities, but is not restricted to them. Figures from the University of Sydney show that the proportion of administrative to academic staff in that university had grown from 23.61 per cent in 1980 to 94.5 per cent in 1994. A great deal of the impetus for these developments results from the busybody interventionism of the last Labor federal government whose sole remaining vestige of commitment to socialism seemed to lie in an obsession with centralist surveillance, and a childish belief in the intrinsic value of collecting social science statistics. A good deal of the mind-set has, however, been adopted by university bureaucracies as part of their own routines.

(2) A particularly irritating aspect of the government-led reforms has been the emphasis on the magical phenomenon of innovation. The preparedness to look at new possibilities in teaching, research and administration is, of course, important for academics; and an openness to the beneficial prospects often involved in change is (as we noted earlier in discussing Newman's outlook) essential to the development of valuable human capacities. But the driving idea behind much of the government-sponsored managerial revolution is that what is

new is necessarily better, and this is just as mindless as the other bright idea that bigger is better. The cult of innovation is well on the way to devaluing proven traditional teaching, research and administration methods, and those who practise them. A few years ago, the *Australian Higher Education Supplement* (14 June 1995) contained a mind-boggling article by three American academics (perhaps significantly, all economists) worrying away at why universities are so slow to adopt innovations. The article first appeared in the *American Chronicle of Higher Education* and was concerned wholly with US universities so there is an initial problem of relevance, but the disturbing fact was that, among the variety of possible explanations examined, the authors at no point considered the hypothesis that some innovations might be rejected because they were unsuitable to the academic enterprise, or less suitable than existing procedures. This hypothesis was, of course, unlikely to surface, given the framework of the investigation, since universities were explicitly treated as industries like any other and the base comparison as to speed of innovation was with such as the coal, steel, brewing and railroad industries. Once we used to joke about universities being degree factories, but clearly the joke has gone sour. Its sourness is likely to linger most in the drive for innovation in teaching, where financially motivated efforts to computerise, mechanise and generally depersonalise education strike at the element of Newman's ideal captured in his comment that a university 'is an Alma Mater knowing her children one by one, not a foundry or a mint or a treadmill'. This is not indeed to deny the legitimate value of computers or the Internet which sensibly used can vastly increase the range and speed of communication, free discussion and debate. Nor is it to deny the supplementary value of various forms of distance education and other types of educational interaction that diverge to some degree from Newman's ideal. In themselves, these are less than ideal routes to education and the inculcation of intellectual virtue and they should be seen as secondary techniques adopted by universities to meet various contingencies. In acknowledgement of the ideal, the best distance education tries to combine periods of face-to-face teaching and personal engagement, and the more remote from the primary paradigm of personal intellectual communication our teaching becomes the less it resembles genuine university teaching. This is an insight that many seem to have lost. A recent statement by one of the newer vice-chancellors (and a former philosophical colleague of mine), Professor Lachlan Chipman, advocating the merits of a 'retail outlet' model of university education illustrates the point (*Australian Higher Education Supplement*, 28 October 1998). Chipman thinks that it is perfectly fine to have course materials, or 'courseware' as he calls it, supplied from a central source but taught at various locations by contracted 'counter staff'. At the 'counter', neither students nor the part-time staff would have any real contact with those who authored the course. No doubt this would be cost-effective but it would be a poor substitute for the education I have been describing. It would produce cheaply many more people who have 'qualifications', but their education would be seriously defective. Once again, if defective education is all we can afford, then it may be better than none at all since some approximation to genuine educational processes may occur, especially through the students' discussion with each other; but we should not delude ourselves about the defects.

(3) The 'big is better' mantra has produced the frequently inefficient and quality-diluting absurdities of the amalgamated mega-universities. One of the chief of these absurdities is the obsession with the PhD, which is driven as much by the need to satisfy government priorities and gain government funding as by any legitimate response to an increase in excellent students. There has been an increase, I believe, and the further extension of educational opportunities to those who can benefit from them is to be applauded. Yet there is also no doubt that the extraordinary expansion of PhD programs in recent years has been

purchased at the cost of seriously downgrading the qualification, so that the relevant employment markets will soon be flooded with doctorates of dramatically divergent quality. As Stewart Sutherland has pointed out (Sutherland 1996: 10), the United States—so often said to be the model here—is much more circumspect about its PhDs. In the USA only ten per cent of institutions with a right to award degrees offer the PhD. State regulations prevent many universities from giving the degree and some prestigious institutions, such as Swarthmore and Tufts, do not bother with it.

(4) All academics are aware of a decline in democratic, consultative and open procedures and an increase in authoritarian, top-down, cursorily discussed decision-making. This will be so familiar to most academics that it hardly needs illustration. Some of these changes have been forced by the pressure of rapid change and a genuine need for speed in decision-making, but all too often such requirements have been irrelevant or invoked in an implausible and sometimes perfunctory way. The abolition of the election of deans at the University of Melbourne is just one example of such irrelevance, and the tendency to neuter or downgrade other representative bodies throughout the system is wellknown. The bureaucratic language of the modern university is the jargon of domination: vice-chancellors have become Chief Executive Officers, academic administration has become governance and leadership, faculty secretaries have become faculty managers. There is much talk of decentralisation but what is decentralised is basically debt rather than power.

(5) Authoritarian structures tend to be hostile to diversity and variety. Hence, uniformity of procedures and practices across the university has become a prime consideration in the new university with the insensitivity to the particular, the special and the detailed that this necessarily involves. In my university, an informal system of student feedback questionaires on teaching had been in existence in many departments and had been used by teachers to improve their course offerings.

The initial move by the new managers was to make this compulsory which was perhaps heavy-handed but arguably justified. The next move was to make the questions asked uniform across the university and to have the results centrally available and tabulated. They could thus be treated as much 'harder' data than they deserved to be and used to prove to the Canberra overlords that the university was engaged in 'quality assurance', and keeping a close watch on their, possibly incompetent, intellectual 'workers'. An irony of all this, as some critics have pointed out, is that the more evidence the universities produce to prove their high quality in teaching or research and thereby to gain competitive titbits of 'quality' funding, the more 'evidence' they provide to Canberra that no real damage has been done to the universities by the vast reduction in funding that the so-called reforms have produced. In fact, measures such as the responses to the student questionaires give little serious information at all about the decline or improvement in teaching conditions and research opportunities that have accompanied the 'reforms'. Experience in the United States makes it clear that a primary effect of such student feedback on teachers is to produce grade inflation since, where university authorities take the questionnaires too seriously, academics respond by courting favour with soft marking.

(6) The changes mentioned in (4) and (5) are part of the erosion of the specific rights and privileges of academics that were once thought to go with their distinctive vocation and its importance for the community. Academic tenure, for instance, has been effectively abolished, though its trappings remain. The introduction and increasing use of redundancy provisions in the academic award adjudications and agreements has been the most striking blow to the significance of tenure. The most recent industrial developments extend even further these draconian powers and there can be no doubt they will be used strategically and politically to the detriment of academic work. A straw in this particular wind may be seen in the fact that a prominent

academic administrator wrote a report for the Australian Vice-Chancellors' Committee a few years back which recommended the retention of tenure only as a 'jewel' (or as he might better have put it, a bait) to attract academic super-stars. This is one further sign of the obsession with status, stratification and hierarchy so characteristic of the new managers and their 'reforms'. It gives me no pleasure to record that, as an 'expert witness' before the industrial tribunal years ago, I predicted the damage that would ensue from even the moderate proposals for redundancy provisions then mooted, and eventually approved. We have gone much further down that particular track now. The obsession with frequent appraisal or assessment of individuals and recurrent reviewing of departments has also added to the sense many academics have that, tenured or not, their jobs are on the line.

I do not support the idea that academic work should be subject to no accountability. I think that in previous eras tenure was given too lightly, and a review of performance over longer periods of time is certainly defensible where it is nuanced and constructive but the point of the tenure system was to ensure (or to make more likely) the exercise of independence of thought by academics in teaching, research and community involvement. These qualities of mind are important for the university to be true to its ideals, and there can be little doubt that they have declined and will decline more in the new universities. Where dissent, eccentricity, forthrightness, or nonconformism marks you out as 'uncooperative', then you have virtually no institutional guarantees of survival and are likely to receive precious little overt support from apprehensive colleagues.

(7) The increased industrialisation of academic life, so enthusiastically promoted by the academic staff associations in the past twenty years or so, and endorsed in a fashion by the High Court's 1983 decision that universities constituted an 'industry' for conciliation and arbitration purposes, has been a natural counterpart to the new managerialism and

has greatly contributed to the deterioration in 'working conditions' discussed in (3). In its wake have come an accentuation of the adversarial attitudes between 'employer' and 'employee' much to the disadvantage of the 'employees', a blurring of the distinctive tasks of academics and non-academics, and too compliant an attitude to the 'reforms' of university education originally promoted by a Labor government to whom the union movement owed (or believed it owed) a great deal.

Ironically, this has led to, or accompanied, a serious decline in (academic) membership of the academic unions which are now amalgamated with other groups that have little in common with the basic interests of university academics. And, into the bargain, there is not much to show for the bottom line, since not only are academic salaries still relatively depressed, but, as a result of government refusal to fund increases, salary improvements now have to be paid for by the severe impoverishment of working conditions, and by the contrived redundancy of one's colleagues. It is an irony of all this that while academics are now viewed as mere employees of the corporation, they are still expected to take their work home and to spend parts of their nights and weekends on research, administration and teaching preparation with no suggestion of overtime rates. The employers get all the benefits of their employees working to the traditional understanding of their own role, plus the benefits of treating them as factory hands with a weak union.

CONCLUSION

The sociologist Thorstein Veblen made a ferocious attack in the early years of this century upon the tendency to turn American universities into 'an arm of business'. Veblen scornfully rejected any place for professional or vocational teaching in universities. His principal target was what is nowadays called 'the Commerce Faculty', but he is almost as scathing about law faculties and would have all vocationally oriented courses relegated to 'the lower and professional schools' (Veblen 1957: 14).

The combination of insight and exaggeration in Veblen's critique is a salutary reminder of both the value and the limits of critiques such as I have been conducting. In pointing to corruptions and faults, one inevitably ignores improvements: contemporary universities are much fairer and more open than their nineteenth-century predecessors; they tread more dangerous paths but sometimes the paths lead to important destinations. This is true, I believe, of the turn towards Asia which, in spite of the many exaggerations and distortions to which this turn has been subject, offers possibilities for a profounder understanding of ourselves and others, and for the eradication of long-standing Australian myths and prejudices. Nonetheless, we need to be alert to the threats that now exist to the integrity of the ideals that make universities worth having. Of course, our universities (like those in Britain and elsewhere that have endured similar onslaughts) will survive the new commercialism in some form or other, just as some form of public broadcasting will survive the gutting, and even eventual abolition, of the ABC. But it is stupid to pretend that all these privatising reforms represent no great loss. And the loss, here as elsewhere in our public life, is a loss of significant and valuable intellectual and cultural tradition.[4]

Notes

1. One point on which I disagree with Newman is his curious rejection of research as an appropriate activity for universities. Newman thought research should go on in special research institutes. This is not the place to pursue this issue, but it is worth remarking that the scope of the term 'research' remains contestable today, and a proper discussion of Newman's position would have to begin by analysing what Newman meant by 'research' and comparing it with its various meanings today.
2. Here I find myself slightly at odds with the suggestion of Stuart Macintyre and Simon Marginson that such experiences were restricted to honours students (see chapter 3) since in my experience they were certainly available to pass students, and not only, I believe, in Philosophy.
3. I owe this apt analogy to Richard Hall.
4. This chapter began life as an article in *Australian Quarterly* (68(4), 1996: 49–62) entitled 'The Very Idea of a University' but it has been refined and much expanded for present purposes.

References

Davis, M. 1991, 'Thinking Like an Engineer: The Place of a Code of Ethics in the Practice of a Profession', *Philosophy and Public Affairs*, 20(2), pp. 150–67.

Newman, J. H. 1960a, *The Development of Christian Doctrine,* Sheed and Ward, London.

——1960b, *The Idea of a University*, Holt, Rinehart and Winston, New York.

Sutherland, S. 1996, 'Universities: Crisis of Confidence or Identity?', Sir Robert Menzies Oration on Higher Education at the University of Melbourne, 28 August.

Veblen, T. 1957, *The Higher Learning in America: A Memorandum on the Conduct of Universities by Business Men*, Sagamore Press, New York.

· 2 ·

Truth and the university[1]

RAIMOND GAITA

In the early days of Margaret Thatcher's assault on the universities, philosophers in the United Kingdom gathered at the University of Leeds to form an organisation they hoped would protect their discipline. One philosophy department had already been closed. The meeting was opened by the vice-chancellor who spoke movingly about why he and other academic administrators had sometimes compromised the integrity of their institutions in (often futile) attempts to accommodate government pressures. I remember clearly his appeal to the philosophers, heartfelt because of his sense of philosophy's noble history. 'Surely', he said, 'philosophy will not offer an extrinsic justification of itself'. Encouraged, the philosophers argued to a junior Minister of Education who was present that no institution could rightly call itself a university if it lacked a philosophy department. A cultured man, he listened carefully, but eventually said impatiently, 'In that case we will call it something else!'.

Many people appear to agree with the spirit of the minister's response. Even vice-chancellors now say, sometimes with astonishing vehemence, that reflection on the concept of a university will yield only elitist nostalgia. Ministers of education and academic administrators are inclined to ask what we want from the institutions of higher education and how we can get it. Those questions, they believe, can be answered without ever mentioning the word 'university'. If we insist on retaining it (their thought continues), we can offer definitions to suit our purposes. They could seek support from the philosopher Sir Karl Popper who argued that questions like, 'What is the essence of a university?' are a sign of muddle that invites obscurantism in reply. He said that we should ask instead, 'What do we want from an institution and how can we get it?'.

That appears hard-headed, but really it is not. We disagree about what we want and some of those disagreements are a function of the fact that our different wants are conditioned by different values to which they are answerable. Some of those values are *sui generis*, that is to say, they cannot be fully explained by reference to facts—biological, psychological, social—which are not themselves values of the same kind. Oversimplifying a little: we cannot explain all our values by reference to our desires and interests (to flourish or to be happy, for example) because our values explain some of our desires and interests, and tell us what counts as a happy or a fulfilled and flourishing life. Acknowledgement of that will drive us back to the question, what *should* we want of the varying kinds of institutions of higher education? Those who have found it important to think about the 'idea of the university' will say that for some of those institutions the answer will come from a reflective understanding of the essence of the university. By a short route we come back to where we started.

And rightly so. When university academics reflect on their obligations to their disciplines, to students, to the university and to the broader community, then if they are educated beyond the confines of their disciplines, they will think with and against a background of reflection that goes back at least to Socrates. That historical depth guarantees the concept of a university its fertility for thought about one historical form of the life of mind—the academic form. Historical depth rather than metaphysical essence secured the concept's distance from the contingent circumstances of time and place, making it possible for thinkers to judge, rightly or wrongly, that their desires, and even the spirit of their times, are faithful or false to 'the idea of a university'. This is thought that may deepen without limit and that can never be exhausted by a set of definitions. It requires inwardness with values slowly apprehended through living the life of the mind in community with fine exemplars of it, and it awakens desires we never had in response to values we had never before seen. To put the point Platonically (but without the metaphysics): the ideals that some people express when they speak of the essence of the university are not the expression of our desires or the objects of our pursuits; they are the judge of our desires and pursuits. The authority and stringency of those ideals do not depend on whether they have been or will be realised in actual institutions. One need not believe in the essence of a university or hanker for a golden age in order to take seriously a conception of the life of the mind whose articulations depend upon a distinction between universities and other institutions of higher education.

Is there comfort for those who lament the passing of an authoritative concept of the university? Yes and no. One reason for saying yes is that we can retrieve an understanding of some of the values expressed in the ideals of a university by reflecting directly on them. Instead of asking what is the essence of the nature of a university? we can ask what are the finest values that have emerged from our traditions of university education? Are there treasures we are obliged to bequeath to future generations? If there are, can we find words that will name them and reveal their value? Which practices will nourish them? Which will undermine them? In all probability what we most value will have arisen quite contingently in the course of our history. That does not diminish it. What matters is not the essence of the university. What matters are its treasures.

Inevitably, any effort to determine what we should most deeply value will excite controversy. But I doubt that anyone will dispute the claim that if we extinguish the conditions under which university staff and students may pursue learning for its own sake, then we will have lost something precious. Two things undermine those conditions. First, pressures and temptations to pursue the life of the mind for its many external benefits. It is hard to exaggerate the degree to which modern universities are subject to them. But the second is more dangerous. It is the continual erosion of the means to articulate a serious conception of the value of learning for its own sake. The conceptual loss we have suffered through the degradation of serious conceptions of the university is partly a consequence of a conceptual loss in characterising its treasures. The managerial Newspeak that now pervades universities is both a cause and an expression of the fact that the language that might reveal that value has gone dead on us. The deepest values of universities can more easily survive periods of severe financial pressures than they can survive the debased ways in which many academics and academic administrators now speak of what they are doing. That is why one might fear that there is to be no comfort for those who are saddened by the demise of a serious concept of the university.

We need to know the vintage of our problems if we are to explain why the universities surrendered virtually without a struggle both to Dawkins and economic rationalism. Managerial Newspeak is only the most recent example of trouble that transcends political divides and began long ago—at least since John Stuart Mill resorted to the notion of a higher pleasure to explain why the life of Socrates dissatisfied was preferable to the life of a pig satisfied. For a long time, we have been unable to speak persuasively of the intrinsic value of learning as something deeper than a higher pleasure or passion. I have a passion for philosophy and also for mountaineering. Both yield higher pleasures but, quite rightly, the taxpayer pays only for one. If the intrinsic value of university studies is nothing more serious than the pleasures that accompany the disciplined exercise of the mind, then it is right that people should look to their extrinsic benefits, be they political or economic, serving the Right or the Left. That is one reason why philosophy, history and physics are mendicants for a respected place in some universities which honour the study of hospitality and gaming.

The reason we find it difficult to argue persuasively for a more serious conception of the intrinsic value of study is not, as we may often be tempted to believe, because our audience is dominated by philistines. Nor is it because of the effects of high unemployment on students or the effects of market-driven policies on staff and courses. Such economic and political factors are important, but their impact on the universities is as much effect as it is cause of our inarticulacy. In the sixties the universities were vulnerable to the call that they serve the requirements of political idealism. They are now vulnerable to the pressures to serve the economic imperatives of the nation. In both cases their vulnerability has been partly a function of the fact that those who defended them, sometimes passionately, could rarely articulate a vision of the life of the mind that would move people to see something serious and deep where they had not seen it before. It went together with the loss of the concept of a university as something more than a high-flying institution, three stages past kindergarten, which excels at research. For a long time we did not notice what we had lost. That is why the vice-chancellor's plea at Leeds was ineffectual and why the minister's rhetorical response to the philosophers was so unnervingly successful.

This is a cultural phenomenon, a quite general conceptual loss, and has little to do with individual failings of character or intelligence. Concepts we need are beyond our reach in the way that we capture when we say that a form of speaking has gone dead on us. The spread of Managerial Newspeak, for example, was facilitated by the replacement of the idea of academic life as a vocation with the idea of it as a profession. At a certain point the concept of a vocation became as anachronistic as the concept of virtue. When that happened our sense of the value of truth and its place in the characterisation of academic life changed. What one makes of talk of the love of truth, of truth as a need of the soul, of the need to be concerned with truth over vanity, wealth, status and so on, will be different according to whether one's conception of academic life and its responsibilities is structured by the concept of a vocation or by that of a profession. In his notebooks, the philosopher Wittgenstein agonises over whether his work is infected by a dishonesty born of vanity. Seen in the light of the concept of an academic vocation, that is no more than should be expected of one who is lucidly mindful of its requirements. In the light of the concept of a career or a profession, it is likely to appear neurotic or precious.

It is no small matter, the ubiquitous success of Managerial Newspeak in the characterisation of university life. Our sense of the reality of values depends on the way we are able to speak of them. The 'linguistic turn' of the latter half of this century, the emphasis on 'language games', 'forms of discourse' and so on, has rightly made us aware of how vulnerable the concepts in our living possession are to changes in language, and how vulnerable language is to changes in our lives. When certain ways of speaking become unavailable to us, we cannot necessarily extract our old thoughts from those ways of speaking and express them in an idiom more congenial to the present.

It would, of course, be absurd to suggest that tracing the degeneration of an idea will give us an explanation of the present state of universities—as absurd as thinking that the demise in religion is a consequence of the fact that people are no longer convinced by the arguments for the existence of God. Both are in deep ways expressions of the way we live. That is why I spoke of the decline of concepts in terms of the deadening of ways of speaking. I hoped to express the complex interdependence between how we live and what we can say, the kind of life we can live with language that lives for us. But a social or historical account of how we have come to be where we are must first describe where we are, and that cannot be done without an analytic description of the degeneration of the concept of a university. Furthermore, most of us interested in this topic are not only curious about the nature and origins of a social phenomenon. We are also trying to understand what matters to us. To try to do that without attention to the fertile history of thought about the university would be arrogant and foolish.

Truth is now a suspect concept in many academic quarters. Debunking the rhetoric that has sometimes surrounded it has some point and justice. But I think that we will have no serious conception of the life of the mind unless we link it to our need of truth. Without that linkage, the ideal of a liberal education degenerates to, at best, an Arnoldian celebration of culture as a means to the adornment of personality.

The concept of truth is important in the characterisation of two aspects of university life. First, in the characterisation of an academic's commitment to his or her disciplines. That commitment can be characterised in many ways, but it is hard to see how it can be done adequately without appeal to an academic's desire to understand things as they are rather than as they appear to be. A consideration as basic and simple as that cannot undercut serious scepticism about truth. However, the distinction between reality and appearance—our sense of what it comes to in any discipline—is interdependent with a set of critical concepts whose serious application should make scepticism about truth technical and unthreatening. There is philosophical disagreement about the connections between the applications of the critical concepts which determine what counts as good and bad thinking in any discipline and this or that conception of truth. But if we attend closely to the way we use those critical concepts, then in my judgement residual scepticism about truth will not lead to a corrosive scepticism about objectivity. Those concepts distinguish legitimate from illegitimate persuasion and they do so because of their connection to the many ways we distinguish seeing things as they are from how they appear. One cannot mount an argument—something that depends upon the distinction between legitimate and illegitimate forms of persuasion—and at the same time debunk the concepts which make that distinction possible.

My concern in this chapter, however, is not with the concept of truth as it relates most directly to the practice of academic disciplines, with the fact that it matters whether what one says in pursuit of them is true or false. It is with the concept's application to the obligation on members of the university to reflect on what they do—to reflect not only on the nature and presuppositions of their disciplines, and on the relations of the disciplines to one another, but also on the place commitment to an academic discipline can have in a human life. That is the second of the aspects of university life that I alluded to earlier. There may be no such a thing as the essence of the university, but there are truths which appear to be basic to any serious notion of a university. One of them is that nothing can rightly call itself a university if it does not impose on at least most of its members an obligation to reflect on the value of the life of the mind.

That truism grounds the claim that there can be no university without a philosophy department, for when it is flourishing philosophy is arguably pre-eminent among the disciplines in the humanities that guide such reflection. Insofar as that obligation to reflection falls on thinkers and scholars in their role as members of a university, I think its existence assumes that they are able to engage with 'the best that is known and thought' in the history of such reflection. That presupposes standards of the kind we now associate with institutions capable of producing first-rate scholarship. A sense of that obligation has, I believe, been part of most serious conceptions of the university, and is one of the treasures that we must salvage. Of course, the two—the practice of the disciplines and reflection on what it humanly means to be committed to them—will come together in a good university. They will come together in a never-ending challenge to academics to make authoritatively living in their practice an adequate response to Callicles' challenge to Socrates: show that a lifelong devotion to the life of the mind can be worthy of any human being who has better-than-mediocre aspirations.

This is some of the marvellous speech that Plato gives to Callicles in the dialogue *Gorgias*.

> It is a good thing to engage in philosophy just so far as it is an aid to education, and no disgrace for a youth to study it, but when a man who is now growing older studies philosophy, it becomes ridiculous, Socrates . . . When I see a youth engaged in it, I admire it and it seems to me to be natural and I consider such a man ingenious and the man who does not pursue it I regard as illiberal and one who will never aspire to any fine or noble deed. But when I see an older man studying philosophy and not deserting it, that man,

Socrates, is actually asking for a whipping . . . Such a man, even if exceptionally gifted, is doomed to prove less than a man, shunning the city centre and market place, in which the poet said men win distinction. He will spend the rest of his life sunk in a corner and whispering with three or four boys and incapable of any utterance or deed that is free and lofty and brilliant.

In my experience, students invariably fail to take Callicles seriously. Confident that they are superior to him in their understanding of the worth of the Socratic life, they smile condescendingly when they hear his speech. They think that Callicles is a philistine. In their hearts, however, 99 per cent of them agree with him, as do many of their teachers. If one leaves aside for a moment his claim that the continued study of philosophy is demeaning to an older man, then what Callicles says in appreciation of the worth of philosophical study is a good statement of the ideals of 'liberal education'. He does not offer an 'extrinsic' justification for the importance of philosophical study by the young. He praises it for cultivating certain qualities of mind—an imaginative appreciation of and concern for what is 'fine and noble'—which is presumably conditional upon an absorption in the subject for its own sake. He believes that the study of philosophy for its own sake is necessary to a certain kind of personal cultivation. 'The pursuit of sweetness and light' is not an expression one would expect to hear from Callicles (although he would applaud 'the pursuit of excellence'), but he thinks, as Matthew Arnold sometimes does, that the chief good of study for its own sake is the cultivation of an intellectually refined urbanity.

Callicles would also agree that the study of philosophy tended to make its students more thoughtful citizens. He would not grant, however, because he would not find intelligible, that a life devoted to philosophical study, or to put it more generally, a life lived in a love of truth, could be a life worthy of a noble spirit. Perfectly aware, if only because of Socrates' example, that philosophy could inspire an absorption which lasted a lifetime, he denies only that it could be a worthy absorption. His praise of Socrates is quite serious as far as it goes. If we find that hard to believe it is because we find it hard to reconcile such praise with his contempt for those who believe that reflection and study could worthily inspire a lifelong devotion. But therein lies the seriousness of his challenge. Socrates took it seriously. He replies to Callicles that 'of all inquiries . . . the noblest is that which concerns the matter with which you have reproached me, namely, what a man should be and what he should practise and to what extent, both when old and when young' (*Gorgias* 488a).

Socrates—not the historical Socrates but the character in Plato's dialogues—developed an argument to respond to Callicles. Plato gives us the character to show what a life committed to philosophy can mean. His point, I believe, is that the imaginatively realised life and the reflective characterisation of it are inseparable. The point has echoed throughout the history of thought about the university. Critical reflection on the example of scholars and teachers who spend a lifetime, 'sunk in a corner' is partly what distinguishes universities from other institutions of higher learning: not the mere fact of such examples and reflection upon them, for these occur elsewhere, but the acknowledged obligation to such reflection. That is why, as I said earlier, it is a conceptual truism that universities impose on most of their members the obligation to reflect on the value of the life of the mind. The value of truth—what it may be to value it 'for its own sake'—is revealed only in the reflective appreciation of the way it deepens the lives of people who care for it. We do not have a sense of it independently of that.

It will be evident that I have appealed to a strand in our tradition that has been under vigorous attack by another strand, now represented by some postmodernists, taking their cue partly from Nietzsche's attack on Socrates and from his debunking of certain conceptions of truth and objectivity. Insofar as I understand postmodernists, I believe they are mistaken for reasons that are too technical for me to discuss here. Nonetheless, it strikes me as natural to a university in these times and proper to its critical function that the rhetoric that has often accompanied talk of objective truth, of our need of it and the forms of our commitment to it should be under sceptical scrutiny. If in

Julien Benda's day it was *trahison des clercs* to attack the notion of objective truth, it may now be *trahison des clercs* not to take seriously the reasons for scepticism about it. But that is not my real concern here. I intend neither to praise nor to condemn post modernism, but to show why it is a lesser threat to any serious conception of truth and truthfulness than the mendacity that is now widespread in university life.

Intellectual eros is an aspect of the inner life—the life of the soul, if we think of the soul as we do when we speak of soul-destroying work or of suffering that lacerates the soul (rather than as a metaphysical entity whose existence is a matter for speculation). The inner life consists of our reflective emotions—love, grief, joy and, of course, intellectual passion—emotions whose very existence is partly constituted by reflection. Their nature is conditioned by the fact that we distinguish their reality from their false semblances; real intellectual passion, real love, real grief, real remorse and so on from their many egocentric counterfeits.

It is hard to imagine anyone who is totally indifferent to whether they feel real love or one of its counterfeits, real grief or sentimental self-indulgence, real intellectual passion or vain posturing, although many people prefer not to think too much about these things, and some think it positively dangerous to the integrity of those states to do so. Superficiality is the undeniable cost of genuine indifference. The requirement to distinguish between the real and the false forms of the inner life seems to arise from the very nature of the inner life. If we remember how basic our inner lives are to our sense of humanity, then the observation that they are composed of states whose nature requires lucidity of us goes some way to supporting one version of the Socratic claim that an unreflective life is unworthy of a human being. And if we remember the natural connection between the concept of the inner life and the concept of the soul when it is not used speculatively, then we can see why it has so often been said that truth is a need of the soul.

Just now I wrote of a requirement to lucidity about the inner life. It would have been equally natural to speak of a requirement to distinguish the true from the false in it. We can say much the same about the concept of truth as it applies to our efforts to understand our inner lives as we say of it elsewhere—it is interdependent with the concepts that mark what it is to think well or badly. At a general level, those concepts appear to be the same whether we are thinking about physics or about poetry. In all inquires we try to see things as they are rather than how they appear to us, strive for reality rather than illusion, try to think clearly and relevantly rather than in ways that are muddled and distracted, and so on.

It is a fact of great importance that these general truisms about truth and objectivity obtain across all forms of intellectual life. But it is equally important to note that such generalities may disguise differences of the first importance. They are differences *in the form of* what is common, rather than just *in addition to* what is common, even when those forms go by the same name or descriptions. In physics and in reflection about poetry we try to 'see things as they are' rather than how we would like them to be, or how they appear from distorting perspectives. We try to resist distorting forms of subjectivity. But what it is to do this will differ from one to the other. The effort to resist sentimentality, jadedness, bathos and cliché is intrinsic to the very nature of reflection on poetry as, of course, it is to poetry itself. Those critical concepts play little part in most of the natural sciences, however, and when they do they function as terms which mark external obstacles to thought— obstacles like hastiness, the desire to protect a pet theory, tiredness or drunkenness—rather than as ailments to which thought is intrinsically vulnerable.

Someone who strives to avoid sentimentality when they are thinking about the life of the mind and their commitment to it, is someone who aims to think what is true and who necessarily aims to think truthfully—necessarily, because as well as being a form of falsehood, sentimentality is a form of untruthfulness. Truth and truthfulness are inseparable in the conceptual structure of sentimentality, as they are in the structure of most of the critical concepts with which we assess our thought about the states of the inner life This shows itself in the way authenticity and integrity are often invoked as concepts which partly characterise the forms of thinking well rather than as the names of virtues which help us to think well. Clearly, this is not so for all forms of thinking. It seems not to be in physics. Truthfulness is important there, of course, but as a means to securing and protecting truth. It is not intrinsic to the conception of truth that is sought and protected.

The concept of truthfulness comes into our thoughts about the university in at least two ways. First as truth's servant, mindful of its needs and loyal in its protection of it. This is the kind of truthfulness that concerns us when we worry that the temptations of wealth or fame may distort scholarship. Second (but to see this we need to note that sentimentality can be a form of error rather than merely a cause of it) as a value intrinsic to the kind truth at stake when we reflect directly on the nature of the inner life, or are engaged in thought that depends on such reflection—thought about history, parts of philosophy, literary studies, parts of psychology, and of course, about the different forms of intellectual eros.

One more step is necessary before I can sketch the relevance of what I have been saying to an assessment of contemporary pressures on universities. Rising to the requirement to be lucid about one's inner life is an effort to be objective—the success of which depends upon the realisation of a distinctive individuality. It is the kind of individuality we refer to when we say that each human being has a unique perspective on the world. Though it might seem paradoxical at first, all efforts to see our inner lives 'as they are' rather than as we would wish them to be, or as they appear from a limited or distorted perspective, require thought to be disciplined by critical concepts that individualise the thinker. That lies behind our meaning when we say that someone has 'something to say' (but when we don't mean that they have a new theory to propound or new facts to report), that they have 'found their voice', that they speak from an authority that is inseparable from the fact that they have lived their own life and no one else's. Putting the thought the other way about should diminish the sense of paradox. If we ask what it means to be someone who has something to say, who speaks with an authority that depends on authenticity, then the answer is that the thought of such people is disciplined by concepts which reveal, for this kind of thinking, what it is to strive to see things as they are rather than as one would wish them to be, or how they appear from this or that perspective.

The air of paradox in the claim that objective thought about the inner life is essentially personal is generated by the common and natural assumption that truth and thought which aims at it are essentially impersonal. Simone Weil expresses that assumption beautifully in her essay 'Human Personality':

> What is sacred in science is truth. What is sacred in art is beauty. Truth and Beauty are impersonal. All this is too obvious. If a child is doing a sum and does it wrong, the mistake bears the stamp of the child's personality. If he does the sum exactly right, his personality does not enter it at all. Perfection is impersonal. (Weil 1977: 318)

Weil's point is characteristically forceful, but the notion of the impersonal is, as I hope I have shown, more complex in relation to truth than she allows. There is some point in saying that even reflection on ethics and on what our lives may mean is impersonal, for here too—here especially!—one must resist the blandishments of what Iris Murdoch (in her *The Sovereignty of Good*) calls the fat relentless ego and struggle objectively to see things as they are. But there is also some point in saying that when truth and truthfulness are inseparable—when we are thinking about the human spirit—thought is essentially personal. Perhaps that is what Kierkegaard had in mind when he said, misleadingly, that truth is subjectivity. It is best, however, to resist saying flatly that thought about value is personal or that it is impersonal. Attention to the critical vocabulary that tells in its various applications what thinking well or badly come to will, in some contexts, incline us to emphasise the way thought is personal and in others to emphasise the way it is impersonal.

Earlier, I said that we fully appreciate the kind of value we ascribe to the pursuit of truth for its own sake only when we see it in lives deepened by it. Those lives speak to us because we acknowledge the truthfulness that is inseparable from their capacity to move us and thereby to claim our trust. We must trust if we are to be open to what we may learn from the lives of others, lives which may enable us to see value where we had not seen it before, or to discover value of a kind we had not known existed, or to hold onto values when our sense of their reality waxes and wanes. When that trust is undermined, by cynicism for example, as it now is in most universities, then we become increasingly closed to the power of example, and so increasingly unable to learn from others the deepest values in the life of the mind. Not even Socrates could disarm the worldly cynicism which prevented many of his interlocutors from seeing in his example the value of the philosophical life.

There is no way, however, to the understanding of such value than one mediated by authoritative example, for there is no purely discursive route, available to any reasonably intelligent person of good will, to the appreciation of the value of anything important, let alone the value of a lifetime devoted to the pursuit of understanding. No proof waits to be discovered and written into text books, encyclopaedias or private notebooks that we can consult whenever we are in doubt and that will assure us which things are really valuable. Nothing merely discursive can assure us once and for all 'what a man should be and what he should practise and to what extent, both when old and when young'. Inescapably, we learn by being moved, and that would be so even in heaven. But we must be open to being moved, and then we must, in disciplined sobriety, sometimes trust the authority of what moves us, and ourselves in doing so. What gives us the right to do the latter? Again, the answer is that we must turn to the critical vocabulary that determines what it is to think well or badly. It will tell us what it is to be rightly moved and what are its many false semblances.

A university community of scholars exists when its members acknowledge their obligation to reflect on the nature and value of the life of the mind, as that has been revealed in the great examples of the past and in their own experience. When it is most true to itself, the academic community is constituted by the ways its members respond to the ideal of an individuality realised through critical, truthful, historically aware reflection on what it humanly means to live an academic life. Then the relevant language of value is most alive, nourished by examples, fertile in historical resonance, often allusive but always rigorous.

Sadly, most universities are now some distance from that ideal, and many of their members appear to be blind both to the fact and why it matters. In common with other institutions which succumbed to great external pressures, universities have been tempted to describe their submission to those pressures as relatively without cost to their integrity. Life in universities is now marked by a pervasive mendacity that disfigures accounts academics and administrators give of what they have done to save subjects and jobs. Hazel Rowley did not exaggerate when she said 'never before has there been so much talk of "excellence and quality assurance" and never before [has there been] so little concern for either' (*Australian* 18 August 1996). We academics tend to deny the extent of the untruthfulness, but everybody knows that it is now widespread—and that knowledge generates a debilitating cynicism about the higher ideals of the university. That cynicism erodes the trust—the epistemic space—in which lives deepened by critical obedience to values *sui generis* may teach us their lessons. Then the language which could reveal such value begins to go dead on us. Managerial Newspeak flourishes.

If what I have said is even broadly true, then it should not be surprising that there is widespread despair among academics. Many of them say that if they had known what was before them, they would not have entered academic life. They are not all old fogies, past doing much, in second and third rate institutions. The despair exists among young academics in the best universities, flourishing in their research. Many of them hunger for the quiet, daily, communal affirmation of the dignity of living a life devoted to the pursuit of knowledge and understanding. Instead they encounter in nearly all aspects of their academic lives the corruption of their deepest ideals as their institutions compete with each other to keep up with the times.

Belief that it is necessary to keep up with the times is now almost universal. It is not, however, as the rhetoric of the corporate university tries to seduce us into believing, a truth written in the heavens that universities should change with the times. Inevitably, they will do so to some degree. And good scholars in them will always find a voice, suitable to each generation, to realise, and make fully living, the deepest values of their institution. It seems to be a truth even about values we call universal and eternal that each generation must appropriate them in its own way and speak them in its own voice. Hostility to relativism should not tempt one to hanker for an eternal and universal voice—a kind of cosmic BBC English—with which to express what matters most to us. But changes which are self-consciously motivated by a desire to be up with the times are, like the slang of teenagers, invariably modish and sometimes, like Managerial Newspeak, modish and ugly. Students who self-consciously speak of their studies in the language of their times, having learnt to speak no other, are likely to be prisoners of their times and will not have the words with which to name, and so to recognise, their inheritance. Sometimes, therefore, universities must resist their times if they are not to betray their students.

In the finest essay I know on the subject, Hannah Arendt wrote of the complex relation to time—to past, present and future—that is required of both teachers and students.

> Education is the point at which we decide whether we love the world enough to assume responsibility for it and by the same token save it from that ruin which, except for renewal, except for the coming of the new and young, would be inevitable. And education, too, is where we decide whether we love our children enough not to expel them from our world and leave them to their own devices, not to strike from their hands their chance of undertaking something new, something foreseen by no one, but to prepare them in

advance for the task of renewing a common world. (Arendt 1977: 196)

Mostly when people say that teachers should prepare the young for their future, they imply that teachers should be prepared to adjust the curriculum and the content of individual subjects according to the best predictions of the 'needs of the future'. One version of that informs the rhetoric of the corporate university. It is not what Arendt had in mind when she said that teachers must 'prepare [students] in advance for the task of renewing a common world'. Her emphasis is not on preparing the young for a conjectured future which would, more often than not, be preparing them to conform to the aspirations of whichever economic and political groupings have the power to shape the future according to their interests. Arendt's emphasis is on a teacher's obligation to ensure *that the future remains in the hands of her students*, to ensure that no one 'strikes from their hands their chance of undertaking something new, something foreseen by no one'. Teachers deny their students 'their chance of undertaking something new' when they persistently change what they teach to make it 'relevant' to their students' future needs, as they are divined by government committees and their academic advisers.

Arendt's remarks are a fine statement of the public duties of a university. When a university provides students with a space that protects them from the pressures of the world—from worldliness, in one of the many senses of that word—and from the pressures which conspire to make them children of their times, then it fulfils its primary public obligation. It is a space in which they form new desires and ideals in the light of values that they had probably not dreamed of and certainly never before fully understood. The unworldly connotations of the expression 'a community of scholars' should not be a source of embarrassment. To the contrary, it should be celebrated as of the essence of a university and its public duty.

And, as Arendt's remarks make clear, it is of the essence of the kind of respect for freedom that should characterise the university. Sir Zelman Cowen tells the story of a visiting dignitary, a politician I think, who addressed the dons at Oxford as employees of the university. One of them responded, 'We are not employees of the university. We *are* the university'. One could seldom now appeal to the common understanding pre-supposed by that rebuke. Sir Zelman took it to express the essence of collegiality and he took collegiality to express the essence of university government. 'When you lost collegiality, then you lost the university', he said. The dismal tendency to authoritarianism among university administrators attests to the penetration of that observation.

To see this, contrast the spirit of Sir Zelman's story with these words by Professor David Robinson, Vice-Chancellor of Monash University, when he explained why he had sought to discipline Emeritus Professor John Legge after he had publicly criticised the university. 'Such staff [as Professor Legge] should confine their interests and actions to focused academic effort and in no way abuse the hospitality of their host' (*Australian*, 12 August 1998). Listen also to the tone of these remarks, again by Professor David Robinson: 'University management will, whether we like it or not, become much more explicit, more corporate, more specialised and more professional' (*Age*, 11 August 1998). That is not the tone of an administrator, reluctantly and regretfully bowing to the times. It is is the bullying tone of someone determined to run with the times, dragging others with him and intimidating those who hesitate by pretending they have no choice.

Academic freedom is not what is most deeply at stake here. At stake is any serious conception of the universities in whose light one can plainly see that sometimes the true champions of a university are those who criticise it, as a matter of conscience. The capacity to be faithful to such a conscience, essential to the very nature of academic practice, is one of the things that academic freedom protects. The demise of any serious concept of the university is the reason why Professor Robinson would probably find unintelligible the suggestion that he heads a university which has betrayed an ideal which it was its respon-sibility to serve. It is also why it probably never occurred to him that he demanded from Professor Legge not gratitude, but servility of a kind inconsistent with the dignity of academic life. Professor Robinson is far from alone in the attitudes he expressed.

It would be unjust to Professor Robinson and his fellow corporatists, and I would not do justice to the difficulty of my topic, if I did not emphasise how natural his attitude is. Or, perhaps more precisely, if I did not make explicit that his attitude is merely a coarse version of one that is natural and pervasive. Callicles expresses it in his disdain for those who are 'sunk in dark corners'. Robert Bolt expresses it too in his play *A Man for All Seasons*. In it Richard Rich seeks Thomas More's patronage for a post at court. More refuses, urging him to become a teacher. If he were a teacher, Rich asks, who would know? More replies, 'You, your pupils, God, not a bad audience that'. Incredulous, and suspicious, partly because More himself has just been made Lord Chancellor of England, Rich turns elsewhere for favours.

The power of Bolt's play is partly a function of his subtle perception of the tensions between Rich's vulgar ambition for fame, More's urbane, worldly enjoyment of high office, the unworldliness of the scholarly life and that 'moral squint' (as Cromwell puts it) that made More a martyr and a saint. Callicles hardens those tensions when he limits his praise of philosophy to the young and shows his contempt for those who would commit themselves to it beyond, say, their mid-twenties. But his belief that a lifelong commitment to philosophy is unworthy of anyone with energy and noble vision is, as I have already suggested, widely shared. Those who share it extend it to the study of any discipline for its own sake, but especially to disciplines in the humanities. There is, to be sure, another tradition that celebrates the scholarly life and its unworldliness. Once strong, it is now weak, and (it has been the burden of this chapter to argue) bereft of a voice which could, in our worldly times, disclose its value. Put these facts together and we could predict something like the situation we are now in, one in which we (decreasingly) pay lip service to the study of disciplines for their own sake while continuously eroding the conditions in which it can honourably be done. Add market and commodity fetishism to those facts and we have Managerial Newspeak and the corporate university.

The vulgarity of the corporate university should not, however, blind us to the fact that it is a corruption of an attitude that is natural, common and in one of its forms (Callicles') consistent with a noble conception of liberal education. It will now be obvious that although I have characterised Callicles' challenge I have done little to meet it. At the closing stage of this chapter, it would be absurd to try. But I wish to give one more example, which I hope will make more concrete what I meant when I referred to the 'treasures' of a university education. Perhaps it will also show up the posture of hard-headedness that derides study for its own sake, as irrelevant to 'the real world'. It is an incident recorded in Primo Levi's book, *If This Is Man*. Levi was an Italian Jew incarcerated in Auschwitz, a Nazi death camp in which more than a million Jews and Gypsies were murdered. One of the finest writers of the century, his writings on the Holocaust are, in my judgement, unmatched.

Levi tells of a time when he was teaching Italian to a French prisoner by way of reciting verses of Dante, the great Italian poet, who is to Italian what Shakespeare is to English. As he recites, and then translates, the Canto of Ulysses, he is nourished by its beauty. He says, '[It is] as if I also was hearing it for the first time: like the blast of a trumpet, like the voice of God. For a moment I forget who I am and where I am' (Levi 1987: 118). Then, at a critical point, he forgets some lines. With mounting panic he tries to recall them, but to no avail. Levi tells us that he 'would give today's soup' to remember. If I had space I would quote Levi's account of what a small bowl of soup meant in Auschwitz. But some of you will know and I am sure that all of you can imagine.

The number of things that could be substituted for Dante in Levi's narrative is small. I want to suggest a simple criterion that anything would have to satisfy if it were to do for Levi what Dante did. It has to be something that can inspire a lucid and worthy love. Love is a word that can be used in many sentimental ways. To give a tougher meaning to it we must have the right examples before us. I have given one. Here is another from the autobiography of the wonderful cellist, Pablo Casals.

> For the past eighty years I have started each day in the same manner. It is not a mechanical routine but something essential to my daily life. I go to the piano and I play two preludes and fugues of Bach. I cannot think of doing otherwise. It is a sort of benediction on the house. But that is not its only meaning it has for me. It is a rediscovery of the world of which I have the joy of being a part. It fills me with awareness of the wonder of life, with a feeling of the incredible marvel of being a human being . . . I do not think that a day has passed in my life in which I have failed to look with fresh amazement at the miracle of nature.

As with Levi's response to Dante, so with Casals' response to Bach—love is the word we need to describe it. And for the same reasons that we knew that few writers could substitute for Dante, we know that very few compositions—Bach's included—could substitute for the preludes and fugues. Works such as these are what I had in mind when I wrote of the treasures that a good university education may offer. People will disagree about which works should be included, but I doubt that after consideration, many would deny that a distinction is to be made between works that may inspire a worthy love and works which, however glorious, cannot. Most university curricula must, of course, be made up of the latter works. They will be the occasion for wonderful adventures in thought, but they could not, as Dante did, nourish a soul—even in Auschwitz. Reflection on the former, especially on examples of them in our discursive tradition, may enable us to understand what sober sense can be made of talk of the love of truth, or as Simone Weil preferred to put it, of the spirit of truth in love (Weil 1978).[2] Such examples do not so much support such talk in the way that evidence supports a hypothesis: they show what it can soberly mean. Levi's story should silence any inclination to ask, what in the real world is the good of it?

Notes

1. Parts of this chapter first appeared in various editions of *Quadrant*, and in my *A Common Humanity*, Text Publishing, Melbourne, 1999.
2. I have written about this in 'Goodness and Truth' in *Philosophy*, October 1992. A shorter version appeared in *Quadrant*, June 1991.

References

Arendt, Hannah 1977, *Between Past and Future: Eight Exercises in Political Thought* (enlarged edition), Penguin, London.

Levi, Primo 1982, *If This is Man*, Sphere Books, London.

Plato 1998, *Gorgias* trans. by Robin Waterfield, Oxford University Press, Oxford.

Weil, Simone 1977, 'Human Personality' in George A. Panichas (ed.), *The Simone Weil Reader*, McKay, New York.

——1978, *The Need for Roots*, Routledge, London.

• 3 •

The university and its public

STUART MACINTYRE & SIMON MARGINSON

Most members of the University of Melbourne learned of the rejection of this book by the Melbourne University Press through newspaper reports (see the Afterword to this book). Many were alarmed by the allegation that senior members of the university had prevented its acceptance because some of the contributors criticised university policies. The Faculty of Arts adopted a resolution to express its concern that the Press board's actions seemed to infringe on academic freedom. The matter was discussed at the subsequent meeting of the Academic Board (which is composed of all the university's heads of departments and professors). One contributor, Tony Klein, had a copy of the letter of rejection which made it clear that the Press decision not to publish the book was not simply a commercial one. Macintyre suggested that the role of the chairman of the Press board, who had assumed that role as a deputy vice-chancellor, seemed to involve a conflict of interest now that he had vacated that office to become the head of Melbourne University Private. Other board members worried about damage to the reputation of the university. In the absence of the vice-chancellor, a current deputy undertook to make inquiries.

At the next meeting of the Academic Board, a month later,

the vice-chancellor was present to defend the conduct of the Board of the Press. He had absolute confidence that its members had acted properly and that allegations made against them were without foundation; he tabled a number of documents to support the propriety of their decision. It was difficult to question his stance since he would not entertain any suggestion that impugned the integrity of his colleagues, and his chief criticism was levelled at inaccuracies in an article by Peter Craven in the *Age* that had opened the controversy. This was not the first time the *Age* had published material critical of the university, he said, and the university needed to resist such attacks in order to preserve its collegiality. With the drawbridge raised, internal criticism was stilled.

Contemporary universities work hard at public relations. Through consultants they burnish the corporate image, through press offices they pump out media handouts, through a host of glossy publications they trumpet their achievements. That Melbourne's broadsheet newspaper should respond to these blandishments with stories critical of the university is surely cause for concern. A high proportion of the *Age*'s writers are graduates of the University of Melbourne and hardly inimical to its fortunes. Like the Premier, Jeffrey Kennett, you might put down the bad news stories to irresponsible obstructionism, but the correspondence page of the *Age* suggests that many readers are also uneasy with what appears to be happening at Parkville. The threats to classical studies, the eager enrolment of full-fee students, the establishment of Melbourne University Private, the proposal to demolish terrace houses in order to extend the campus—that these and other stories are frequently garbled only emphasises the extent of the unease.

The *Age*'s readers have a close interest in the university. Whether as former students or as parents of children who hope to study at Melbourne, they follow the changes occuring there with disquiet. Rather than dismiss the adverse reportage for its inaccuracy or exaggeration, those in charge of the university should heed it as a warning. The *Age* publishes such stories because they tap a public apprehension that the University of Melbourne is no longer meeting expectations. Those expectations are a compound of self-interest and altruism. They speak to its customary role as a place of professional training for doctors, dentists, lawyers, architects, engineers and business managers. The beneficiaries of this vocational function might recall their experience warmly or critically, but they fear that the transformation of a familiar metropolitan institution into a research-intensive international one might mean that the facility from which they benefitted will be neglected or made less accessible to their children. Their expectations do not finish there, however. There is also an attachment to the university as a place of learning and intellectual inquiry, a place where new friendships are formed and horizons widened, a place that sustains a range of studies and activities not directly related to vocational training but valued nevertheless. Even those who do not study classical languages or read the publications of the Melbourne University Press are concerned that the reorientation of management goals might threaten its capacity to serve as such a place.

The misgivings of middle-class Melbourne about its oldest and most privileged university are both particular and general. Threats to Australia's other sandstone universities generate similar anxieties. While the newer metropolitan universities do not usually possess constituencies of the same depth and influence, their travails are periodically deplored. The strain on regional institutions, which are subject to more intense scrutiny, causes an intense concern. In Britain, the United States and elsewhere, changes to higher education have produced extensive debate. At its wilder extremes this debate is fuelled by allegations of culture wars and denunciation of tenured radicals who impose an intellectual tyranny of political correctness on the clasroom and the curriculum. There are echoes of that here in the assault on 'black armband history' but it is peripheral to the predicament of the Australian university. It is hardly plausible to blame academic historians for failing to help us feel relaxed and comfortable about the national past when the history profession is fast shrinking to the point of extinction in the majority of Australian universities.

As part of the present dispensation, academics are encouraged to communicate their work to the public. Commentary on public issues, contributions to the opinion and editorial pages of the newspaper, write-ups of research discoveries and appearances on radio and television are all set down in the individual *curriculum vitae* and listed in university bulletins as measures of performance. Yet academics have been singularly unsuccessful in communicating what is happening to the university. Certainly they complain about underfunding, overcrowded lecture theatres, obsolete equipment, inadequate libraries, deteriorating staff–student ratios and compulsory redundancies; but these are familiar complaints. Particular assaults bring particular responses, as in the closure of a department, the victimisation of an individual or interference with a publication. But the logic of the present system of higher education and the implications of the far-reaching changes made over the past decade are seldom publicised.

Most public discussion of Australian universities occurs within the specialised pages of the *Campus Review Weekly*, the Higher Education supplement of the Wednesday *Australian*, or its state equivalents. All of these are dominated by the press releases of the institutional advertisers that sustain them; the dissident voices are swamped by the puffery. The National Training Education Union (NTEU) sustains an important critical forum but the impact of its publications is restricted to the membership. Even some of the most cogent criticisms of present university policy and management, moreover, are self-referential. They draw out the educational and intellectual consequences of turning higher education into an industry, the inequities, the wastage of talent, the degradation of standards, the threats to intellectual freedom. They are far less likely to establish the public implications of this transformation. With their attention fixed on what they know best, they treat the university as a closed system, its contribution to the larger society a self-evident good.

Why should those outside the universities care about what is happening within them? What call should the universities have on the support and concern of society at large? What does it matter if the conditions of those who study, teach and conduct research are reshaped along with the rest of the public and private sectors? One way of responding to these questions is to return to the ideals of the university, as some contributors to this volume do with their defence of intellectual inquiry, the academic vocation and the pursuit of truth. An alternative path is to consider the university as a civic institution. Universities were established and developed in this country along with parliamentary democracy from the middle of the nineteenth century as a particular kind of public corporation, autonomous but accountable, state-funded yet fee-charging, open to all yet selective, enjoying special privileges but expected to fulfil a range of functions for the public good.

Throughout their subsequent history Australian universities have expanded greatly in size and complexity, but two relationships have remained critical: those with government and the citizenry. As the result of changes in government policy from the mid-eighties, it is the second of these relationships that is now in doubt. The shift from the old civic university to the new market-oriented, semi-public enterprise has thrown in doubt most of the expectations associated with its operation.

In drawing out the nature of these relationships it is instructive to look back at the operation of the civic university and consider its dealings with government and the public. This can be only an outline sketch, in part because we lack a proper history of Australian universities. The only comparative study was written twenty years ago and stopped short of the twentieth century (Gardner 1979). The deficiency is itself indicative of a failure to reflect critically on the place of universities in this country. Most universities have one or more official or authorised history which provides a narrative of its institutional and intellectual life. Some of these are substantial and accomplished works of scholarship, but they are written from within for an internal readership. They operate in the biographical mode of the institutional life-story. They tell of the foundation, the recruitment of staff, the building of the campus, the changing patterns of teaching and research, student life and protest, the influence of lay governing bodies, the early professorial oligarchies and the regimes of the vice-chancellors who supplanted them in the last half of this century.

Singular in their institutional concern, these university

histories seldom compare their own institution with others or ask why this disciplinary emphasis differed from that one elsewhere. They acknowledge the expectations of the outside world in the decision to create a university, and sometimes in the addition of new faculties. Government is admitted to the story as the *deus ex machina* that created the university, then injected or withdrew resources, occasionally interfering until the recent past when it became constant in its demands. We no doubt exaggerate (see Poynter and Rasmussen 1996) in order to make the point that these histories are presentist. They trace a journey from primitive innocence to high modernity, reached some time around the Murray and Martin reports (of 1957 and 1965 respectively), that then falters after Dawkins and ends in the current condition. With allowance for particular controversies, the treatment of context is fragmentary and episodic. The world that the university inhabits in these accounts is initially negligent, then appreciative, and finally importunate. Nevertheless, together they do provide insight into the changing conditions of the civic university.

The first universities were those of Sydney (established in 1850), Melbourne (1853), Adelaide (1874), Tasmania (1890), Queensland (1909) and Western Australia (1910). Sydney and Melbourne originated as statements of colonial aspiration, marking the advent of self-government with an institution of liberal education that would 'reclaim the character, create the taste, form the manners and confirm the loyalty' of a restless agglomeration of individuals (Macintyre 1991: 146) and fit them 'to discharge the duties and offices belonging to the higher grades of society' (Turney et al. 1991: 4). To this end both began with a classical curriculum that would provide 'mental culture and improvement' (Turney et al. 1991: 41). They survived, since the initial enrolments were so meagre, by offering professional degrees, first in medicine and law, then science, engineering and later agriculture, commerce, architecture, education and other fields.

Even before this reorientation, the distinctive features of the Australian university were formed. They were secular, since religious difference was a source of conflict; and they were urban, largely non-residential and meritocratic, in order to attach themselves to their clientele. They were staffed by a teaching professoriate, which taught across a broad range of subjects and, even in the professional courses, placed a generalist emphasis on a systematic body of knowledge. And they were small, the six of them teaching less than 5,000 undergraduates on the eve of the First World War. Lay governing bodies, dominated by the professional élites, kept a close rein on the personal conduct and extra-curricular activity of the professors. The intention was to protect the university from adverse publicity in order to safeguard its annual grant; the effect was to seclude it from the life of the community that sustained it.

The nineteenth-century university was not popular. In 1881 the *Bulletin* described the University of Sydney as 'coldly isolated, deriving its inspirations from antiquated systems, and scarcely returning appreciable benefits for the support extended to it' (Turney et al. 1991: 170). Ten years later the *Sydney Morning Herald* suggested that the annual appropriation for the university should be withdrawn and asked, 'When will the lesson be learned that above all things a University to be truly useful must be really popular?' (Turney et al. 1991: 201). In 1906 the *Age* condemned the University of Melbourne as a 'feeble imitation' of Oxford and Cambridge (Rich 1990: 31).

Some of the limitations were beyond the university's control, some self-imposed. There was little demand for higher learning in a society that placed a high value on practical qualities in the pursuit of wealth. The economy was based on the export of primary commodities and reliant on the importation of capital, labour and technology, which were adapted to local needs. Local industries grew by import replacement of a limited range of manufactures together with construction and service activities. The high standard of living and the keen demand for skilled labour provided little incentive to undertake extensive career preparation. The great majority left school in their early teens and acquired occupational skills in employment by pupillage, apprenticeship or informal instruction. Secondary education was meagre, and schools of mines, technical colleges and teachers' colleges provided specialised training. The universities were slow to adapt to these conditions. With their emphasis on character formation, they were initially reluctant to allow part-time study, and evening classes came late in the nineteenth century. Both the tuition fees and the opportunity cost placed the university beyond the reach of all but a tiny minority.

Yet by the turn of the century the universities had reoriented themselves to secure their role as public institutions. Control of professional registration and public examinations consolidated their influence—and the latter mechanism restored the centrality of the humanities to a liberal education (Smith 1991). The move into extension studies broadened their reach: initially professors offered public lectures off the campus; subsequently the state governments provided special grants for the employment of staff to conduct tutorial classes in suburban and regional centres. The admission of women affirmed the principle of accessibility. Public endowments, scholarships and free places gave it greater meaning. Together with government establishment of new chairs in agriculture, industry and other fields regarded as contributing to the national benefit, these developments strengthened the utilitarian orientation of the civic university. Its distinctive qualities were noticeably apparent in the creation of the University of Queensland and the University of Western Australia, both bearing the state title; there was also the shift from the freestone quadrangles and sylvan setting of the original foundations to the functional brick laboratories and classrooms of the later period.

Yet the university remained a place apart, self-contained and conscious of its difference. For the staff it was part of the wider world of learning from which it drew its new appointments, procedures and customs. However cramped and impecunious they might be, these provincial universities insisted on the maintenance of their own intellectual standards: in the late nineteenth century the University of Melbourne warned that it would not recognise the law degree of the University of Adelaide because students there were given a purely legal training with no general education (Duncan and Leonard 1973:

31). If Australia was to share in the world's knowledge, it must maintain these standards and also keep up with the increasing pace of research. Some of its professors did—there were more than a score of Fellows of the Royal Society in Australian universities before 1939—but chronic indigency, heavy teaching loads and distance from intellectual centres drove some to leave and others to fall back on recycling old lectures. For the students, the undergraduate experience was an interval between childhood dependence and the responsibilities of adulthood, a time of licence. The excesses associated with the annual Commencement and Commemoration ceremonies, and irruptions of privileged adolescents onto city streets, were a regular cause of public complaint and the most common occasion for questioning taxpayers' support of the university.

The six small, often beleaguered, civic universities that served Australia up to the middle of the twentieth century did not encourage freedom of intellectual inquiry. The professors, originally appointed for life and later until retirement, were expected to conform to community expectations. Unlike teachers and the staff of technical colleges, however, they were not public servants. Control was vested in the governing body. It used its disciplinary powers widely: at Melbourne in the 1880s professors were fined for assault, suspended for drunkenness (Blainey 1957: 103). Above all, the university sought to avoid controversy: again at Melbourne the professor of Medicine was instructed not to lecture on 'protoplasm' lest he offend the churches and the professor of Philosophy was warned that his lecture on morality in state schools should not broach party politics or sectarianism (Blainey 1957: 117). In the most celebrated enforcement of these conditions at the end of the nineteenth century, the Melbourne University Council dismissed a professor of Music for the immorality of his poems; his claim that the charge 'resolves itself into the question of freedom of thought and public speech' was to no avail before the insistence on respectability (Blainey 1957: 118; Rich 1990).

His was an exceptional case and the capacity of governing bodies to proscribe the activities of academics was coming under challenge. Senior academics already drew on their public prestige to speak out on extracurricular subjects. Collectively they had begun to claim and eventually established an entitlement to comment on university business. In 1916 the Council of the University of Tasmania rebuked a lecturer who had criticised the provision for his language teaching, and reminded him he was its 'paid servant'. In objecting to the misrepresentation of their status, the staff appealed to a 'recognised right' to discuss university affairs. The Council rescinded its censure of the lecturer (Davis 1990: 71–2).

A series of episodes marked out the boundaries of political dissent. In 1902 the professor of history at the University of Sydney, Arnold Wood, was forced to resign from the presidency of the Anti-War League after calls for his dismissal for criticism of the Boer War (Crawford 1975). During the First World War German staff were dismissed from the University of Melbourne (Blainey 1957: 137–8, Poynter 1997: 377–80). The archaelogist, Vere Gordon Childe, was forced to resign from a college at the University of Sydney and denied appointment to a staff position in Ancient History because of his criticism of the war (Evans 1995), and Guido Baracchi was forced to declare himself 'a loyal member of the British Empire' or face expulsion from legal studies at the University of Melbourne (Blainey 1957: 140). The economic historian, Herbert Heaton, was warned by the Council of the University of Tasmania in 1915 to abstain from expressing personal opinion reflecting upon national policy (Bourke 1990: 65). Other staff engaged in extension studies for the Workers Educational Association came under fire after the war for alleged left-wing sympathies at Adelaide (Bourke 1990: 66–8) and Queensland (Thomis 1985: 142). Adultery allowed the removal of the dissident economist, R. F. Irvine, from Sydney in 1922 (McFarlane 1966). There were calls for the dismissal of the Sydney geographer, Thomas Griffith Taylor—and bans on the use of his publications by the University of Western Australia—because he questioned the country's development capacity (Powell 1993).

Taylor survived to move to the United States in 1928, and the University of Sydney Senate also resisted public demands in 1931 that its professor of Philosophy, John Anderson, be dismissed during his phase of communist notoriety. The Senate, while affirming 'the principle of free speech in the University', found he had 'used expressions that trangress all proper limits' and severely censured him (Kennedy 1995: 96–9). Between the two world wars a claim for academic freedom was increasingly asserted in Australian universities. Academics began to speak out on a range of domestic and international issues: Aboriginal rights, immigration policy, the rise of fascism and the dangers of appeasement. They were active in the Book Censorship Abolition League, formed in 1934, and then in the creation two years later of the Australian Council for Civil Liberties—though its founder, Brian Fitzpatrick, was unable to obtain a permanent academic post (Watson 1979). University governing bodies generally tolerated staff involvement in such activities, though they were still concerned to avoid public disputation that might damage the institutional reputation.

Against that established concern there was the emergent idea of the university as a place of open inquiry that should lead and inform public discussion. This was the middle ground for academic participation in such international bodies as the League of Nations Union, the Institute for International Affairs and the Institute of Pacific Relations, which connected Australians to their overseas counterparts and sustained local research. Here professors joined with men and women of affairs to provide press and radio commentary on current issues. A similar domestic role was played by the emergent economics profession during the depression and recovery, and by the Australian Institute of Political Science, as government began to tap specialist expertise (Alomes 1988).

The same changes affected student life. Prior to the First World War the university's pastoral role imposed limitations on those *in statu pupillari*. Political societies were prohibited. In the mid-1920s students at the University of Melbourne established a Labor Club, and soon the anodyne Public Questions Society gave way to a spectrum of political clubs on most campuses. Direct party affiliation was discouraged, but the chief opposition to local branches of the Communist Party at the universities of Melbourne and Sydney came from conservative students

(Macintyre 1998: 232). Conflict and disturbance, rather than disloyalty, was now the principal argument for official restriction of student political activities. The change is nicely illustrated by reaction to the celebrated debate of 1937 in Melbourne's Public Lecture Theatre, where three Catholic champions of Franco debated three defenders (two of them communists) of the Spanish republic before an audience of a thousand. The ageing lay Chancellor was appalled that such a debate should occur on university grounds; the newly arrived academic vice-chancellor insisted that it was appropriate for students to take an interest in such an important issue, providing order was maintained (Blainey 1957).

The appointment of full-time, academic chief executive officers, which began at Sydney in 1924, signalled the growth of the university and the decreasing influence of lay council officers. Where they continued, as at Queensland where the former head of the state public service served as honorary vice-chancellor until 1960, there were much greater restrictions on staff and student freedom. He acted as the 'government minder' (Thomis 1985: 226); other universities reduced the number of graduates on their governing bodies and increased the government appointees, but secured greater autonomy from outside control. As the civic university increased in scale and complexity, it outgrew its dependence on local professional élites. As it broadened its activities, it was able to cultivate the values of academic freedom. The successor to the vice-chancellor who had defended the Spanish civil war debate in 1937 disposed of a Council demand in 1940 that all staff take an oath of loyalty (Poynter and Rasmussen 1996: 63).

It was the earlier vice-chancellor who urged in 1937 that 'the boundaries of the State should be the boundaries of the University' (Brown 1990: 74). He was struck on his arrival from Cambridge by the poverty of the Australian universities, the narrowness of their activity and the marginal position they occupied in the community. He sought to revive the liberal mission of the civic university by placing it at the centre of national life.

Almost immediately, the Second World War gave the universities a new importance, recognised in the establishment of the Commonwealth Universities Commission in 1943 and the Australian National University in 1946. After the temporary injection of federal funding as ex-service personnel passed through the universities, the Commonwealth began providing annual grants. The reports of the Murray Committee in 1957 and the Martin Committee in 1964 increased the provision, the Whitlam government increased it again. In the late 1940s seven universities taught some 30,000 students; by the early 1970s there were seventeen universities and more than 200,000 students. New universities, new disciplines, proper libraries, modern laboratories, tutorials, research funds, academic presses, journals and systematic provision for study leave and overseas travel—these were the bounty of the new dispensation.

The dramatic growth was made possible by sustained economic growth. The long boom that lasted from the end of the Second World War to the OPEC oil crisis of 1973–4 saw rapid expansion of the secondary and tertiary sectors of the economy, and rapid increase in white-collar employment calling for higher levels of education. The post-war demographic bulge and migration program brought new demand for education. The states were unable to fund the expanded educational requirements, the Commonwealth took over the task. In 1939 the universities drew half their income from state government grants, and the rest from fees and bequests. By 1951 the states provided just over two-fifths and the Commonwealth one-fifth. Ten years later the Commonwealth contribution of 43 per cent surpassed that of the states (Marginson 1997: 29). Furthermore, expenditure on education as a proportion of Gross National Product doubled between 1951 and 1961, and doubled again by 1975, the last year of the Whitlam government (Marginson 1997: 26).

Why did the universities receive so much of this public largesse? Partly in the cause of greater equality: the idea that universities should be accessible to all qualified to enter them was significant, and led from the Commonwealth scholarship scheme to the eventual abolition of fees. Partly for reasons of greater national efficiency: the notion of public outlays on universities as an investment in human capital was also compelling. And partly, no doubt, in response to the political pressures of overcrowding, quotas on entry and rising expectations. These influences came together in what Simon Marginson has described as the incorporation of the universities into the 'nation-building' project of the post-war era (Marginson 1998).

In itself the nation-building goal was not new: universities had been seen as contributing to it from the early Commonwealth period. It gained special meaning and force after the Second World War when new techniques of government gave augmented confidence in public policy and global circumstances lent unprecedented urgency to national tasks. Hiroshima, the Cold War and Soviet successes in the space race made the advance of Australian science paramount. Denied access to American military technology, Australian governments—both Labor and Liberal—were committed to the development of a nuclear capacity in collaboration with Britain. The formation of the Australian National University and the recruitment of Marcus Oliphant to head its school of physical sciences were direct consequences: the parsimonious Ben Chifley told the doubtful H. C. Coombs that 'If you can persuade Oliphant to head the school we will do whatever is necessary' (Foster and Varghese 1996: 21).

Science, engineering and medicine were the key to national security, economic competiveness and welfare. Economics, psychology, sociology and the social sciences would contribute to the solution of social problems. The humanities and arts also had a place in a civilised modern nation. The Murray Committee provided the rationale for the expansion of the civic university. Australia needed 'a very large number indeed of highly educated men and women'. This should be 'a full and true education', and only the university could provide the 'breadth of education' to produce 'rounded human beings'. Government alone could provide the resources needed to remedy the overcrowded facilities, build honours programs and postgraduates studies, and sustain enhanced research activity, but the Committee saw little danger in this relationship. It recognised that the public and 'even statesmen' could be vexed by the inconvenient exercise of academic freedom, but this was inherent in the duty of the universities as 'guardians of intellectual standards and intellectual integrity'. Their duty was to 'seek the truth and make it known'. Hence the committee was 'confident that no Australian Government will seek to deny them their full and free independence in carrying out their proper functions as universities' (Poynter and Rasmussen 1996: 181–3).

Seven years later the Martin Committee sought to cope with the consequences of this blueprint as the further increase in demand outstripped supply. It continued to affirm the civic model and indeed pushed the claims of the university further. The chairman, a physicist, was insistent on the academic purpose of the university as a place of intellectual inquiry where teaching and research were inseparable. Furthermore, this research should not be constrained by utilitarian pressures. Martin assumed a connection between the advancement of knowledge and the national interest but did not pursue it. No such justification was needed, nor should it be allowed to interfere with the pursuit of knowledge 'for its own sake' (Davies, 1989: 47). If applied research was required, it should be done elsewhere along with the narrowly vocational training needed to remedy the shortages of skilled personnel. From this redefinition came the binary divide (that prevailed for the next two decades) between the universities and the technical and teachers' colleges, the one sector affirming the research–teaching nexus and funded accordingly, the other assigned a subordinate role.

Martin's conception of the university as a scholarly, research-oriented institution remote from the mundane concerns of society bore little relationship to the actual circumstances and practices of Australian academic life in the post-war period, but it serves some critics of the present predicament as a romanticised golden age. It should not. This was not an age of plenty. The older metropolitan universities struggled to cope with constant expansion and recurrent financial difficulties. The new ones, which were created in Sydney and Melbourne in the 1950s, then in the other state capitals and regional centres during the 1960s and 1970s, typically began with pioneering energy before growth was capped, leaving substantial deficiencies. Public provision was strategic, not unconditional.

The initial rationale for government expansion of higher education also created new conditions for those who worked in it. The crucial importance of science for military and strategic aims saw first the imposition of political surveillance over the CSIRO, then its extension to the universities. In 1952 the Australian Security and Intelligence Organisation (ASIO) conducted an appraisal of academics in every Australian university. Oliphant's work at the Australian National University (ANU) gave that university particular sensitivity. The Director-General of ASIO warned Menzies of 'subversives there', and the two met with the Vice-Chancellor who thought it might be possible 'to ensure that persons who are suspected of being a security risk will not be appointed to responsible positions' (McKnight 1994: 147). The ANU qualified several academic appointments and the Commonwealth government placed restrictions on the work of existing staff (Foster and Varghese 1996: 126). The historian Russel Ward, who had left the Communist Party in 1949, was refused appointment at the University of New South Wales in 1955 because he had been 'active in seditious circles in Canberra' while a doctoral student at the ANU (McKnight 1994: 154).

The interference of the security state was accompanied by public invigilation of the loyalty of staff and students. The experience of Max Crawford, professor of History at the University of Melbourne, provides an illustration. In 1946 a Liberal member of the state parliament named him as one of the 'pink professors' responsible for the propagation of communism in the university and schools (Crawford 1946–7). When the attack was renewed in the following year Crawford wrote to the Vice-Chancellor to dissociate himself from communism and resign from the presidency of a Soviet friendship society. Yet ASIO drew on this episode to advise the United States embassy when he applied for a visa to visit an American university three years later, and he was denied entry. ASIO also continued to obtain information about his political sympathies from colleagues and students (National Archives 1961).

The confidence of the Murray Committee that government would respect the full and free independence of the universities was conditional on their governing bodies withstanding direct and indirect political pressure. In the case of the University of Melbourne, the Council policy was that so long as members of staff taught their subjects objectively, the university did not require adherence to any standard of political or religious belief (University of Melbourne 1947). Yet the Council forbade meetings on campus after Crawford and other professors addressed five hundred students to urge a negative vote in the 1951 referendum to ban the Communist Party (Poynter and Rasmussen 1996: 117–18); and similar restrictions existed at other universities. In the climate of the Cold War, some governing bodies acceded to pressure while others revived their claim to regulate the conduct of staff. The dismissal of Sydney Sparkes Orr in 1956, recently re-interpreted as a case of sexual harassment (Pybus 1993), aroused the ire of staff associations because it bore on this contested ground.

Yet the right of academics to control their affairs was itself coming under dispute from within. During the 1960s student protest presented a sharp challenge to the expectations that accompanied the growth of higher education. It commonly took the form of a rejection of the material progress and instrumental reason associated with the post-war expansion but, as with other aspects of modernism, it also drew on the very values of the modern civic university to contest its purpose. Student radicals employed the autonomy of the university against service of government objectives and in opposition to national policies. They thus applied the Murray Committee's notion of the university as a place of open inquiry to the university itself, and reversed Martin's idea of a university aloof from mere training and practical application of knowledge to insist that the university be relevant and engaged. This in turn brought confrontation with the hierarchical collegiality whereby the modern university conducted its affairs.

For senior academics it was a time of painful readjustment.

For the conservative politicians who had provided for the transformation of public provision, the insurgents were biting the hand that fed them. When the oil crisis of the mid–seventies ended the long boom, taking with it the circumstances that had fuelled the expansion of the universities, there was little inclination to build them further. On the other hand, there were strong political pressures to maintain access to higher education and satisfy the broader demand for university places. The Fraser government did not reintroduce fees. It reduced funding per student and squeezed economies from the universities to allow a modest growth in enrolments. Between 1975 and 1983 Commonwealth expenditure on higher education remained static while student numbers rose by 28 per cent, from 273,000 to 348,000 (Marginson 1997: 191, 218). In its first four years the Hawke government enrolled a further 45,000 students with a slight increase in financial support. Then came Dawkins.

Other contributors to this volume describe the changes that have accompanied Dawkins' creation of the Unified National System and their effects on teaching, research and the conditions of academic life. The emphasis here is on the wider context of this transformation and its implications for the civic role of the university.

As Marginson has noted, the reconstruction of the Australian universities was part of a larger reconstruction of the public sector (Marginson 1998). With the end of the post-war long boom and the collapse of Keynesian techniques of national economic management, there was a move to reduce public outlays, deregulate and seek greater competitive efficiency by exposing public institutions to market forces. The new orthodoxy affected health, telecommunications and other utilities as well as education, and it subsumed the distinctive features of public policy—such as maintenance of wage levels and the complementary welfare system—that had served national goals. The expectation was that such changes would assist Australians to compete in the global economy, and the country's earlier techniques of public policy were treated as encumbrances rather than advantages.

With the retreat from the older belief that government could play an active role in nation-building went the commitment to the university as a custodian of national science and culture. Government no longer understands the universities as instruments for nation-building. Continued public funding is seen more as a cost than as an investment. The university is now expected to serve national objectives in new ways: as a teaching institution engaged in vocational training of a far more direct and systematic nature, as a place of research where the production of knowledge is much more closely linked to practical and commercial uses, and as a business with the potential to generate foreign income. Occupational skills and research outcomes are now commodities, their costs of production and monetary returns both carefully calculated. They have both public and private value, so the government funding is supplemented under the principle of 'user pays' by student fees, joint enterprises and charges for intellectual property and consultancies. Government assumes that the closer universities move to full cost recovery, the more efficient they will become, the better able to survive and prosper in the global market.

From this come the new techniques of university management, the corporate practice of the academic enterprise, the emphasis on executive leadership and line management, the transformation of governing bodies into corporate boards, the program budgeting, output measurement and mechanisms of quality control. As academics respond to and internalise these practices, so they redirect their own activities to applied fields where market demand is strong at the expense of core disciplines. It is not just classics, philosophy and history that feel the pinch: physics, chemistry and mathematics are also weakened. Similarly, as the students who are enrolled into these universities accept the logic of the market, they respond accordingly. Recent surveys reveal that the great majority of school-leavers see higher education as a means to a better income. One study found that 78 per cent of students in Years 10 to 12 who said they were planning to go to university nominated employment-related reasons. Non-instrumental reasons such as interesting courses or the social benefits of university life were nominated by less than three per cent of respondents (Gibson and Hatherell 1997: 125).

The effects on the university itself are all too apparent, as the contributors to this volume make clear. Perhaps the most striking feature of the university itself is the loss of confidence in the academic mission. In their adoption of the language and values of the enterprise, academics seem almost embarrassed to affirm the values of intellectual inquiry. As Hilary McPhee discovered when she returned to a university fellowship: 'It's as if the imperatives from the so-called "real world" are more urgent and more grownup, more modern—and any notions of a creative and intellectual life are to be spoken of in low voices and engaged with only in private'. She notes also the capitulation to apparently inexorable external pressures: 'I keep hearing the word They. As in "They won't let us do that or say that in public", or "They'll cut our funding if we do"' (McPhee 1998: 1). The minatory presence of They has as damaging effect on the collegiality and independence of today's university as the restrictions on academic freedom had on the older one.

The principal They is government, and the failure of university administrators to defend the civic university from assault by Commonwealth and state ministers is conspicuous. The vice-chancellors have accepted the fiscal constraints on public funding as a given, while they have embraced the competitive opportunities of Higher Education Charges and full-fee enrolments as a source of independence from reliance on Canberra. But in so doing they have made the university less secure, less coherent, more vulnerable. The vice-chancellors take the increasing proportion of non-government income as an index of autonomy. But as universities become more imitative of the private sector, and as competition policy forces universities to become more commercial in pricing their 'products', we are entitled to ask if this is a proper use of public facilities. As those who work in universities become service providers, and those who make use of them are treated as customers or clients rather than students, their public nature is eroded and their contribution to citizenship diminished. As they manoeuvre for global advantage, they diminish their contribution to national culture. As they become slicker in their marketing, they become indistinguishable from private corporations.

It is this transformation of education into a business that most seriously erodes its civic capacity. The Australian university began as a public institution serving public purposes: the preservation and advancement of knowledge, the preparation for professional careers in a broad intellectual setting designed to foster inquiry, the pastoral approach to the formation of personality, a capacity to reflect on public issues and an explicit role in building national institutions and national identity. It was given public support and a substantial degree of autonomy in order to do these things. It did not always do them well. It was sometimes too remote and sometimes too solicitous of public opinion, sometimes complacently mediocre in its intellectual standards, sometimes arrogant in its pretensions. Yet for a century and a half it survived, adapted and prospered. The university is a resilient institution, founded on the accretion of knowledge and with a strong sense of obligation to a common purpose. It would be a pity if those who are its present custodians betrayed their responsibilities to maintain it.

References

Alexander, Fred 1963, *Campus at Crowley: A Narrative and Critical Appreciation of the First Fifty Years of the University of Western Australia*, Cheshire, Melbourne.

Alomes, Stephen 1988, 'Intellectuals as Publicists 1920s to 1940s', in Brian Head and James Walter (eds), *Intellectual Movements and Australian Society*, Oxford University Press, Melbourne.

Blainey, Geoffrey 1957, *A Centenary History of the University of Melbourne*, Melbourne University Press, Melbourne.

Bourke, Helen 1990, 'Herbert Heaton and the Foundation of Economics at the University of Adelaide, 1917–29', in F. B. Smith and P. Crichton (eds), *Ideas for Histories of Australian Universities*, Division of Historical Studies, Research School of Social Sciences, Australian National University, Canberra, pp. 58–71.

Brown, Nicholas 1990, 'Aspirations and Constraints in Australian Universities in the 1950s', in F. B. Smith and P. Crichton (eds) *Ideas for Histories of Australian Universities*, Division of Historical Studies,

Research School of Social Sciences, Australian National University, Canberra, pp. 72–93.

Crawford, R. M. 1946–7, File on F. L. Edmunds, Crawford Papers, University of Melbourne Archives, Melbourne.

——1975, *A Bit of a Rebel: The Life and Work of George Arnold Wood*, Sydney University Press, Sydney.

Davies, Susan 1989, *The Martin Committee and the Binary Policy of Higher Education in Australia*, Ashwood House, Melbourne.

Davis, Richard 1990, *Open to Talent: The Centenary History of the University of Tasmania 1890–1990*, University of Tasmania, Hobart.

Duncan, W. G. K. and Leonard, Roger Ashley 1973, *The University of Adelaide, 1874–1974*, Rigby, Adelaide.

Evans, Ray 1995, '"Social Passion": Vere Gordon Childe in Queensland, 1918–19', in Peter Gathercole, T.H. Irving and Gregory Melleuish (eds), *Childe and Australia: Archaeology, Politics and Ideas*, University of Queensland Press, Brisbane.

Foster, S. G. and Varghese, Margaret M. 1996, *The Making of the Australian National University 1946–1996*, Allen & Unwin, Sydney.

Gardner, W. J. 1979, *Colonial Cap and Gown: Studies in the Mid-Victorian Universities of Australasia*, University of Canterbury, Christchurch.

Gibson, Dennis and Hatherell, William 1997, 'Reflections on Stability and Change in Australian Higher Education', in John Sharpham and Grant Harman (eds), *Australia's Future Universities*, University of New England Press, Armidale, NSW, pp. 121–36.

Kennedy, Brian 1995, *A Passion to Oppose: John Anderson, Philosopher*, Melbourne University Press, Melbourne.

McFarlane, Bruce 1966, *Professor Irvine's Economics in Australian Labour History*, Australian Society for the Study of Labour History, Sydney.

Macintyre, Stuart 1991, *A Colonial Liberalism: The Lost World of Three Victorian Visionaries*, Oxford University Press, Melbourne.

——1998, *The Reds: The Communist Party of Australia from Origins to Illegality*, Allen & Unwin, Sydney.

McKnight, David 1994, *Australian Spies and Their Secrets*, Allen & Unwin, Sydney.

McPhee, Hilary 1998, 'Challenges for Universities and University Leaders', unpublished address to AVCC Leadership program, 31 August.

Marginson, Simon 1997, *Educating Australia: Government, Economy and the Citizen Since 1960*, Cambridge University Press, Cambridge.

——1998, 'Harvards of the Antipodes? Nation-building in a Global Environment', Winter Lecture series, University of Auckland, 21 July.

National Archives 1961, ASIO file on R.M. Crawford, AA A6126/16, item 16.

Powell, Joseph 1993, *Griffith Taylor and 'Australia Unlimited'*, University of Queensland Press, Brisbane.

Poynter, John 1997, *Doubts and Certainties: A Life of Alexander Leeper*, Melbourne University Press, Melbourne.

Poynter, John and Rasmussen, Carolyn 1996, *A Place Apart. The University of Melbourne: Decades of Challenge*, Melbourne University Press, Melbourne.

Pybus, Cassandra 1993, *Gross Moral Turpitude: The Orr Case Reconsidered*, William Heinemann Australia, Melbourne.

Rich, Joe 1990, 'The Liberal–Democratic Bias of Melbourne University and its Community around 1900', in F. B. Smith and P. Crichton (eds), *Ideas for Histories of Australian Universities*, Division of Historical Studies, Research School of Social Sciences, Australian National University, Canberra, pp. 31–47.

Smith, Bruce 1991, 'Crime and the Classics: The Humanities and Government in the Nineteenth Century Australian University', in Ian Hunter et al. (eds) *Accounting for the Humanities: The Language of Culture and the Logic of Government*, Institute for Cultural Studies, Brisbane, pp. 67–116.

Thomis, Malcolm 1985, *A Place of Light and Learning: The University of Queensland's First Seventy-Five Years*, University of Queensland Press, Brisbane.

Turney, Clifford, Bygott, Ursula and Chippendale, Peter 1991, *Australia's First. A History of the University of Sydney. Volume 1, 1850–1939*, Hale & Iremonger, Sydney.

University of Melbourne 1947, Council minutes, 14 April.

Watson, Don 1979, *Brian Fitzpatrick: A Radical Life*, Hale & Iremonger, Sydney.

· 4 ·

Australian universities today

JOHN MOLONY

An understandable obstacle to our conversation on the state of the universities is the natural tendency to look to immediate concerns and interests, thereby limiting our ability to see the whole. The case of the vice-chancellors being unable to speak effectively with the one voice on the wider issues affecting the university sector is an example. Recently, the former executive of the Australian Vice-Chancellors Committee (AVCC) said that the vice-chancellors have never been able to arrive at a strategy for higher education, which surely handicaps them in enunciating policy. On the other hand, the various ministers responsible for higher education have been unwearied in their utterances. Lacking experience, and the wisdom that sometimes comes from it, they have had to rely on the advice they receive. The failure of the West Committee of 1998 to come forward with advice deemed to be either useful or acceptable must result in the further reliance of ministers on departmental bureaucrats. The determination of such people to see the whole is unquestioned given that, in effect, they control it. To decide whether their judgement of the whole and the advice they have given to their ministers has been to the good of higher education is impossible because that byzantine bureaucratic world remains hidden from our gaze. Our one remaining right is to judge its fruits.

STANDARDS

Given the problems in the university sector it is no wonder that morale is generally low among staff. A professor of Psychology at the University of Melbourne said recently, 'there is a deep anger among most academics at the way their lives have become as a result of the "supermarket" policies of successive federal governments. I don't know anyone who isn't depressed.' We witness each university concentrating inwardly on its own future without regard for the well-being of the whole sector. Added to that, decisions of the most astonishing kind are regularly made by administrators without reference to the staff and this has been consistently the case in all our universities for some years now.

The savage cutbacks in funding have resulted, among other things, in redundancies, either forced or voluntary, in higher proportions of untenured staff, the closing of departments, less choice of courses in many instances, a rapidly deteriorating tutorial system, hastily marked essays and reduced accessibility of teachers to students. With the incessant quest by many universities for student numbers in order to keep up the flow of government funds and the consequent lowering of entry requirements, it is axiomatic that standards at the point of entry have suffered. All these have a flow-on effect through to the highest level, as will soon become apparent. I will substantiate that point from my perception of several of the seven higher-degree theses I have examined in the past few years.

STUDENT FEES

It is idle to look back to the past as a kind of lotus land to which we long to return. That land no longer exists, except in some ways in a few of the very small institutions, which surely indicates that big may not necessarily be better and that big is not less costly. In the 1950s, before the binary system was introduced, there were less than 40,000 students in our universities. Now there are over 600,000. We cannot return to the ways of that earlier period, indeed some aspects of university life we were happy to see disappear. In the 1950s the rich, but rarely the dumb—given the need to matriculate—obtained entry to our universities, together with others whose parents skimped and saved to get them there. There were also others whose intellectual capacity and hard work made them candidates for scholarships, bursaries and the like. With the current proposals for fees, leading inexorably to a full fee-paying student body, the outcome is an inevitable return to the rich, perhaps the dumb-rich also, being first served. Even if fees are combined with scholarships, especially if such scholarships are funded directly by particular sectors such as industry, the likelihood is that the poor, and even the clever among them, will suffer.

Recently, two academics went further and suggested a system of higher fees for students repeating courses because they take up more of their teachers' time. The hope was that such a sanction would ensure more study and less partying by the students. This deplorable suggestion shows the widening gap between present and past. In the past the rich were often more inclined to partying than the poor, but an added fee will not deter the rich if they fail. The poorer student, who frequently has to work part-time as well as study, is often worn out and exam results may suffer. Thirty years ago or less a suggestion putting a strict monetary value on our labour as teachers, would have been scorned and summarily rejected. The case is different now, even were we to react negatively. We would have little impact on the outcome.

COMMONALITY

To speak of the past is to speak of ideals that could only be striven for and never completely achieved. No one would deny that many of us fell down in our responsibilities from time to time. Nonetheless, it is still useful to pause on two basic principles that guided us in our work and in our membership of an academic community. One is illustrated by the use of the words 'academic community'. The well-being of the university demanded of us a constant response to our responsibilities and relationships within the academic community. That attitude implied, and most often succeeded in achieving, a commonality of purpose. Mission statements were not needed because we knew that the higher education of our students on the one hand, and our dedication to research and the dissemination of its fruits on the other, were our essential purpose. Those who did not understand our purpose were unaware, ignorant or perverse. The vast majority of fair-minded students, their parents and friends, as well as most of the general public knew what the purpose of a university was. Indeed, they respected that purpose and they treasured their universities as fundamental to the core of a society in which the values of our civilisation were cherished, nourished and taught.

To achieve our purpose we all had differing tasks and responsibilities. Some of us were academics, others administrators, others secretaries, laboratory assistants, accountants, and library staff, together with whoever else was needed by the enterprise. The academic staff knew full well that without the help of the others their prospects of success would be slight. The administrators, including the Vice-Chancellor, and others engaged in similar support activities knew that without the academics they had no purpose whatever. They realised that their power came from the whole university community and that the one element without which the enterprise would become meaningless was the academic. All of us, in our moments of greater clarity, knew that we were mere phantoms without the students, who were the embodiment of our immediate purpose and thus part of our community. Such, with its strengths and weaknesses, was the principle of commonality. Its concomitant structures were geared to achieve our purpose. That a percentage of academics and others within the university community did not live up to the ideal is not a comment on the principle, on the university itself or on its purpose, but on human nature.

ACCOUNTABILITY

The other principle is accountability. Today, it seems to mean that the university must be openly responsible to those who provide its financial support. In an alleged secondary sense, accountability is owed to the government that decides the measure of funding and, increasingly, the way in which funds are to be used. Finally, accountability also includes the university's readiness to serve 'the national interest'. There was no mention in the past of that particularly totalitarian concept, so frighteningly abused in this century, nor of our responsibility to certain sectors of the wider community, in particular to industry.

How then did we conceive of our accountability? I suggest that we saw it as exercised within our community on the grounds that if we were effectively accountable there, we would be accountable elsewhere. Principally, we accepted that we had to be accountable to, and for, those whom we taught. They were not mere numbers or even simple names, but real people with all the strengths and weakness shared by humanity. They had come to the university so that we might share with them our knowledge of, and experience in, our respective disciplines. To seek and understand the truth, the nature of things, is to inculcate also the virtues of justice, tolerance, decency and much else that makes up civilised behaviour. To be accountable to our students was to demand much of ourselves as we tried to stay at the forefront of our discipline in our reading and research, to prepare lectures, to guide students in their reading, to assess their written work with care and to return it to them personally. We knew that we had to demand certain standards of intellectual rigour from our students, in default of which we would betray them, the wider community and ourselves.

This understanding on our part meant accountability to the academic community in all its component parts. It extended to our peers, on whom we relied for the friendship, the example and the day-to-day encouragement that lightened our burden; to the head of department, the Dean, the Vice-Chancellor and whomever else relied on us doing our part. Was it not the case that a librarian, a secretary, a gardener, all those who were part of the community, generally took pride in our pursuit of the noble purpose of education at the highest level? Did they not rejoice in the good name of the university and regret its failings? And, if we as academics pursued our purpose with resolution, were we not thereby accountable to the wider community that made our work possible by financing it? Should this not have been sufficient to satisfy government?

THE NEED FOR REFORM

The critics who have undertaken to reform us reveal their own mental poverty by calling us 'nostalgists' who lack an understanding of the real world, based on economic rationalism. No one denies that the universities needed a degree of reform. They will always need reform because every institution suffers deformation and therefore requires reformation. Nevertheless, in undertaking reform, was there clear evidence, for example, that the public had become concerned about the paucity of universities and wanted them doubled in number to thirty-seven separate institutions? Why was the academic status of universities diluted by changing funding structures so drastically? The effect was that some of the new ones became universities in little more than name while the others suffered from a lack of funds; of which the proportion provided by government has fallen from ninety per cent in 1981 to fifty-five per cent today. Why has there been such an unseemly scramble to be one of the top eight (or whatever number makes up the inner club of universities) except to ensure survival and standing? Was it advisable to create suddenly a need for so many new university staff that general competency became questionable, to encourage them to offer courses in every conceivable area of interest to the human imagination and to offer degrees in areas of knowledge that no one had hitherto associated with higher education?

To question the number of courses and degrees now offered is to invite being branded as an elitist who lacks a true perception of students' needs. We are told that in the university of today the students are entitled to demand courses and subsequently receive degrees, preferably paid for, which will give them the vocational training that suits their perceived needs. Even were that argument granted, would it not remain the responsibility of the vendor, the university, to decide on the suitability of the goods it offers? If not, are we to conclude that no area of human endeavour is outside the scope of the intellectual formation, even if we call it training, that any given university ought to offer? No one would wish to deny that it is a useful social skill to know how to mix a cocktail. Would anyone propose that it is the business of a university to teach such a skill and, if so, would they wish to extend the range by suggesting that the skills required in the sex industry should also become part of the curriculum? It could surely be argued that such an industry helps satisfy the demands of the national interest financially, and that tourism and hospitality courses would benefit from inclusion of such skills on the curriculum.

WHO DEMANDS REFORM?

However, more serious matters help us get a sense of where responsibility lies. Did the general public make an outcry for the constant denigration of universities by attacks and belittlement, with often unrestrained assertions about élites and privileges? Who called for the undermining of academic standing and personal confidence by loss of tenure (that continues to drop—from 82 per cent of staff in 1982 to 58 per cent in 1995) as well as the comparative downgrading of salary levels? Who asked that there be a 'teaching only' and 'research only' categorisation of staff? Why has it been necessary to demand of the universities, and especially of the academic staff, seemingly endless reviews at all levels to prove accountability? Who invented and foisted on us citations, the judging of a book as 'substantial' if it has eighty pages and the comparison, without any evaluation of substance, of one work with another? Did industry demand the subservience of universities to its alleged requirements and the subsequent chasing of research dollars to do what is called applied, rather than pure, research? If so—and it is much to be doubted—can it be proved that industry would not be content with our awarding doctorates to scholars whose credentials rest on the fact that we have educated them to the highest level in their chosen disciplines?

THE NATIONAL INTEREST

What was, or is, the concept termed 'the national interest'? Who decides its nature, how is it to be achieved and what, apart from doing the work for which they were founded, have universities to do with it? Indeed, if there is to be a national interest will it have a moral dimension? For example, will students being trained in MBA programs, because the national interest demands them, be taught the moral dimension of employment as a universal right? On the grounds of the national interest, did the public demand that effective control of universities be taken into the hands of managers, themselves controlled by government through draconian financial measures and an incessant stream of injunctions and cautions issuing from DEETYA (the Department of Education, Employment, Training and Youth Affairs) and its minister? Is it possible that the move to managerialism was intended as a step towards control and the achievement of other aims that unfold month by month? Without clear and unequivocal answers to these and a myriad of related matters the question still remains: Why did the controllers of public funds take the steps they have taken, and are still taking, to change, radically, rapidly and forever the nature of the universities?

In effect, we are not talking about reformation but a wholesale change in the nature of universities. The most effective way to subvert an institution is to change the principles upon which it is based. To take an institution, the essence of which is commonality, and change the structure of authority within it is ultimately to destroy it. If it remains in existence, in name at any rate, it is because it has become a different entity. In the university of the past authority came from below. Now it comes from above. In the past we were directly responsible to the community to which we primarily belonged. Today we are responsible to government, even though government would claim speciously that we are responsible to the public. To make a university community principally accountable to centralised forces without its walls is to weaken accountability to students and confreres within and, eventually but rapidly, to change its very nature. That is exactly what happened in all totalitarian societies, of which the most recent examples in the West are Fascist Italy, Nazi Germany and the Soviet empire.

A DESTRUCTIVE REVOLUTION

It is tedious to restate the jargon-filled language pouring from the lips and pens of politicians, bureaucrats and administrators in relation to the university and its purpose. Suffice to say that it all points to a collapse in commonality; and those who changed, deliberately, the relationship that made commonality work knew what they were doing. They wanted control and there can be no commonality in a system that is controlled from outside. The result of this destructive revolution, for such it was, is obvious. As academics we are now employees; the politicians and their servants are our employers and the purpose of the university is production. Production means supplying a market. Management means directing production. Excellence means producing goods the market will buy. Meanwhile, high ideals are eroded, morale suffers drastically and purpose translates into quotas. In short, whereas we once had a purpose we strove to fulfil, often mightily, now it is being lost and worse still we are being forced to lose it and we no longer know what we are to do. Some universities will remain and retain, partly at least, their purpose. They will be self-funded through endowments and fees. Others will be obliged by market forces to close, and others again will become colleges on the American model at its lower levels, without a commonality of purpose within themselves. Their accountability will be to their pay-masters. It is our responsibility, not someone else's, to start the revitalisation of our purpose. Otherwise, the system of higher education as we have known it will disappear.

'TREASON OF THE CLERKS'

It is appropriate to use the expression 'treason of the clerks' in the circumstances in which we find ourselves, provided we ask who was guilty of that treason. Treason must be judged on what has been betrayed and the higher the values, the more worthy the institution, the graver the treason. Were the universities of the mid-eighties so grossly negligent in the pursuit and upholding of their purpose that not some mere measure of reform was advisable, but change of a kind that would affect their very essence? If that kind of change was not necessary, if it could not then or now be proved to have been necessary, the universities were betrayed and grievously so. Who betrayed them?

One answer is so stark as to bear no more than enunciation. The Hawke government betrayed the universities but the Prime Minister, in an entirely craven way, took no responsibility. No, it was done by the Department of Education headed by the Minister, John Dawkins. The same department presided over, and does so today, the worst period of unemployment that has wounded the nation, especially the young people of the nation, since the Great Depression. The historians of the future will take note of the fact that Dawkins' department had responsibility for education, employment and training while the current one is also responsible for youth affairs but no longer responsible for employment. It is not the universities alone: our whole society bears the marks of the department's policies. We know little of the motivations of the various ministers responsible for the Department. We do know that they are advised by servants of the public who are responsible to no one but them.

WE ARE RESPONSIBLE

What we must confront in all this is our own responsibility. Are we not the ones who stood by and witnessed the erosion of our hopes and ideals? Did we do anything with determined purpose when we saw our universities being turned into factories in all but name? Did we refuse to fill in the endless questionnaires, to participate in the review committees, to allow ourselves to be measured and quantified, to accept demands that we spell out the path of our future endeavours with ambitious plans to do this and that, write this, research that and so on *ad infinitum*? Did we recoil from competing for the dollars held out to us, to become the servants of industry or whatever other segment of the public weal allegedly demanded what our masters called relevance? Did not some of us rejoice jealously in the alleged excellence of our own institutions while deploring its lack in others? The litany of our supine compliance in the face of manifest tyranny is endless. Nonetheless, I must ask one final question. What did we do to stop our being turned into helots serving a state bent on reducing us to facsimiles of factory workers turning out a product to suit the ends of that state? Did we ask ourselves how long it would be before the most gifted among us would flee elsewhere, or whether the day would come when we would hesitate long before advising the best of our students to follow our path and join us in the academic community?

FALSE TRUST

I grieve that I cannot answer the above questions with a quiet conscience. There is little I can comfort myself with except to plead that I trusted. Was it wrong to trust those we saw rise from our academic ranks, rarely after any consultation with us to take responsibility for the well-being of our universities? We had our work to do, our students to teach, our research and writing to get on with, as well as the personal concerns of our lives. We were not invited, perhaps we were not even capable, to meet with ministers, to discuss the future of our institutions with the bureaucrats and to canvass members of Parliament. We did not see it as our province to read the endless pronouncements of ministers, editorial writers, TV commentators, letter-writers and all those who purported to have the interests of higher education at heart.

In the end, green and white papers were published which we scarcely comprehended, couched as they were in the language of the market place. Perhaps in our innocence we did not even consider them to be our immediate concern. What we did was to go about our tasks trusting in our vice-chancellors and senates and councils to take care of our universities and to preserve their purpose and ideals. Let us leave aside the apparent equanimity with which the senates and councils allowed themselves to be reformed, to acquiesce in the reduction of their numbers, including students and staff members, and to see representatives, drawn from private enterprise and other similar areas, replace them. All of this was said to be in the name of efficiency, but who questioned what results they were expected to achieve? Did anyone ask whether those same managers, leading executives and others, had made such a success of their own enterprises that they could promise to do the same for the universities? The state of the economy may be a partial answer to that question. In any event, it is probably the case that, today, the majority of the people who made up those new bodies, many of them there still, even understood what they betrayed.

CHIEF EXECUTIVE OFFICERS

I cannot leave this analysis of treason without putting before you those, with too rare but honourable exceptions, whom I am convinced are principally responsible, both as individuals and as a body, for our betrayal. They are responsible precisely because they were the ones whose sacred duty it was, and still is, to defend the universities. Why do we still grant them the high title of Vice-Chancellor? They permit themselves to be called Chief Executive Officers and, for the most part, they behave as such. Is there a shred of evidence that any of them ever refused or questioned their transformation from the collegial to the managerial role? Are they prepared to shoulder responsibility for the acts which are, in truth, theirs? They have taken immense pains to surround themselves with a breathtaking phalanx of deputies, pro vice-chancellors, assistants, and such, all of whom, with them, enjoy the emoluments of high office. It is to these colleagues and other lesser lights, for such is now the reduced state of collegiality, that the Chief Executive Officers look when the time comes to take a painful decision, after which pronouncements are made, piously but falsely, that a proper process of consultation has been followed.

The result is that, today, the Chief Executive Officers are our employers. We are their employees and they treat us exactly in the fashion of employers in any large industrial or business firm. That includes their right to sack us not, mind you, because we are necessarily unequal to, or unworthy of, our responsibilities, but because we have been declared redundant, or because our area of expertise has been judged as no longer useful to the purpose of the university. The grounds for such decisions, rarely expressed in academic terms, is normally that the government has cut back on funds. The thinly veiled intention of privatising the universities, like a myriad of other public institutions of the state, is not mentioned.

RETURN TO BASIC PRINCIPLES

Some people in our universities today may accept that the present state was unavoidable. They will argue that the forces determined on change were so powerful, and of such a nature, that resistance was impossible. Others may hold that radical change of the kind we have witnessed was necessary for the survival of the universities. Probably there are even some who, never having shared an understanding of commonality and accountability as we understood them, are happy to foster the changes that are under way and to mouth the new language of the economic rationalists.

Nonetheless, there are many who do not accept that a return to basic principles is impossible and they hold that we have an obligation to lay down the guidelines for an alternative future. The past, however, teaches us an important lesson. It has so often been the case that would–be reformers have embarked on their task without having any agenda other than the need for reform. Equally often their attempts at reform, undertaken in a piecemeal and unprincipled way, led to chaos and destruction. Those who wish to stop the destructive process witnessed in Australian universities during the past decade must have an agenda that lays down the guidelines for a way ahead. Those guidelines must stand firmly on the principles of commonality and accountability. Otherwise, any effort we may make will prove futile.

• 5 •

Ends and means in university policy decisions

BRUCE LANGTRY

Here is a sign of the times. Melbourne University Private Limited was established early in 1998 by the University of Melbourne, with the support of various corporate partners. It 'will be structured as a tax-exempt body', though its constituent schools 'will operate on a fully commercial basis'.[1] The new university is directed towards a different constituency from existing public universities.

> Its programs will be designed essentially for an emerging
> domestic and international market demanding high quality
> educational [sic] and training to meet the professional
> up-grading and re-skilling needs of early to mid-career
> technical, managerial or executive clients already in
> employment. Corporate and individual professional clients will
> measure its success in terms of the real present value it adds to
> the people it educates and trains.

Its 'major competitive advantages over most new private universities' will include 'an established brand—the "Melbourne" trade mark, backed by accreditation from the University of Melbourne'.

The foregoing expressions of the new institution's aims and values contrast dramatically with those voiced when the University of Melbourne was opened in 1855. The Chancellor, Redmond Barry, while recognising the need for instruction in what is 'useful' as well as what is 'speculative', talked mainly in terms of cultivating the minds of young men, and the introduction of learning, wisdom and virtue. He spoke of education as 'adopting the great moral duty of assiduously cultivating that learning, wisdom and virtue, not to be inherited as worldly wealth descends'. He described education as something 'without which worldly riches sit, like undeserved honours, gracelessly and unprofitably on the possessor' (*Argus*, 14 April 1855).

The difference between the two statements of aims and values is not merely stylistic. Why did the people who wrote and approved the material about Melbourne University Private Limited leave out the sort of points that Redmond Barry made? It was not because they thought that the fundamental importance of these points could be taken for granted. Surely it was rather because mention of learning, wisdom and virtue would have been irrelevant, a distraction from the message that the new university wanted to convey.

THREE CONCERNS ABOUT UNIVERSITIES TODAY

Other contributors draw attention to major positive achievements of Australian universities and lament current deficiencies and dangers. Let me list three of the problems that worry academics about the current state of higher education.

1. *Distortion of research and teaching priorities.* Such distortion frequently occurs as a side-effect of financial incentives and disincentives put in place by budget committees at university and faculty levels. Consider four examples. First, many academics who would have been perfectly happy to get on with inexpensive projects central to their intellectual interests have come under considerable pressure to apply for large ARC grants, and therefore to devise projects which require

major financial expenditure. Either the application is unsuccessful, in which case there has been significant waste of
time, or it succeeds, in which case the academic is committed to a research topic and research strategy which she or
he has chosen not for its intrinsic scholarly merits but rather
for its potential to attract ARC money and to feed into
funding formulae which determine the level of resources
available to the department for basic items like photocop-
ier maintenance. Second, there is reason to believe that in
some institutions recent professorial appointments have been
heavily influenced by grant-getting capacity and achievement, as a factor alongside research publication record.
Third, the measures used in funding formulae are crude,
over-simplified measures of research achievement, and their
influence on both the form in which people decide
to publish their work and rewards to departments for
their work results in both inefficient allocation of resources
and perceived unfairness. Fourth, there is grade inflation,
resulting from giving higher marks for tactical reasons.

2. *Erosion of tenure*, combined with financial pressures of various
   well-known kinds, is having two bad consequences. First,
   in some cases the selection of individuals to be declared
   redundant seems to have been influenced by who has or
   has not been critical of those in power, rather than purely
   by comparisons of research and teaching contributions; and
   belief by colleagues that this has been, and might in the
   future be, so provides a significant threat inhibiting policy
   debate. Second, the absence of secure career paths even for
   very bright young researchers has led to low morale and a
   considerable loss of talent from many discipline areas. As
   Gustav Nossal recently said, 'The issue that concerns me
   most is the plight of the younger Australian university
   academic' (*Australian Universities' Review*, 40(2), 1997: 11).

3. *Steadily increasing teaching and administrative workloads.* There
   is less time to prepare a lecture, less time to mark an essay,
   less time to chat informally with students about their work

and their intellectual interests. But time is the single most important input to the quality of teaching.

THE *TELOS* OF THE UNIVERSITY

Identifying certain practices as distorting a university's research and teaching priorities presupposes some conception of what those priorities ought to be. Some people have thought that the very nature of the university embodies a set of central scholarly goals whose continued achievement constitutes the university's supreme good. It would be a mistake to saddle ourselves with such a view here. Let us rather think specifically of long-established institutions like the University of Melbourne and the University of Western Australia, and concentrate on these questions: What aims and values ought these universities pursue? What aims and values for these universities ought governments approve, protect and nourish?

There are many of them. No doubt universities should seek to train professional people needed in the working of the economy. No doubt they should seek to work in partnership with industry to devise new products and services which Australia can sell overseas. But these goals are not at the heart of what universities should be doing. As in any big enterprise, some aims and values have a central role, supporting and giving coherence to the others. Three of these spring to mind. First, universities should provide a liberal education for their students. Second, they ought to engage in research aimed at increasing our depth of understanding of the world, including human beings and human activity: we seek not merely an accumulation of items of information, but theoretical insight. Third, they should contribute to their society's critical self-evaluation.

These points would be platitudinous if they were not, at the end of the twentieth century, so controversial.

By a liberal education I do not mean a course in the humanities as opposed to a degree in science, engineering, agriculture or whatever. For science, engineering and agriculture should be taught in such a way that the course constitutes one way of obtaining a liberal education. Such an education is defined not by its subject matter but by the intellectual virtues, skills and values that permeate it and that students acquire through it. Of course even a far-from-liberal university course will seek to do more than convey facts, routine procedures and practical knacks. Many of these will be left for the graduate to acquire on the job. The rapid pace of innovation has led to emphasis on the understanding of underlying principles and the development of analytical and critical ability as the crucial accomplishments of a university degree. But a liberal education offers more. A liberal education involves inquiry into the intellectual credentials of the principles, and the moral justification of the institutions and practices into which the student is being initiated. For example, are the claims made in scientific medical journals more worthy of belief than the claims of naturopaths and other alternative therapists, and, if so, why? Are medical experiments which involve deceiving patients morally acceptable?

A liberal education seeks to cultivate an interest in significant questions independently of any payoff to oneself in terms of professional advancement. It involves caution or scepticism about claims to authority; respect for truth, objectivity and rationality; skill in argument and an openness to follow argument where it leads—and these not only in some limited field but broadly, in all areas of one's life. It involves awareness of the intellectual, cultural and social context within which one thinks and acts as a professional. It involves awareness of serious alternatives to one's own personal and professional values, and reflection on one's reasons for working and living as one does.

There is no need to fill out this sketch any further. Rather, let us turn to consider in broad terms the justification of the value-judgments that have lain behind what I have been saying. Why is it desirable and important that accountants, chemical engineers and pharmacists receive a liberal education? Are there reasons to which governments, entrusted with the good of society as a whole, ought to attach great weight?

A convincing answer must do more than say that certain things are good in themselves, independently of their connection with anything else. Rather, the advocate of a liberal education should appeal to the central role that critical thought, an interest in significant questions for their own sakes, respect for truth and so on have in the good life for a human being, and so in a good society. Human good is not to be exclusively identified with happiness or the fulfilment of desires; after all, the intellectually disabled may, if they are very lucky, be contented and have most of their desires fulfilled. Try a thought-experiment. Consider a person devising a plan for his or her life, a life which is to operate successfully as an organic whole. Our planner will no doubt include being fairly happy as a desideratum. What else? There is no unique answer: there will be a lot of variation between individuals. Perhaps significant professional achievement. Perhaps marriage and children. Certainly friends. But any successful life plan will also provide for various personal qualities, without which the other specifications cannot be made to work: health, intelligence, courage, honesty, social skills, and so on. Jews and Christians will endorse such items as contained within traditional religious goals and values, but add some further elements: a meaningful relationship with God, along with qualities whose value becomes clearest in the context of a relationship with God. The resulting life plan needs to involve a workable and harmonious package of such elements. Of many of these elements, such as health, it can be said both that they are good for their own sake and that much of their value comes from the contribution they make to the person's life as a whole.

Now the ingredients of a liberal education have a very strong claim to be included in such a life plan. I have not seen this argued comprehensively in a satisfactory manner. But it is fairly clear in broad outline how to do so. For example, why do we have reason to seek understanding beyond what we can see to be relevant to our professional advancement? Partly because we may have a mistakenly narrow view of what is relevant to our professional advancement. Partly because participation in the broader intellectual life of society opens our eyes to options for living that we would not have otherwise considered, and increasing this awareness is in general a wise strategy. Partly because seeking general understanding contributes to our autonomy; autonomy is a character ideal which many people regard as underpinning their sense of themselves as moral agents.

Some people will be sceptical about the value-judgements appealed to in the foregoing sketch. Increasing options and developing one's autonomy, they will say, cannot be justified as culture-transcendent human goods. Other people will argue that even if you yourself happen to think the value of these things can be rigorously demonstrated, surely you will agree that not all your value-judgements about society ought to be used as a basis for public policy. For purposes of public policy-making in a pluralist society such as our own, they will say, governments and their agencies must abstract from particular, contested beliefs about value. They should keep their basic assumptions about what is good for human beings as sparse as possible, leaving it for individuals to decide for themselves as to what will enhance their lives.

Not so. In assessing the justice of laws, the social desirability of institutions, and the effectiveness of government programs, we need a rich, thick account of what is good for individual human beings and for society as a whole. Judges and state-employed social workers making decisions about particular cases involving mental illness, adoption and child custody after divorce need elements of such an account. If it is substantial enough for *their* work, then surely it will also suffice to ground arguments in favour of the goals of a liberal education.

Some writers today try to debunk objectivity with respect to truth and rationality and thereby attack the foundations of traditional university education. They say:

> Of course discipline areas have conventions which label certain procedures and arguments as rational and objective. But these conventions are not themselves grounded in independently valid rules or values of reason. So there is no justification for saying that taken as a whole modern astronomy has better rational credentials, or is likely to be closer to the truth, than the beliefs about the make-up of the heavens held hundreds of years ago by Australian Aborigines. If we prize methodological rigour in physics, then our doing so has much the same

standing as our prizing methodological rigour in the composing of madrigals.

This is a philosophical attack on specific values. I think it needs to be—and indeed can be—fought off with philosophical weapons, wielded with professional skill.

ECONOMIC AND MANAGEMENT PRINCIPLES MISAPPLIED

Now why would a so-called 'economic rationalist' or a 'managerialist' want to quarrel with the goal of a liberal education? Indeed, why would they be unhappy with the further idea that universities ought to have a strong internal ethos of academic collegiality and freedom of inquiry? The key doctrines of the so-called traditional model of universities seem perfectly compatible with the view that universities exist to promote the prosperity of society within financial constraints imposed by government budgetary priorities and the ability of universities to raise money from non-government sources. They are also compatible with the recognition that the university's success requires efficient management, to ensure that research and teaching outcomes are optimal relative to the available resources.

Why, then, does higher education today often seem to involve a profound clash between two cultures? Why do bureaucrats in Canberra, and within the university itself, often talk about policy in ways that seem to profoundly threaten the values traditionally embodied in research and teaching?

Coming to think of the university as selling courses as products in the higher education market is a bit like coming to think of a diocese as hiring priests in the labour market. In a way, the new descriptions are accurate. Nevertheless, they may reasonably be deplored. There is more involved than jarring symbolism. From the standpoint of traditional values, if we start conceptualising roles and activities in the new way, then their aims and guiding principles may undergo a drift in ways which undermine the mission of the university, or of the church. By and large the contributors to this volume believe that this is what has happened in Australian higher education over the past decade.

Just as economists may find it illuminating to treat marriage as an economic transaction, so they may find it illuminating to treat a university as a firm supplying services to individual consumers, or to the state. But marriage partners would typically be unwise to treat their relationship as primarily consisting in the trading of services in order to fulfil the mutually disinterested desires of each. And management consultants would be silly to recommend that they treat their relationship in this way. Similarly, it would be a misuse of economics and management theory for governments or universities to be overly preoccupied with the economic contribution that universities make to society, or with economic analyses of their internal functioning.

Politicians and bureaucrats are in two minds about this truth. On the one hand they acknowledge—at least, they sometimes *say*—that research and learning have value to society which cannot be reduced to effects on the gross national product or international trade balance, and they support the continuation of 'pure' work in the natural sciences and humanities. On the other hand, they frequently ram through major policies which have predictable bad side-effects on research and learning, in order to advance what they identify as economic objectives for society as a whole; and they push for internal university resource-allocation methods which again have predictable bad side-effects—of the sort outlined above. (By 'bureaucrats' I mean not only people in government agencies like Department of Education, Training and Youth Affairs and senior 'general' staff of universities, but also academics such as vice-chancellors and the chairs of faculty budgets committees. As various contributors to this volume have pointed out, the integrity of universities has not only been attacked from without: it has sometimes been betrayed from within. The federal government does not dictate to faculty budgets committees how they will distribute funds between departments and centres within the faculty.)

There is no doubt that universities need efficient management practices. There is no doubt that internal funding formulae, transparent to all and adopted for the right reasons, can be a vast improvement on older hidden processes, which sometimes amounted to wheeling and dealing in which the most skilled operators won the most booty for themselves and their dependants. But the management practices which have brought about or worsened the problems identified above cannot be described as well-devised and well-implemented.

Efficiency involves the optimal achievement of one's goals relative to the available resources. Achieving efficiency in a large organisation can become a matter of purely technical expertise—if we understand 'technical expertise' to include skill in persuading and motivating people—provided that one has adequately identified what one's goals are, and what trade-offs between them one is prepared to make. Unfortunately, this is one of the tricky bits, where it is easy to go wrong. Sometimes, for instance, a company's directors can be heard saying, 'The aim of our firm is to maximise long run profits; everything else is subordinate to that', but close examination of actual decisions by the board and senior executives reveals that the firm's behaviour is driven by much more complex aims.

In some cases senior managements of universities and faculties seem to be operating with drastically oversimplified conceptions of what the goals of their institution are (or ought to be), and therefore with drastically oversimplified measures of efficiency. For example, consider just two ultimate goals: deserved prestige for excellence in research publications, and production of many highly skilled, sought-after graduates. To construct and work with a strategic model which recognised only these two goals as ultimate would be crude indeed, and likely to lead to serious misallocations of resources. For a management strategy which delivers genuine efficiency must give independent weight to many other *product aims* and *process aims* (as I call them).

Among the university's product aims are that graduates should not only be skilled and sought-after but also people possessing the disposition to be alert and critical thinkers concerning theoretical and policy-related issues well outside their work. Among the process aims are, surely, that decisions made by universities, faculties and departments about what research projects are to be permitted and funded are to respect academic autonomy and collegiality, and are not to be influenced by personal or factional loyalties. I have already provided arguments for a justification of the view that universities ought to aim at the key qualities contained in the idea of a liberal education. In chapter 7 in this volume, Seumas Miller offers a defence of academic autonomy.

There are times when cumbersome decision-making structures should be stripped down, and the authority of individuals in certain key positions increased. But in deciding whether proposed streamlining will indeed promote efficiency, attention has to be paid to the totality of the ends to which the best means are to be found. Open, rational debate in setting curricula should be valued not merely as a candidate way of finding courses that will be successful—whatever counts as success—but also as an independent end, valued for its role in making the university as a whole an academic community that embodies and nourishes liberal values in education. In many situations, it may well turn out that the slower and more elaborate processes deliver a much better cost–benefit performance than the proponents of streamlining think.

During war or other times of national emergency, governments are apt to downgrade the weight they normally give to considerations like liberty and due legal process, to more effectively deal with the threat to the country's well-being, or even its very survival. Perhaps some universities believe that in the late 1990s they face major threats to their well-being, or even their survival, resulting from inadequate government funding— for instance, to meet salary increases—and from pressures of national and international competition to attract students. Perhaps their academic boards, in line with Melbourne University Private, think, 'Constructing and marketing popular courses, entering into research partnerships with industry, and cutting costs which will be relatively unproductive over the next few years, are the preconditions of achieving our other aims. So these concerns must be given top priority. We have little choice: the rules of the game have not been set by us.'

I think that this defence of short-term thinking and the

betrayal of traditional values is fairly feeble. For example, funding difficulties and pressures of competition cannot be blamed for the way that university public relations and marketing rhetoric often assumes and so promotes, rather than resists, the idea that the main reason for going to university is to enhance career prospects. What is true is that the conduct of university administrations needs to be seen in the context of constraints and temptations arising from government higher education policy over the past decade.

Evidently the federal government and university administrators have been working with an oversimplified understanding of the contribution of higher education to the good of Australia, and so an oversimplified view of what constitutes efficiency in resource allocation.

Redmond Barry and his colleagues saw themselves, correctly, as founding a modern, secular university which would contribute both to the broader community's intellectual life and to its long-term material prosperity. Their self-understanding deserves our respect. Of course, it would be foolish to allow nostalgia for a selectively remembered past to distract us from clear-headed focus on urgent, practical concerns of the present. But it would be equally foolish to allow preoccupation with misconceived urgent, practical concerns to distract us from clear-headed focus on our mission. What institutions like the University of Melbourne and the University of Western Australia should be doing, if they are to allocate resources well, should be understood in terms of the goal of liberal education.

Note
1. This and related quotations are taken from a brochure issued by Melbourne University Private Limited on 16 February 1998.

PART II

SPECIFIC CONCERNS

• 6 •

The value of fundamental inquiry: the view from physics

TONY KLEIN

INTRODUCTION

To complement Janet McCalman's exposition on problems facing humanities research in the future (chapter 8), I aim to concentrate on the value of *scientific* inquiry, though by no means denying the possible value of *other* forms of fundamental inquiry. More specifically I will concentrate on physics, or *natural* philosophy, simply in order to avoid straying too far from my home territory.

Scientific inquiry, though having its origins in ancient Greece, really took off around the sixteenth or seventeenth Century. It may be interesting to remark that almost from its inception there was a divergence of opinion, or even latent conflict, between scientists and society regarding the purpose of their endeavours.

Gallileo Gallilei (1564–1642) emphasised pure knowledge for its own sake—for the intellectual development of humanity, for the sake of Truth with a capital T. (Mind you, this did not stop him from making a few florins by selling telescopes to the Venetians!) On the other hand, Francis Bacon (1561–1626), his contemporary, argued for more or less immediate, practical benefits to society. Echoes of this dichotomy have rumbled down the centuries and persist to this day. In fact the issue flares up in an acute form from time to time and it is with us again, in a pretty severe form.

VALUES? WHAT VALUES?

It is quite clearly a question of values and the conflict between types of values. On the one hand are the pure, cultural and aesthetic values which bring joy and satisfaction—and occasionally, dare I say it, immortality—to individual creators, and kudos and international standing to their nations (as well as their universities). Unfortunately, such values appear to be beyond the scope of economists—they dismiss them simply as 'externalities'.

On the other hand we have the economists' tangible, material values produced by the application of basic knowledge, usually by means of some new technology. Although immense in value, the applications of basic scientific inquiry are almost always far in the future, in the case of physics separated by about 25 years from their moment of creation as pure, basic science. The usual example is electric power, the work of Michael Faraday, the fruit of which he did not live to see but the value of which is said to exceed the capitalisation of all the shares on the London Stock Exchange.

A more recent example is the laser. Invented in 1960, it spent decades as 'a solution looking for a problem'. It took the usual quarter of a century before it penetrated our households. (Every CD player, for instance, has one in it.) Even if we could predict the winning application, economists will tell you that it is not worth investing a dollar today hoping to reap profits in 25 years' time. They want a much shorter time-frame, one that basic science can almost never deliver. One might as well spread the risk and play the stock market.

On the same argument, educating one's children is an equally unprofitable exercise. Isn't it ironic that both education and basic research or fundamental inquiry (I am using the terms interchangeably) are beyond the reach of market economics?

So who should support basic research? The government, of course, meaning the nation as a whole. The cost should be shared by all, in the same way that we share the cost of educating the next generation. In this way, looking back in time, by discovering the nature of matter and its fundamental forces, or the nature of life and heredity, we have not only gained knowledge and insight but we have also been able to attain a standard of material welfare and a level of health and life expectancy which would have been unimaginable a century ago.

Well, then, why don't we just continue along the same magic road? Why does the nation not continue to pick up the tab for basic research as well as for universal tertiary education? For very similar reasons—the economists tell us that we cannot afford it.

THE FUTURE OF TERTIARY EDUCATION

In the case of education, we have, in our time, witnessed the extraordinary expansion of higher education for an essentially doctrinaire reason, namely equality of opportunity (which we all support). Unfortunately, it was coupled to the idiotic proposition of equal outcomes—a doctrine which flies in the face of facts regarding the distribution of human abilities. It also flies in the face of rudimentary economics. We simply cannot afford to educate everyone to the same standards of attainment— it would take too long and too much effort, if possible at all. [Quote from a colleague at a Dawkins University: 'If their knuckles clear the ground, given enough time we can teach them calculus! Is it worth it?'.] Alternatively, must we then reduce the quality of education to the lowest common denominator?

That being clear nonsense, we have two alternatives. One is to 'smash the system' by deconstructing all knowledge. Unfortunately, whatever its merits elsewhere, that does not work in the pure sciences—the stone of reality will kick back. Or the second is to allow (or force) the system to stratify. Let us all get a university degree—but not in the same field and not to the same standard of attainment. I think we are clearly witnessing this in our times. The 'unified national system' is turning into the 'stratified national system'. However, we are not there yet; the better universities are currently forced to under-educate some of their students because of a lack of resources, in order to pay for over-resourcing the education of the less able.

My guess is that, given a few more years, the system will reach some kind of equilibrium; some form of just and justifiable differential funding will evolve and, if we are clever as well as lucky, that equilibrium will be an equitable one—more in the direction of meritocracy than of aristocracy. Let me declare a strong bias in favour of a Menzies-type of Commonwealth scholarship system (of which I am a product), not too different from that proposed by Peter Karmel in chapter 10 of this volume. The only loss will have been the devaluation of the words 'university', and 'professor'—but that has happened already and besides, the Americans got there a long time ago!

THE FUTURE OF RESEARCH

I hope most readers will agree that fundamental inquiry is an unalloyed good thing, with immediate cultural values and assured economic rewards—albeit some 25 years later. Of course, you may not agree: a neo-Luddite attitude to new knowledge is, alas, all to prevalent today but it simply does not withstand rigorous scrutiny. Finding the way out of our problems will surely need more knowledge, rather than less. Unfortunately, with fundamental inquiry, as with the case of mass tertiary education—or even more so—no nation can allow the indefinite proliferation of basic research, no nation can afford to pay for it all.

The seemingly indefinite growth of science has been apparent for quite a long time. More than 35 years ago, Derek da Solla Price published a book, *Little Science, Big Science*, in which he documented the fact that, using whatever measure, scientific activity has been growing exponentially, and at a very fast rate, for the last 300 years. Extrapolating his graphs, it seemed that in a few more decades we would all have PhDs in science.

Clearly, something had to give and a steady state had to be reached. The activity had to level out, but how? The examination of that question is turning out to be quite painful. This is well documented by John Ziman, a noted solid state physicist and (later) Head of the Science Policy Group in the UK. In his book *Prometheus Bound—Science in a Dynamic Steady State*, he argues that science has reached its 'limits to growth'. While deploring the intrusion of managerial machinery and jargon [accountability, performance indicators, appraisal, efficiency and so on] he recognises and explains the various administrative devices for controlling the number of re-searchers—including the killing off of weak research units in order to enhance the survival of others. A grim but real blueprint!

In all areas of fundamental inquiry this has meant a substan-tial loss of jobs—not so different from what has happened in other walks of life, particularly in areas of the public service. In some fields of research, however, substantial installations, apparatus and research facilities were shut down also, leading to massive upheavals, loss of morale and reduced incentive for people to choose research as a career.

At the same time, we have witnessed a great scarcity of *industrial* money for research, caused by the current ethos of short-term thinking and watching the bottom line (all blamed on economic rationalism—perhaps erroneously). A large number of industrial research laboratories have closed in the last decade, in many Western countries. Not that industry has ever been a great supporter of fundamental research, with a few noble and notable exceptions, (they are too impatient for tangible returns) but the effect was to restrict a possible escape route for 'refugees' from basic science into industrial research.

The problem was compounded by the ending of the Cold War and the curtailment of military funding for research. This happened not only to applied research directed at weapons development, but it also led to very large reductions in support for basic research.

The use of military funds for the support of basic research has a very long history, all the way back to Archimedes and his (possibly apocryphal) 'burning mirrors'. It is characterised by the fact that the military have always been much more patient in waiting for a 'breakthrough' from the basic into the (militarily) useful. Perhaps they had much more money to 'squander' or perhaps they were more prepared to countenance money-no-object solutions to problems. In any case, they have in recent times supported 'blue sky' research in many esoteric areas (even in the general theory of relativity). Some have indeed paid off spectacularly and led to extremely valuable spin-offs in non-military applications, such as the Global Positioning Satellite Navigation System, but that is another story.

So, the 'drying up' of Cold War money, mainly in the USA, although not total, has aggravated the stringencies in many areas, with worldwide repercussions. We see, therefore, a bleak time for fundamental research.

In Australia we have, on top of this, the recent shrinkage of government funding, obliging universities to seek additional funds from fee-paying students, from contract research and from any other means that their beleaguered managers can think of. But the trouble is that none of the proposed solutions to the university funding problem is of much help to the departments which pursue *fundamental* research. *They* are not the ones which are in great demand by fee-paying students, nor are they the ones which attract sizeable industrial funds.

ARE THERE ANY SOLUTIONS?

In sum, it is becoming clear that we have to limit the growth of the fundamental inquiry industry, as much as we have to come to a new equilibrium with educational expenditure. But there is a real danger that we will over-compensate and become a nation of uneducated philistines with a third-rate research capability; or that working conditions in universities will become so unattractive that we will fail to attract first-rate minds into academia. Can we avoid these undesirable outcomes? Are there any solutions?

The British solution to the tertiary education funding gap is, partly, the introduction of a flat tuition fee of £1,000 (ironically by a Labour government), although it is not yet clear whether and how any of this money will be spent on universities. The Deering Report, which was the precursor of this decision, identified a funding shortfall of £350 million in 1998–99 and £565 million the following year. The solution to filling the research funding gap in the UK is quite drastic: whole departments (of Physics, in particular) have been shut down and only a select sub-set of university departments are *allowed to* conduct research (or, to be more precise, receive any research funding)—the rest are supposed to engage in teaching only. The effects of this policy, draconian in its sudden onset, are yet to be evaluated. My great fear is that, as usual, well before its consequences are apparent, the policy will be blindly copied by *our* masters in Canberra, if not by our vice-chancellors, who may yet be cornered into not giving *any of us* any *time*, let alone money, for research. (This being an egalitarian country, we risk having the British Solution imposed on *all* the universities!) Worst of all, the Deering Report leaves the implementation in the hands of Whitehall bureaucrats—they are the ones who will ultimately decide who should be funded to do research.

By way of contrast, let us look at the American solution; it has been in place for a very long time. It is not a centrally or bureaucratically driven solution but rather a Darwinian, evolutionary process. The result is that not all tertiary institutions are engaged in research in the USA: for example the majority of two-year community colleges are not. Not all departments, even in some of the proper universities, award PhDs, so that staff may do research only by way of a hobby. However, I know some very fine scholars who live like that, that is by teaching alone, in their regular jobs, and who do their scholarly work in their own time or during vacations. The good ones among them attach themselves to research groups at rich and successful institutions during the summer vacation and supplement their income as well as indulging in their scholarly hobby. (A less obvious advantage of this *modus vivendi* is that these people are free from the rat-race of research performance appraisal, grantsmanship and so on. From this distance, it is starting to look attractive.)

The Japanese solution is a very interesting one—they are going the other way. For a long time, Japanese researchers (in the sciences, anyway) concentrated on applied science and produced fabulous rewards for their industry. Only in the last few years have they come to the realisation that they cannot live like this indefinitely. In fact they recognise that the reserve of available and exploitable basic science (produced mostly by the West) will run out sometime in the twenty-first Century and hence, in 1995, the Japanese Diet passed (unanimously) a new law, the Science and Technology Basic Law. It guarantees comprehensive funding for basic science in universities, industry, and government research laboratories. In practice, the sudden appearance of sizeable funds has led to a certain amount of wastage and opportunism, but I have no doubt that in the long run the policy will pay off. A similar ethos, for the expansion of basic research, exists in Korea also. I am sure that the irony of its counter-cyclical nature will not have escaped the reader's attention.

The European solution, to the extent that any exists as such, is to form multinational research groupings (with membership determined by peer review) which hand out research funds on a highly competitive basis. The money comes from a central pool filled by national contributions and the net effect is that each nation is shamed or goaded by the others into adequate research spending. This applies only to a fraction of the basic research expenditure of each nation, but it identifies the best and most worthy work in each EU member state. Thus it is not clear to what extent it is a solution to the problem faced by each member nation in their support of all its basic re-searchers and research institutions. Germany, for example, had to be quite ruthless in shutting down inferior institutions in the former East Germany and in retrenching the unproductive or inefficient people on their staff.

In Australia, the nearest to an original solution to the research funding problem is represented by the Cooperative Research Centres (CRCs)—one of the most innovative pieces of science policy to have emerged in recent years. The CRCs have mandatory industry participation, along with government research organisations (such as CSIRO), in joint projects with one or more universities. Although they are aimed mostly at applied research, there is nevertheless scope for undertaking basic inquiry and thus extracting industry support for longer-range, less specifically targeted projects. There should, of course, be more of this kind of thing but not many industries are willing to take a longer-term view. The resource industries are perhaps more easily persuaded, because their activities involve longer horizons. Nevertheless, the CRCs do not contribute greatly to the funding of basic science. On the contrary, their establishment was meant to divert some effort from less productive areas of pure science into more (immediately) valuable applied science. While this has relieved the pressure on the 'basic science' purse to some extent, it has not really solved the problem.

So, in order to solve the funding problem for pure research, or basic inquiry, I am afraid that Australia is likely, as usual, to follow the British model, 'down-sizing' the sector by more and more stringent managerial tactics, involving centralised bureaucratic intervention. Alternatively, we may be forcibly directed towards the American model of reaching the same ends—that is cutting down research—by simply tightening the purse-strings and allowing attrition to occur by 'natural selection'. Either way, British or American, the process is likely to be painful and potentially destructive, especially if carried out too rapidly or taken too far. In the CSIRO the process is almost complete—hardly any pure science is left—and, I am sorry to say, the same trend is visible in many of our universities: pure science is being phased out and many science departments (Physics in particular, as in the UK) are being reduced, amalgamated, destroyed. That this should be the course of action in the erstwhile technical colleges, which were never meant to do research, let alone basic research, may be understandable, if they have no ambitions to rise in academic status. Unfortunately it is happening also in institutions which claim to be proper universities, with all the intellectual pretensions of being 'high quality' universities.

Is this good? Is it necessary? It seems to me that there ought to be an alternative tactic for ameliorating the plight of the fundamental disciplines. Leading universities, such as the University of Melbourne, which do have the potential for raising fees from students undertaking professional courses, or for earning external funds from applied research, could take steps to cross-subsidise the basic disciplines in some sort of equitable way. This would involve undoing the long-standing arrangements of numbers-based funding which, over the last several decades has led the deans of professional faculties to act like robber-barons, tending to enrich their own fiefdoms at the expense of the faculties and departments which foster the basic disciplines.

A fair system of cross-subsidisation, based on the teaching of service courses did exist, once upon a time; it would only need farsighted leadership at the local level to restore it or reinvent it. To do so would not be easy but it might work and might lead to the preservation of one of the greatest glories of the university as an institution: the freedom and the opportunity to pursue fundamental inquiry. After all, what else distinguishes a university from a mere trade school or business college?

CONCLUSION

I do not think there is a conclusion, but let us try a summary. The twin financial problems brought about by universal tertiary education and by the worldwide proliferation of scientific activity both impinge upon the university system. Both are real and both need solutions. The problem of financing mass education at the tertiary level will, perhaps, be solved by the (re-)introduction of tuition fees but in any case it is leading us rapidly towards stratification—towards what I have called the 'stratified national system'.

The 'limits to growth' of scientific research (which arguably applies to all fundamental inquiry) will also result in a stratification of tertiary institutions, only a sub-set of which will be allowed or able to conduct fundamental inquiry—they will be the research universities. The rest will be forced to revert to being teaching institutions (perhaps with a small number of research departments), as was largely the case before the 'binary divide' was suddenly abolished by the Dawkins reforms.

We could hope that it would not be whole institutions but rather individual departments which will be able to (or licensed to) conduct research: clearly it would be fairer. Would the system of peer review cope equitably with the problem of deciding which departments? Could we arrive at a balanced and fair system without government intervention but purely by 'natural selection', as in the USA, or must we suffer from bureaucratic and managerial meddling as in the UK?

And, finally, could an equitable system of cross-subsidisation between faculties or departments be reinvented? This would re-unite universities which are otherwise doomed to be divided into the haves and the have-nots: those who can earn fees and research income by being immediately relevant, and those whose preoccupations are with the long-term, fundamental, cultural, aesthetic values, essential to the future welfare of society but, alas, of no immediate market (or marketable) value.

References

da Solla Price, Derek 1963, *Little Science, Big Science*, Columbia University Press, New York.

Ziman, John 1994, *Prometheus Bound—Science in a Dynamic Steady State*, Cambridge University Press, Cambridge.

• 7 •

Academic autonomy

SEUMAS MILLER

Hybridisation and transmogrification of the university[1]

In this chapter I offer a philosophical exploration of the notion of academic autonomy and its relation to freedom of intellectual inquiry.[2] Academic autonomy is a so-called traditional academic value. Other such values include institutional autonomy, collegial conceptions of governance, academic freedom, tenure and ownership of intellectual property, and the centrality of academics and of academic matters in the life of the university. These values are part and parcel of a particular conception—call it the traditional model—of the university and of the role of the academic. Roughly speaking, according to this model universities have as a purpose the acquisition and dissemination of knowledge, for its own sake as well as for the benefits that such knowledge brings to the wider community. Here knowledge is broadly conceived so to embrace not only information, but also understanding and the skills to acquire information and understanding, including the skills needed by the professions.[3]

It is quite common to hear people say that this traditional conception is outdated and irrelevant, as are its associated values.

My own view is that in fact there is no viable alternative conception to the traditional view as I have described it.

Evidently many universities in the English-speaking world—and certainly in Australia—are being pushed by government, bureaucratic and market forces in the direction of a very different institutional model, namely that of the large bureaucratic business corporation. One argument for this is that universities need to be privatised and corporatised so as to enable them to become more competitive and better able to contribute to the growth of the economy. This kind of argument is open to question on a number of counts. First, while universities have a role in relation to the national interests of the communities which fund them, they have wider supranational purposes, such as the pursuit of knowledge for its own sake, the dissemination of that knowledge internationally and the pursuit of knowledge in the service of human, as opposed to national, needs. Is the cancer or AIDS research undertaken in (say) the US undertaken simply for the good of sufferers who happen to be US citizens? Is research into global warming undertaken by Australians undertaken simply to benefit Australia?

Second, the assumption that corporatisation and privatisation of the universities is in fact ultimately going to assist the economy is extremely doubtful. If the problem is economic competition and growth, surely it must be business organisations (and government economic policy) that are in need of reform.

Third, notwithstanding the rhetoric, many of the recent developments in the higher education sector amount simply to bureaucratisation, rather than the establishment of a set of efficient businesses functioning in a competitive market. This bureaucratisation has taken the form, in part, of ongoing and ever-changing requirements to collect data, contrive mission statements, put in place (often counterproductive) accountability mechanisms, and satisfy bureaucratically defined quality audits. Such initiatives—whatever their initial impact—are now beginning to lead to a loss of genuine efficiency in teaching and research. For one thing, they are resulting in overadministration. For another, the incessant changes in bureaucratic demands on academics breaches the first law of good administration, namely, stability of procedures and processes.

At any rate, thus far the result is the spawning of a hybrid institution comprised of incongruous elements of the bureaucratic corporation on the one hand, and the traditional university on the other. The emergence of this hybrid beast both threatens academic values and generates significant institutional confusion in relation to the appropriate culture, governance and purposes of universities.

Hybridisation also has the effect of transmogrifying—in the sense of magically transforming—academic issues into resource, financial, market and bureaucratic issues. This process is caused by, and in turn contributes to, the shift in the status of academics from autonomous professionals to industrial employees, and the concomitant shift in power from academics to administrators. Transmogrification also contributes to the erosion of academic values. For example, in Australia the undermining of institutional autonomy vis-à-vis government and market forces, taken in conjunction with the weakening of collegial processes and the watering down of academic tenure threatens individual academic autonomy and, therefore, freedom of inquiry in Australian universities.

If hybridisation is problematic, full-blown corporatisation—whatever its short-term economic benefits might be—would signal the death of the university as an institution. On the full-blown corporatisation model, universities transmogrify into business operations training students for jobs and conducting research for business and government. In place of universities we have glorified training colleges servicing the immediate needs of the job market, and research centres doing the bidding of whoever has the money to pay. This conception is both facile and dangerous. It is a conception fixated by short-term economic needs, and utterly bereft of any understanding of the nature and extent of knowledge, the means by which it is acquired and transmitted, or of the importance of knowledge over the long term in the maintenance, reproduction and transformation of societies, and the institutions and individuals that comprise them. The intellectual capital accumulated by generations of classicists, Asianists, physicists, philosophers, scientists, mathematicians, literary writers, historians, linguists and, for that matter, economists—ironically in Australia students are fleeing economics in favour of business courses—is far too important to be surrendered to market forces comprised of the preferences of eighteen-year-olds and the current needs of, for example, the tourist industry.

Those who attack the traditional conception are fond of painting its supporters as Luddites unable to respond to a rapidly changing (and therefore presumably exciting) world. Here, as elsewhere, they are unable to differentiate issues. First, nothing I have said is inconsistent with the notion of a privately funded university. Whether or not an organisation is a university is a matter of its activities, structure, culture and purposes, not its funding source. (Although the structure of funding can under certain conditions have an important impact on the nature of universities.)

Second, supporters of the traditional conception do not need to reject every particular new development that has taken place. There may have been a need to strengthen the accountability of individual academics in relation to their teaching and research performance. Again, the new entrepreneurism has assisted laudable new projects such as, for example, the provision of tertiary education to some occupational groups that need it, and were formerly denied it. More generally, there is, and always has been, a need for interaction between universities and industry, the professions and the wider community. It might be that some parts of some universities had insulated themselves to an unacceptable degree from the wider community, and there was a need to re-invigorate these external relationships.

However, none of these acceptable new developments—as opposed to the unacceptable ones—are inconsistent with the traditional model. For example, initiatives in higher education for police ought to be viewed as a continuation and extension of the traditional role of the university in professional education. Indeed, historically universities have proved themselves immensely flexible, not only in respect of developing education programs for new professions, but also in relation to pursuing research in applied science and technology.

It has to be said that academics are to some extent responsible for the problems, or the extent of the problems that they now confront. In Australia in the face of attacks on institutional autonomy, collegiality, tenure, intellectual property and so on, they seem to have fallen victim to a kind of collective paralysis. They have failed to speak out and failed to mobilise opposition. In some areas of the humanities this is in part the result of an abandonment of these academic values. For example, many postmodernists are contemptuous of academic values such as truth, reason, knowledge and individual academic autonomy (Freadman and Miller 1992; Coady and Miller 1993; Miller 1995).[12]

To an extent academics have failed to rationally address some of the genuine academic issues—as opposed to artificially induced problems, such as competitive neutrality and enterprise bargaining—that confront universities, and one important result has been the transmogrification of these problems into resource, financial and market problems to be dealt with by managers. One such academic issue is redundancies. Whether or not there ought to be redundancies in some areas of the university is in large part an academic issue to do with the academic value and centrality of the area of intellectual inquiry in which redundancies are being proposed. The main effect of financial strictures ought to be to concentrate the collegial minds of universities on what, academically, the most important areas of inquiry, and seek to protect them by, for example, providing them compulsorily to students.

Another related problem concerns research. What ought to be the priority areas for research and how much genuine intellectual progress is being made in these areas? This is a complex academic question which perhaps the collegial decision-making bodies of universities have not adequately addressed in the past, preferring to allow individual academics to go their own way and discipline groups to follow intellectual fashions. It might be that the intellectual specialisation and compartmentalisation resulting from the so-called explosion in knowledge, but also from the pluralist and competition-inducing structure of faculties and departments, might have worked against the possibility of especially large universities (multiversities) dealing adequately with this question. At any rate, the general result is that this important academic issue has been in large part transmogrified into a bureaucratic/competitive market issue. Universities are now busy competing with one another in a race that begins with a frenetic attempt to identify pots of money and second-guess political agendas, and ends with an adjudication based on research dollars won and numbers of publications produced. The important academic task of attempting to determine what sorts of research really need to be done and genuinely assessing intellectual progress has been sidelined.

FREEDOM OF INQUIRY AND KNOWLEDGE AS AN END IN ITSELF

The significance of academic autonomy is relative to a particular conception of the university as an institution, and more specifically, to a particular view of the purpose of universities. As stated above, I do not believe that there is any viable alternative conception to that of the traditional one. To my knowledge none has been propounded which can withstand even the most obvious objections. As argued above, the model of the bureaucratic business corporation is certainly not adequate.

If the fundamental purpose of the university is the acquisition of knowledge for its own sake, as well as the dissemination of that knowledge for the sake of the community, then we need to consider the conditions under which these purposes could be realised. There are two general conditions, namely, freedom of inquiry and publication on the one hand, and intellectual honesty and competence on the other. It is obvious that without intellectual honesty and competence knowledge will not be attained and disseminated. Self-deceivers, liars and epistemological incompetents will not assist in the realisation of so difficult and uncertain a goal as the acquisition of knowledge and its dissemination. What of freedom of intellectual inquiry and publication?

There are two especially salient traditional arguments for

freedom of intellectual inquiry, the first associated with the English philosopher John Stuart Mill, the second (loosely) associated with the German philosopher Immanuel Kant.[4] (I do not mean to imply that these arguments are the only ones advanced by these philosophers, much less that the versions of them I propound below are precise renderings of their work.)

According to Mill, new knowledge will only emerge in a free market place of ideas (Schauer 1981: 16ff). If certain ideas are prevented from being investigated or communicated then the truth is not likely to emerge, since those suppressed ideas may in fact be the true ones. Since universities have as a purpose the acquisition of knowledge, presumably a university must in part consist of a free market place of ideas.

Let us look more closely at this argument, restricting ourselves to ideas in the sense of putative knowledge, for example, hypotheses, unsubstantiated claims, interpretations, theories, requiring a complex process of reasoning and justification—the sort of knowledge pursued in universities. Here Mill appears to rely on a distinction between rational inquiry and justification on the one hand—(a possibly solitary activity)—and freedom of communication on the other. This argument needs to be unpacked. I suggest the following rendering of it.

(1) Freedom of communication is necessary for rational inquiry.
(2) Rational inquiry is necessary for knowledge.
Therefore (3) Freedom of communication is necessary for knowledge.
The argument is valid and premise (2) is plausible in relation to the sort of knowledge pursued at universities. What of premise (1)?
The justification for (1) is evidently that rational inquiry requires: (i) a number of diverse views or perspectives (possessed by different persons and different interest groups); (ii) a substantial amount of diverse evidence for/against these views (available from different sources); (iii) regarding (i) and (ii), there is no single infallible and reliable authority.

Notice that Mill's argument for freedom of inquiry— understood as rational inquiry in a context of freedom of communication—is instrumentalist or means/end in its form. The claim is not that freedom of inquiry is good in itself, but rather that it is a means to another good, namely knowledge. (It is then an open question—as far as Mill's argument is concerned—whether or not knowledge is an intrinsic good, or merely a means to some other good. By contrast, I have already assumed that knowledge is an intrinsic good.) To this extent the moral weight to be attached to freedom of inquiry is weaker than it would be by the lights of an argument which accorded freedom of inquiry the status of an intrinsic good or fundamental moral right.

The second argument for freedom of inquiry is not inconsistent with the first, but is nevertheless quite different. Specifically, it accords freedom of inquiry greater moral weight by treating it as having the status of a fundamental moral right. This second argument—or at least my own neo-Kantian rendering of it—relies on a wider sense of freedom of intellectual inquiry, one embracing not only freedom of thought and reasoning, but also freedom of communication and discussion (Kant 1979: 43ff; Dworkin 1979). The argument begins with the premise that freedom of intellectual inquiry thus understood is a fundamental human right.

Thus conceived, freedom of intellectual inquiry is not an individual right of the ordinary kind. Although it is a right which attaches to individuals, as opposed to groups, it is not a right which an individual could exercise by herself or himself. Communication, discussion and intersubjective methods of testing are social, or at least interpersonal, activities. However, it is important to stress that they are not activities which are relativised to social or ethnic or political groups; in principle, intellectual interaction can and ought to be allowed to take place between individuals irrespective of whether they belong to the same social, ethnic or political group. In short, freedom of intellectual inquiry, or at least its constituent elements, is a fundamental human right. Note that being a fundamental human right it can, at least in principle, override collective interests and goals, including national economic interests and goals.

If freedom of intellectual inquiry is a human right, then like other human rights, such as the right to life and to freedom of the person, it is a right which academics as humans possess along with all other citizens. But how does this bear upon the specific institutional purpose of the university to acquire, transmit and disseminate knowledge? Before we can answer this question we need to be clearer on the relationship between the human right to freely engage in intellectual inquiry on the one hand, and knowledge or truth on the other.

The term 'knowledge', as used in this context, embraces not only information, but also understanding, as noted by several others in this volume. Note also that in order to come to have knowledge in this sense, one must possess rational capacities, that is, capacities that enable not only the acquisition of certain kinds of information, but especially the development of understanding. Here the term, 'rational' is broadly construed. It is not, for example, restricted to deductive and inductive reasoning.

Freedom of intellectual inquiry and knowledge, in this extended sense of knowledge, are not simply related as means to an end, but also conceptually. To freely inquire is to seek the truth by reasoning. Truth is not an external contingently connected end which some inquiries might be directed towards if the inquirer happened to have an interest in truth, rather than, say, an interest in falsity or (à la Derrida) playfulness (Freedman and Miller 1992: ch 5). Rather truth is internally connected to intellectual inquiry. An intellectual inquiry which did not aim at the truth would not be an intellectual inquiry, or at least would be defective *qua* intellectual inquiry. Moreover here, aiming at truth is aiming at truth as an end in itself. (This is not inconsistent with also aiming at truth as a means to some other end.) In other words, an alleged intellectual inquiry which only aimed at truth as a means to some other end would not be an intellectual inquiry or would be defective *qua* intellectual inquiry, since for such a pseudo-inquirer truth would not be internal to his or her activity. Such a pseudo-inquirer is prepared to abandon—and indeed would have in fact abandoned —truth-aiming if, for example, it turns out, or if it had turned out, that the means to his or her end was not after all truth, but rather falsity.[5]

Further, to engage in free intellectual inquiry in my extended sense involving communication with, and testing by, others, is to freely seek the truth by reasoning with others. Intellectual inquiry in this sense is not exclusively the activity of a solitary individual. Moreover, here reasoning is broadly construed to embrace highly abstract formal deductive reasoning at one end of the spectrum and informal (including literary) interpretation and speculation at the other.

There are, of course, methods of acquiring knowledge which do not necessarily, or even in fact, involve free inquiry, for instance, my knowledge that I have a toothache, or my knowledge that the object currently in the foreground of my visual field is a table; but these taken by themselves are relatively unimportant items of knowledge as far as universities are concerned. (Obviously other items of knowledge of the same species can be very important in the context of some intellectual inquiry, for example, an inquiry into whether a recently developed drug eases pain or an inquiry into ordinary perception.)

Given that freedom of intellectual inquiry is a human right, and given the above-described relationship between intellectual inquiry and truth (or knowledge), we can now present our second argument in relation to freedom of intellectual inquiry. This argument in effect seeks to recast the notion of freedom of intellectual inquiry in order to bring out the potential significance for conceptions of the university of the claim that freedom of intellectual inquiry is a human right.

(1) Freedom of intellectual inquiry is a human right.
(2) Freedom of intellectual inquiry is (principally) freedom to seek the truth by reasoning with others.
(3) Freedom to seek the truth by reasoning with others is a fundamental human right.

This section began with the assumption that the university has as its fundamental purpose the pursuit of knowledge, both for its own sake and for the benefits such knowledge brings the wider society. Subsequent discussion has yielded the following additional plausible propositions. First, the kind of knowledge in question is attainable only by reasoning with others. Second, to engage in free intellectual inquiry is to seek truth (or knowledge) for its own sake. Third, freely seeking the truth (or knowledge) for its own sake, and by reasoning with others, is a fundamental human right.

Let us grant the existence of a human right to freely pursue the truth by reasoning with others. What are the implications of this right for universities and for academics' freedom of inquiry?

Given such a right of intellectual inquiry, it is plausible to conclude that the university is simply the institutional embodiment of that moral right. In short, the university is the institutional embodiment of the right to freely seek the truth by reasoning with others.

The notion of an institutional embodiment of a human right is multiply ambiguous.[6] For our purposes here, it is important to distinguish an institutional embodiment of a moral right from an institution such that persons have a right that it be established or a right to be members of it or to have access to it, or both. Perhaps citizens have a right that institutions of criminal justice, including courts of law, be established, and perhaps they have a right that schools be established and right of access once they are established. But I am not claiming that persons or citizens have a right that universities be established, or that once established everyone has a right of access to them, or even that universities ought to be established because they produce a good to which people have a right. What I am claiming is that once a justified decision has been made to embody a moral right institutionally—a decision which is not necessarily based on the existence of a right to have that institution established or a right to the good it produces—then various things follow concerning the nature of that institution. One of the main things that follows is that the exercise of that (institutionally embodied) right by members of that institution ought to be facilitated and given special status and protection, and certainly not allowed to be infringed, either by other members of that institution or by external persons or groups.

At any rate, in the case of the institutional embodiment of

the right of free intellectual inquiry there are at least four claims that seem warranted. First, universities have been established as centres wherein independence of intellectual inquiry is maintained. This flows from the proposition that the university is an institutional embodiment of the moral *right* of the inquirers to freely undertake their intellectual inquiries. Universities are not, for example, research centres set up to pursue quite specific intellectual inquiries determined by their external funders. Nor should particular inquiries undertaken by academics at universities be terminated on the grounds that some external powerful group, say government, might not find the truths discovered in the course of these inquiries politically palatable.

Second, the free pursuit of intellectual inquiry is not simply a right for academics, but also a duty. This follows from the fact that the university has been established to ensure that the right to intellectual inquiry is actually realised in practice. Failure to exercise this right would eventually lead to an inability to exercise it. The right would then cease to exist in any meaningful sense.

Third, universities must have a teaching function to enable the preservation, not only of knowledge, but of the activity of free intellectual inquiry. In so far as students go on to become academics, then knowledge and intellectual inquiry are preserved.

Fourth, universities have a duty to transmit intellectual skills and values to the wider community, and also to disseminate scholarship and research to that community. Intellectual inquiry is not only a human right, it is an activity which produces external benefits. For example, knowledge is a means to other goods, including economic wellbeing. Accordingly, and notwithstanding the rights of academics to freely inquire, it is reasonable that, *qua* community supported institutions, universities take on an obligation to ensure that their intellectual activities have a flow-through effect to the wider community in terms of such external benefits. In so far as students enter the wider community as, for example, members of the professions, the wider community benefits from knowledge and at least some of the methods and values of intellectual inquiry.

Again, dissemination of research has obvious benefits to the community, including economic benefits.

On the view of the university under consideration, interference in the process of the free pursuit of knowledge in universities strikes at one of the fundamental purposes for which universities have been established. Such interference could not be justified, for example, on the grounds that whereas free inquiry might be necessary for the acquisition of knowledge in many instances, in some particular instance free inquiry was not leading to knowledge, and therefore in this case free inquiry could be interfered with without striking at the basic purposes of the university as an institution. To this extent the neo-Kantian argument affords greater protection of freedom of inquiry than does Mill's market place of ideas argument.

Moreover, the university, in so far as it pursues this purpose, can so pursue it, even if so doing is inconsistent with the collective goals and interests of the community or government. In this respect the right of intellectuals to pursue the truth is akin to the right of the judiciary to pursue justice even in the face of conflicting collective goals and interests, including the national interest. The *Mabo* decision of the High Court of Australia to uphold certain land rights of Australian Aboriginals might prove not to be in Australia's national economic interest. But in so far as judges were entitled as a matter of law and justice to recognise native title, then they were entitled to make the decision that they made. Similarly, Australian academics researching political or ethical issues in, say, China or Indonesia have a right to publish that research notwithstanding the damage it might do to present diplomatic relations and economic prospects. This is not to say that there might not arise some contingency, such as war, which would override the duty of an academic to speak the truth. But such contingencies are extraordinary. They do not form part of the day-to-day economic and political problems confronted by a wealthy democracy in the late twentieth century.

We also saw, above, that academics do not simply have a right to freely inquire, they have a duty to do so. In accepting an academic position a person accepts an obligation to the fundamental purpose of the university as an institution, and the purpose of universities is free inquiry. The duty to freely inquire has certain implications. For one thing, it will entail maintenance of an appropriate level of competence in the disciplinary area in question; and if for some reason an academic is no longer capable, psychologically or otherwise, of free inquiry in the disciplinary area in question then they ought not to draw the salary provided for this purpose.

For another thing, this duty to freely inquire generates the further obligation to preserve knowledge and reproduce the rational capacities necessary for the preservation and extension of knowledge. In the final analysis, academics have an obligation to preserve, for example, Classics as a field of study.

And this duty to freely inquire brings with it the justification for certain kinds of institutional accountability mechanisms to ensure that this duty is satisfactorily discharged.

Importantly, academics not only have a right to inquire into, also to discuss and communicate, certain possibly controversial or otherwise difficult issues, they have a duty to do so. The analogy with the judiciary is again relevant. In relation to the *Mabo* decision the High Court judges not only had a right to make the decision that they made, but also a duty to do so, given that the specific decision made was the one dictated by law and by justice. Again, academics inquiring into political or ethical issues in relation to Indonesia and China not only have a right, but also a duty, as Edward Said puts it, to 'speak the truth to power' (Said 1994). The fundamental obligation of academics is to the truth, as opposed to its consequences, as the fundamental obligation of judges is to justice and the law, and not to economic or other consequences. Moreover, in so far as consequences need to be taken into account, it is not the business of academics to give overriding weight to the interests of their country, or their community, or, indeed, their university. Certainly, it is not the business of academics to discount the human rights of the East Timorese, or incarcerated Chinese dissidents, or for that matter, the interests of members of other nations in a clean environment or, in the case of the Pacific

Islanders, the preservation of coastal towns from rising sea waters.

Even if freedom of intellectual inquiry for academics is the institutional embodiment of a basic human right, the corresponding right for academics is somewhat specialised and raises a host of problems centring around the relationship of the individual academic to the university institution in which he or she is housed, the disciplinary group to which he or she belongs, and of course to the wider community. What is in question here is by no means simply the relatively individualistic notion of free intellectual inquiry that might be characteristic of the ordinary citizen in her or his community or even of the intellectual existing in a community outside a university or like institutional context. Specifically, the right and duty of freedom of intellectual inquiry in universities immediately raises more detailed issues of so-called academic autonomy, and academic freedom. To some of these I now turn.

ACADEMIC AUTONOMY

Freedom of intellectual inquiry among academics is a central element of academic autonomy. Academic autonomy also comprises the institutional autonomy of universities.

Autonomy is a philosophically problematic concept, and indeed an essentially contested one, as is its species, academic autonomy.[7] However, there are four relatively uncontroversial things that need to be said about autonomy—including both institutional autonomy and individual intellectual autonomy— relevant to our purposes here.

First, the existence of autonomy depends in part on independence from external control. So, in the case of the intellectual autonomy of an individual, this requires (at least) the absence of unjustifiable customs, laws and ideologies of a kind or prevalence that an individual could not reasonably be expected to resist. It would also require the absence of other individuals possessed of powers of control in respect of an individual which that individual could not reasonably be expected to resist. The latter might include powers of psychological intimidation or of indoctrination.

In the case of the autonomy of an institution, the requirement would be the absence of external coercion or undue influence, including certain forms of financial influence. Obviously, during the Nazi or Eastern European communist periods universities lacked institutional autonomy by virtue of the coercive forces deployed by governments to ensure that they taught particular subjects. Again, the use of control at a distance by administrative mechanisms, such as those which ensure that research funds provided to publicly funded universities are for government-specified purposes only, is inconsistent with institutional autonomy in respect of research. A related kind of mechanism for control at a distance is one which devolves responsibility while maintaining control of funding. An example of this is enterprise bargaining in publicly funded Australian universities at this time.

Second, autonomy consists in part in the presence of various internal features. In particular, the autonomous intellect has the capacity and will to pursue truth by reasoning. Institutional autonomy consists in part in the possession of structures and procedures for collective decision-making that are both coherent with one another and rational in the light of the purposes of the institution. The process of hybridisation mentioned above might tend to erode the autonomy of universities. For such hybridisation tends to generate internal institutional incoherence. This incoherence is twofold. First, there can be an increasing lack of fit between university structures and procedures of governance on the one hand, and their institutional purposes on the other. Putting it simply, traditional collegial structures and processes can become emasculated, and universities can come to adopt more hierarchical top-down bureaucratic structures and processes. But the latter are inimical to the fundamental institutional purposes of universities; purposes such as free inquiry. Second, there can be an incoherence and increasing tension between the collegial structures within universities and the more hierarchical bureaucratic structures. Therefore, institutional autonomy is at risk.

Third, and relatedly, autonomy consists in part in the capacity and will to seek truth by reasoning in relation to one's own purposes, ends, dispositions, character and so on. In short, the autonomous agent is self-reflective in a manner that is both preservative and re-invigorating of the valuable features of the self, but also potentially self-transformative. By analogy, institutions are not fully autonomous unless they are collectively self-reflective in relation to their purposes, structure, culture and activities. Such institutional self-reflection is necessary to ensure that what is good and important is preserved and re-energised, but also to enable desirable transformation.

Fourth, individual autonomy presupposes an enabling framework of social forms, including conventions of language, accepted moral norms, and so on. For example, an individual person cannot think other than in a language; and cannot communicate other than in a community which adheres to moral principles of truth-telling and of trust.

Freedom of intellectual inquiry presupposes an even richer enabling framework of conventions and norms, such as those governing the acquisition and testing of putative knowledge. Disciplined conformity to procedures of testing, including peer analysis and criticism, and repetition of experiments by others, far from undermining free intellectual inquiry of the sophisticated kind undertaken in universities, is a condition for its existence. Daydreaming unmotivated by truth, but only by pleasure, is not free intellectual inquiry.

Once again, by analogy with individual autonomy, institutional autonomy presupposes an enabling framework of social forms and moral norms and especially a framework of other institutions. This framework of other institutions has an enabling role with respect to a given institution. For example, universities function, whether autonomously or otherwise, within a framework of other institutions such as schools, the legal and economic system, and so on.

Having thus characterised in general terms the concept of autonomy, and the conditions for its existence, with special reference to both institutional autonomy and individual freedom of intellectual inquiry, I want now to say something about the relationship between these, and the special threats to individual freedom of intellectual inquiry posed by particular social, political and university environments. In what follows there is a presupposition that the necessary background framework of socio-intellectual and institutional forms—referred to above as the fourth condition for both individual autonomy and institutional autonomy (respectively)—are in place.

Let me first introduce a quote from the scientist-cum-philosopher Michael Polanyi:

> The existing practice of scientific life embodies the claim that freedom is an efficient form of organisation. The opportunity granted to mature scientists to choose and pursue their own problems is supposed to result in the best utilisation of the joint efforts of all scientists in a common task. In other words: if the scientists of the world are viewed as a team setting out to explore the existing openings for discovery, it is assumed that their efforts will be efficiently coordinated if only each is left to follow his own inclinations. It is claimed in fact that there is no other efficient way of organising the team, and that any attempts to co-ordinate their efforts by directives of a superior authority would inevitably destroy the effectiveness of their cooperation. (Polanyi 1951: 34)

Polanyi's point is that each acts freely and independently, but does so, first, on the basis of the work of past (in this case) scientists, and second, with constant reference and adjustment to the work of other scientists. He emphasises the importance of individual freedom in a context of interdependence (not simply dependence). While this description is brief, and there are no doubt differences between scientists and other academics, it is a useful general characterisation of how high quality academic work typically proceeds.

Given this characterisation, and in the light of our discussion of autonomy, what can now be said about the relationship between autonomy and individual freedom of inquiry, and the ways in which they are or can be threatened? The first point is that an oppressive or unduly interfering institutional environment—whether in the form of the university's administrative or academic hierarchy (oppressive structure), or in the form of peers (oppressive culture), or both—has the potential to undermine freedom of inquiry, and hence the possibility of attaining knowledge. Academics confront enemies from within the universities, as well as without.

The second point is that the existence of an oppressive and unduly interfering internal university environment is very often brought about, or at least in part sustained, by the university's own lack of institutional autonomy vis-à-vis government or other external organisations. For example, in the recent experience of many Australian universities governmental interventionist policies have themselves triggered (usually successful) attempts on the part of senior administrators to more tightly control the activities of academics.

The third and consequent point is that freedom of inquiry is threatened in a university which itself has (1) little institutional autonomy vis-à-vis government or business (or both); (2) (a) a hierarchical non-collegial internal structure or oppressive internal culture, or both; and (b) limited protections for individual academics and for their control over their work, including weak forms of academic tenure, and lack of control of the dissemination of their work as a result of the undermining of ownership of intellectual property.

The above argument concerns itself with threats to academics' freedom of intellectual inquiry (and protection against those threats), irrespective of whether those threats emanate from within or without the university.

However, as the discussion of autonomy indicated, the removal of threats to freedom of inquiry is not sufficient for the exercise of the wider notion of individual academic autonomy. The conditions for freedom of inquiry are necessary if an academic is to possess individual academic autonomy, but they are not sufficient. In order to generate sufficient conditions we need to at least consider certain further conditions that we earlier described as internal. These features are both individual and institutional in character.

The first point to be made is that the preservation of the institutional autonomy of universities requires consistent university policies, stable administrative structures and procedures, and decision-making which serves the purposes of the institution. In the absence of such internal institutional features academics will be unable to adequately undertake their teaching and research roles.

These internal institutional features are not simply administrative in nature. There is a need for coherence in relation to the subjects to be taught and the areas to be researched, and indeed, at the university level, in relation to the disciplines to be established. This situation calls for collective rational reflection, negotiation and (finally) agreement on the part of the knowledgeable via collegial structures. In relation to the establishment or maintenance of disciplines, decision-making needs not only to be collectively rational in the narrow sense of realising existing purposes and meeting coordination requirements, it also needs to be (collectively) critically self-reflective. For example, it should take place in part on the basis of judgements as to the foundational disciplines or skills or knowledge, such as (in my view) linguistic communication, literature, critical reasoning, ethics, history, mathematics and general science.

The second point is that individual academics need to possess not only the relevant intellectual competence, but also the appropriate intellectual moral virtues, including intellectual honesty, scholarly diligence, the will to pursue the truth in the face of intellectual fashion and ideology, and so on.

Moreover, academics need to be critically self-reflective in relation to their intellectual work lest they fall into one or other of the twin traps of what might be termed 'active ossification' on the one hand, or of 'trivial technicality' on the other. The state of active ossification is when academics continue with their scholarly or research work, but do so in a cocoon of their own making which the rest of the intellectual world has long since passed by. By contrast, the state of trivial technicality is often achieved by researchers who are 'on the cutting edge' of some line of inquiry, but unfortunately it is an inquiry that is fundamentally trivial.

The third, and consequent, point is that in the absence of

both sets of institutional and individual internal features, it is unlikely that academics will vigorously and competently pursue significant intellectual inquiries. If so, the fundamental purposes of the university will not be realised, notwithstanding the existence of conditions of free inquiry.

Notes

1. This first section of this article is a much shortened version of my 'The Transmogrification of Values', *Meanjin* vol. 56 nos. 3&4 1997.
2. Two useful collections on this and related issues are: Edmund L. Pincoffs (ed.), *The Concept of Academic Freedom*, University of Texas Press, Austin, 1975; and Richard T. De George, *Academic Freedom and Tenure: Ethical Issues*, Rowman and Littlefield, New York, 1997.
3. This view is more or less that proferred by John Henry Newman in his famous work, *The Idea of a University* (any edition) which is also discussed in chapter 1. See also Karl Jaspers, *The Idea of the University*, Peter Owen, London, 1960, and also Jaroslav Pelikan, *The Idea of the University: A Reexamination*, Yale University Press, New Haven, 1992; Tony Coady and Seumas Miller, 'Australian Higher Education and the Relevance of Newman', *Australian Universities' Review*, 36 (2), 1993.
4. J. S. Mill *On Liberty* (any edition) and Immanuel Kant, *Groundwork of the Metaphysics of Morals* (any edition) and *The Conflict of the Faculties*, trans. Mary J. Gregor, Abaris, New York, 1979.
5. For this kind of point see Michael Dummett, *Frege: The Philosophy of Language*, Duckworth, London, 1973, ch. 10, 'Assertion'.
6. For one account of the manner in which the university as an institution embodies intellectual values by way of what he calls constitutive rules, see John Searle, 'Two Concepts of Academic Freedom' in Pincoffs (ed.) op.cit.
7. See, for example, Gerald Dworkin, *The Theory and Practice of Autonomy*, Cambridge University Press, Cambridge, 1988.

References

Coady, Tony and Miller, Seumas 1993, 'The Humanities Without Humans', *Meanjin* 52 (2).

Dworkin, Ronald 1979, 'Academic Freedom', *Philosophical Papers* viii (1).

Freadman, Richard and Miller, Seumas 1992, *Rethinking Theory: A Critique of Contemporary Literary Theory and an Alternative Account*, Cambridge University Press, Cambridge.

Kant, Immanuel 1979, *The Conflict of the Faculties*, Abaris, New York.

Miller, Seumas 1995, 'Postmodernism and its Influence on the Humanities', in David Myers (ed.) *Re-Inventing the Humanities: International Perspectives*, Australian Scholarly Publishing, Melbourne.

Polanyi, Michael 1951, *The Logic of Liberty: Reflections and Rejoinders*, Routledge and Kegan Paul, London.

Said, Edward 1994, *Representations of the Intellectual: The 1993 Reith Lectures*, Lecture V, 'Speaking Truth to Power', Vintage, London.

Schauer, Frederick 1981, *Free Speech: A Philosophical Inquiry*, Cambridge University Press, Cambridge.

· 8 ·

Blurred visions

JANET McCALMAN

Forty years ago the Humanities Research Council published
the first review of the humanities in Australia (Price 1959);
and the Academy of the Humanities has just published the
second—its strategic review of humanities research for the Australian Research Council. The current strategic review under the
leadership of Emeritus Professor Anthony Low decided that
it was time to take stock, to see how far we have come in the
four decades since that first review and since the Murray Report
of 1957.

It's an historical perspective we sorely needed, for it brought
home not that there has been a *renaissance* in Australian scholarship and high culture, but that there has been a *naissance*.
Australia had produced distinguished scholars by the 1950s, but
their distinction was largely acquired overseas, characteristically
in England, and few of them had established 'schools' in Australian universities which had become intellectual powerhouses.
The 1955 review discussed research in just seven fields, listed
('characteristically for its day', notes Anthony Low) in the order
of Classical Studies and Archaeology, English, Modern European
Languages, Philosophy, History, History of Art, Oriental and
Pacific Studies. As Anthony Low has commented, there was no

mention of anything Australian under Archaeology, 'Oriental Studies' was nothing like modern Asian Studies, 'Pacific Studies' was the lone area studies, Visual and Performing Arts comprised only Music and the History of Art; and of course there were no Women's Studies, Gender Studies, Cultural Studies, Media and Communications Studies or Postcolonial Studies (Low et al. 1998: vol. 1, 9–10).

What is equally important is that all seven disciplines of the 1950s had scarcely any Australian content: no Australian litera-ture, rudimentary Australian history, no Australian art, little philosophy directly drawn from the moral issues engaging the Australian people, no Oriental or Pacific Studies which assumed Australia to be an oriental continent sitting between the Indian and Pacific Oceans. And if you scanned a bookshop or a local library you would find no Australian scholar, apart perhaps from Walter Murdoch and W. K. Hancock, who was being read by ordinary readers. In the schools there were few Australian texts for senior students; in the universities, scarcely any educational texts in any subject were by Australian authors and published in this country.

Even from the time that I was an undergraduate student in the late 1960s, there has been a growth in serious Australian writing, both fiction and non-fiction, and in Australian schol-arship that one could scarcely imagine possible thirty years ago. This, of course, has extended far outside the universities: to writing, film and all branches of the performing and visual arts. So much of Australia's high culture has been the product of just the last three decades. And taking a leading part in the great national conversation about what we have been, what we are now and where we may be going, have been humanities scholars. Our national cultural life has been transformed and the universities have played an essential part in that transformation.

They have done so not only as producers of scholars but also in the creation of a critical audience for high cultural production. The explosion of Australian writing, both scholarly and creative, has found a ready audience, for Australians are among the keenest book readers in the world. More Australians read for pleasure than play or go to watch competitive sport.

The post-war expansion of secondary and tertiary education has equally expanded the cultural consumer market. On trains, on beaches—everywhere there are people reading books, many of them demanding books and many of them Australian books.

And if you look at the candidates for ARC fellowships, as I did for three years as a member of the Research Training and Careers Committee, you see there also an extraordinary intellectual achievement: we are producing outstanding scholars in a spectacular range of disciplines. Not only are there the literary scholars, historians and brilliant young philosophers that you would expect, but we are still producing stunning classical scholars, historians of all sorts who can read Thai, classical Chinese and Japanese, old Javanese and Burmese; anthropologists who can work in languages which few outside those cultures know; cultural studies scholars who can hold their own at Berkeley and in Chicago; music scholars, art scholars; world-class linguistics scholars across the full range of world language groups including the Aboriginal, Indo-Pacific and Austronesian languages of our own region. And there are still outstanding Medievalists and early modernists, young people with a suite of classical and ancient European languages. The archaeologists work from Latin America, throughout our region, to outstanding research in the Middle East and the Mediterranean. Australian archaeologists in New Guinea and the Fertile Crescent are leading players in the theorising of the evolution of agricultural civilisations. I list these because not only have these early career academics mastered their primary discipline, but they have mastered new and difficult languages, technical skills and extra-academic expertise of high quality. They are so very good, and yet many of them have little future in university life.

What is also significant is the geographical range of their work. A striking theme in the 1955 review was the tyranny of distance, the sense of isolation from the places 'over there': the UK, Europe and the USA, where real intellectual life went on. Not so now. Australia provides for most of its intellectuals a rich and stimulating base, and cheaper air travel and email have brought the international university world to our doorstep. The cultural time-lag has shortened markedly. Now we can relish the advantages of being a small country of small importance, for our intellectual life is not swallowed up by parochial self-absorption; our own culture does not consume most of our energies; we are in fact able to be more international and cosmopolitan than the Americans or the British or the French. And we can now draw on our own multicultural resources. All this makes Australia a great place to live and work.

The result is that Australian humanities scholars are among the leading earners of international academic repute for this country. As the international citations fall for our scientists, Australian humanities scholars in philosophy, linguistics, archaeology, medieval and classical studies, early modern studies, British historical and literary studies, American and Latin American history, cultural studies, gender studies, anthropology and especially Asian Studies, are in the front rank internationally. Even some who work on Australian history attract international repute, but this substantial international reputation has largely been built at a distance from the sources of the subject. Moreover, increasingly the postgraduate training has been obtained in Australian institutions. Fewer and fewer outstanding students now make the Oxbridge pilgrimage.

So what have been the conditions which have enabled Australian letters and Australian scholarly life to come of age? They have not just come out of the air like some sort of cultural El Niño effect. When you look closely at who has done what, and where and when, it is clear that the *naissance* happened because money was spent on certain strategic institutions. And it is by looking as these that we can assess the nature of our present plight.

First the Australian National University. It is fashionable to criticise the ANU, especially the Institute of Advanced Studies, and while state universities pursue the perfectly legitimate goal of becoming world-class research universities, we do need to remember that this country already has one: except that it is being strangled financially. But it is all the more worthwhile asking where Australian scholarship would have been without the ANU. Without it we would not have done what we have in economic history, in federal law, in archaeology, in Asian studies, in development economics or in demography. The disciplinary boundaries have moved onwards, but the forced association of traditional humanities and social sciences in the two research schools speeded up the lateral thinking of inter-disciplinary work decades before the older universities would themselves have got round to it. The stream of international visitors during the 1960s and 1970s through the Coombs Building in Canberra could not be matched by any other Australian campus. It became a great university because for a time it had the money to be one: its postgraduates were the most fortunate in the land, studying under world-class conditions. Fieldwork was generously supported; there was money for projects and collections. There was money for people to be given the chance to innovate and create: you could go to the Vice-Chancellor with a big idea, and if good enough, it would be supported. In 1964 the ANU produced fully 50 per cent of the nation's PhDs in humanities and social sciences. And it was ANU-trained scholars who built Asian studies and archaeology and anthro-pology in universities all over Australia in the 1970s and 1980s (Foster and Varghese 1996).

The new universities of the 1960s and 1970s have been another institutional source of this explosion of activity and talent. These were the fruits of what Hugh Stretton called 'the noble revolution', the result of the Menzies government's moral courage in implementing everything the Murray Report recom-mended. The young and the brave, and often very bright, formed the new faculties. Much of what they did, they did in reaction to the sandstone universities which had trained them. Many became outstanding at undergraduate teaching, often because they had to work harder with their students, often because they were not of the older establishment themselves and were scholarship people who had been school teaching before entering academic life. In research they went into new areas, were more daring, and often overtook the older depart-ments. The La Trobe History department has had more prize-winning and internationally renowned scholars on its staff than any other in Australia, and than many in England or the USA. Some of those 1960s and 1970s universities, however, have lost their edge because the young staff stayed until they were venerable, and the money for new recruits dried up.

But there was a third generation of universities—the Dawkins universities of the 1980s; and here again the institutions formed from old inner-city technical colleges or in culturally deprived outer urban or regional areas, where no university had ever been before, in some cases became intellectual power-houses: the University of Technology, Sydney, the University of Western Sydney, James Cook University, to name the obvious ones. From the ARC vantage point you see wonderful scholars all over the country, and you realise that the centre of gravity is not in Sydney or Melbourne, no matter how vibrant and active they now are. A tiny English department like that at the Australian Defence Force Academy is outstanding in scholarly editing and Australian literary studies. Macquarie University is the national leader in dictionary and reference work, not Melbourne or Sydney Universities, despite their traditions and library collections. Macquarie is also a national leader in classical and ancient textual studies.

All of these things—things which earn this country substantial international standing and which do feed into the wider culture—have depended on people having real, safe jobs, and the time and support to be daring and take risks. They have needed time from teaching, money to travel overseas, research assistance, equipment and, above all, the infrastructure of library collections. The safety and security are not to be underrated. There is a relationship between the waning of the Cold War, at least in Australia after 1972, and the expansion of intellectual life. Many academics on the Left were cautious during the fifties and early sixties; the Menzies government might have valued universities and been putting money into them for the first time in Australian history, but there was a climate of fear for those on the Left. If academics contributed to the women's movement, gay liberation and the growing pluralism of Australian life, they also were direct beneficiaries of it. Security of tenure gave scholars both freedom from fear of persecution for their ideas and the time to reflect and be creative.

New creative work also depends on the entry into academic

life of new creative people—young people coming from all sectors of the Australian community and from overseas. It depends on creative people being able to move in and out of university employment at odd periods of their lives: entering in their fifties; leaving in their thirties to come back later; going elsewhere for a couple of years; changing institution or discipline or department. But above all, there was time. Study leave could be for up to a year. Teaching loads were lighter. There were more tutors, fewer research students to supervise. Most of all there were fewer meetings. And fewer conferences, fewer demands, fewer deadlines, fewer expectations. It was safe to have a fallow time: to dry up for five years, provided you went on with your teaching. It was possible to sit down and rewrite a manuscript which had turned out not as you wanted, or which had been made out of date by a new archival find. It was possible to justify your scholarly existence with one very good, big book for your career. It was possible to be simply a good teacher. Of course, there were people who did not justify their salaries, but that happens everywhere, even in governments and private enterprise.

Australians and their universities have a great deal to thank Sir Robert Menzies for. He may not have liked left-wing academics, but he did understand what made good universities and that good universities were vital to the nation's wellbeing both culturally and economically. It is a tragedy that his successors have lost their nerve. Just at the time we are being transformed from a country that rode on the sheep's back to one whose future depends on the brains of its people, we are governed by a political élite from both sides of politics which fundamentally distrusts academics and dislikes much of what they do. Labor may pay lip service to the importance of education, but in government successive ministers responsible for tertiary education and research have betrayed a hostility to universities as sources of alternative power and criticism. Labor ministers were just as reluctant as later Coalition ministers to sign off on research funding which was outside their control and for projects they could not understand. Universities were seen to be unaccountable, indulgent and wasteful on the one hand and bastions of élitism on the other: they had to be humbled and refashioned to fulfil a new democratic, rather than a meritocratic, mission.

Labor's successors have an even harsher agenda. Universities, along with the arts community, the 'alternative' society and the bureaucracy, were seen by then as subversive and wasteful parasites on the hard-working tax payer. These 'parasites' were the most strident voices of Labor's bandwagon: the non-producers who lived off the businesses and farms which were the real producers. 'These people' were free-loading, making comfortable livings doing 'research' which more often than not confirmed, and restated in impenetrable language, the obvious. They were a Labor-voting parasite middle class whose wealth and power depended on the state. 'Research' for many Coalition ministers became a dirty word to be expunged from documents and programs. The only 'research' that made sense was applied research that transformed science into products and tangibles: pure research was mostly a waste of Australian time and money.

This very real hostility to research and its needs has now reached a crisis. The federal bureaucracy, like the government it advises, has long resented the universities, again as sources of criticism and alternative power and influence. Even though the administration of the nation's leading research programs through the Australian Research Council and the National Health and Medical Research Council has been cost-efficient by international standards, there is a significant body of opinion in the bureaucracy which wishes to divest the Commonwealth of its role in the national research effort. The administrative gains from giving universities block grants are seen to outweigh the intellectual and national gains of retaining a competitive system monitored by international peer review. That intellectual standards must fall, and nepotism within institutions must increase, matters not, let alone that Australia's reputation among the researching nations of the world will be gravely compromised.

This is not to deny that governments of democratic states at the end of the twentieth century face a fearsome funding crisis: they are running out of the tax income to sustain the welfare state as it has evolved since the Second World War.

But in withdrawing from funding education and research, as both sides of politics have since the late 1980s, they are choking off Australia's most important means of growth and survival. Our economy increasingly will depend on endogenous growth generated by our own intellectual capital, yet we are forcing universities to turn to private funding which is too often capricious and self-serving. Of course, private corporations have to be capricious and self-serving: that is the nature of commerce. They cannot be asked by society to be entirely disinterested, for if they do not put their shareholders first, they will not survive. They cannot be expected to expend vast sums of money without some tangible benefit to themselves; they cannot be required to invest in social institutions with the same moral commitment as must the state. Why should they be called upon now to supply the social goods which are really the business of the people?

Universities likewise are of the people and of the world rather than of private business. Their focus is on the distant future, not this year's bottom line; their responsibility is to the training of fine and professional minds for the world to come and to pursue the pure knowledge that will make the applied possible. Certainly they have responsibilities to the here and now, and applied knowledge is within their brief; but their ultimate responsibility is to the pure knowledge and the training for the long run. Therefore they inevitably look like 'bad investments' which bear little immediate result; and their infrastructure costs seem to grow exponentially. But such investments do pay, and have paid handsomely in this country over the past forty years. Nonetheless, the universities have been called to account; required to submit to the disciplines and preoccupations of the commercial world. They too must become 'competitive', not in the old intellectual sense, but in the new business sense.

I scarcely need to describe the corporatisation of the university which has undercut all those basic securities and decencies which gave creative people the space, both physical and mental, to do good work. Yet the sheer pressure of competitive intellectual production in this era of bench-marking, peer review, student satisfaction surveys, research quantums and constant insecurity has seen an apparent increase in productivity. At the same time there has been an increase in personnel: a net increase in the number of fine minds fighting for the same, tiny, shrinking, fickle space in the sun. And we need to start asking about the quality of the work that rushes from conference to conference, from grant application to grant application, that is driven by fear and ambition rather than intellectual curiosity and passion.

But these are matters that can be changed. What is far graver in the long term is the decline of the national research infrastructure in our libraries. That was the other institutional driving force behind our national cultural *naissance*. Until the 1950s, we had lived off the vision and generosity of the nineteenth-century creators of libraries, above all Victoria's extraordinary State library. Only Sydney University developed a great library; Melbourne came very late to investing in a respectable facility and to commence its collection-building. Again, government money, especially visionary money which built the National Library of Australia and funded it so that it could purchase key collections, changed everything. And the funding of specialist libraries at the ANU built collections that had not existed anywhere else in Australia before. But as we approach the end of the century, only a handful of university libraries are buying widely, and not one state library is building its collection adequately. The decision of the National Library to no longer be a universal library, but to concentrate only on Australia and its region, means that not one library in the country is building a comprehensive collection, or taking every significant serial. If the ARC were strict and adhered to the rules about research environment, only a minority of Australian universities would have the library resources to support postgraduate students, fellowships and large grant projects and therefore be eligible for ARC funding. The costs of library collections and information technology are rising exponentially and not one institution is placed to fund and provide for the long-term future a library able to support world-class research. The cuts which have already come mean that great gaps are now appearing in our collections, gaps that can never be repaired, gaps which will only get wider. The electronic library is not going to solve these problems: it is only creating new ones. Just as our electronic needs are growing, more books are being published in the English language than ever before in human history. We will need to be inventive and bold to make a Distributed National Collection work and we will need to be very smart with our electronic facilities. And we will still need to find the cash and the will to defend and build great collections and archives.

We also face an immediate crisis in the escalating costs of scholarly publications. New copying and disseminating technology threatened the financial viability of traditional print publishing, so that those who were placed internationally to retaliate have done so. Academic journal publishers have universities worldwide by the throat, demanding crippling subscriptions and embargoes on electronic access to compensate for the increasing loss of control over copyright in the electronic and photocopying age. Australia, and other nations whose currencies have deteriorated, have been acutely affected, and in just two years our library collections have declined even further so that in many centres of learning, world-class teaching and research are no longer possible. Publishers and libraries have also reacted savagely to the explosion of print and electronic teaching materials by charging exorbitant reproduction fees. Universities are retaliating by seeking to claim ownership of all their staff's intellectual property. This includes literary copyright, which has hitherto always resided in the author as a moral right and bulwark of intellectual freedom. Loss of literary copyright can only accelerate the brain drain which is already evident: in 1998, six of the leading scholars in mind in this essay have taken prestigious appointments overseas, ranging across cultural studies, social theory, anthropology, ethics and Asian history. Neither can we hope to replace them with other leading scholars if we cannot assure outstanding minds that they will still own their own words.

Great learning has never come out of thin air, but out of talented people being given the intellectual space and institutional support to work to their full capacity. Everything that our high culture has achieved since the Second World War came about because a handful of people had a vision and the will and courage to make their vision happen. The founders of the Australian National University had a vision of a great national university which would transform the research life of the nation and which would explore the recent developments in science and the formal knowledge of human relationships to help solve the world's problems. The Murray Report had a vision which convinced a conservative and suspicious government to invest generously in Australia's intellectual and cultural future. The founders of the National Library had a vision that this country had a unique responsibility to build a world-class research collection not just for itself but for its region. The Australia Council and the Whitlam government had a vision that the creative arts could not flourish in this small, geographically dispersed country without direct subsidy both to creative work and publishing. The framers of Australian Research Council had a vision that world-class research came only through world-class funding and international peer review. And in every case, that vision in time produced outstanding scholarship, writing, and creative work which has enriched both us and the outside world.

References

Foster, S. G. and Varghese, Margaret 1996, *The Making of the Australian National University,* Allen & Unwin, Sydney.

Low, Anthony et al. 1998, *Knowing Ourselves and Others: The Humanities in Australia into the 21st Century,* 3 vols, Australian Research Council, Canberra.

Price, A. Grenfell 1959, *The Humanities in Australia,* Angus and Robertson (for the Australian Humanities Research Council), Sydney.

· 9 ·

Competition and collegiality

JUDITH BRETT

Government policy toward higher education over the past decade or so has been influenced by the belief that exposing the institutions within the sector to increased competitive pressure will enhance the efficiency and productivity of the sector in various ways. This has been in line with the general neo-liberal reform agenda in which governments attempt to create competitive markets for the distribution of various social goods by devolving power and choice to self-managing individuals or institutions, while at the same tightly controlling the terms in which this power and choice can be exercised. Governments withdraw from the direct control of outcomes in favour of 'steering from a distance' (Marginson 1997a).

A clear example of the neo-liberal agenda at work in higher education reform is Dawkins 'clawback' reforms in which money given to universities to fund their research activity was clawed back by the government and given to the Australian Research Council for distribution to individual researchers on the basis of a system of competitive tendering. The autonomy of individual researchers was thus enhanced, while at the same time the government was able to exercise more direct control over the direction of the national research agenda through various incentive schemes. Universities' internal mechanisms for the distribution of research funds were thus bypassed and university research management increasingly focussed on getting research staff to the finishing line in the annual race for grants, themselves introducing various systems of incentives to achieve a 'competitive outcome' for the institution as a whole. Such reforms all assume that increased competition will lead to increased productivity; that the enemies of productive work are laziness, complacency, and various forms of mutual protection racket. Behind this is an assumption of a particular form of human subjectivity—the rational, opportunity-maximising, self-interested individual of market liberalism.

This chapter is concerned to argue that the faith in the powers of competition to enhance academic productivity is misplaced and that much academic work depends for its success on quite different forms of human subjectivity. Further, it argues that the enhancement of the mechanisms of competition in fact threatens the psychological and social conditions necessary for certain aspects of academic work. In particular it threatens our ability to work cooperatively, to think creatively and to teach generously.

I will argue here that institutionalised competitiveness threatens the forms of human subjectivity embodied in three aspects of academic work: our professional collegial relations; the psychological conditions necessary for creative work; the gift relationship embodied particularly in pupil–teacher relations.

PROFESSIONAL COLLEGIAL RELATIONS

Collegial relations have had a hard time from recent university reformers. In the main they have been regarded as barriers to reform, making it harder for university managers to reshape their institutions for the new, more competitive environment being created by the federal government. 'Effective management at the institutional level will be the key to achieving many of the Government's objectives for the unified national system', said Dawkins, but standing in the way of all those vice-chancellors and deputy vice-chancellors bending to the direction of the chill winds outside the ivory towers were the forms of collegial organistion which derived from the idea that the university was a community of scholars—professors with deluded ideas about their traditional authority; faculties who believed in peer review; departments who wanted elected chairs; students who thought they were more than customers (Marginson, 1997a: 69).

Collegial traditions were scorned as at best things of the past standing in the way of universities' necessary modernisation; at worst, the protection practices of a closed shop. 'One must suspect that at times people who wrap themselves in the flags of collegiality and academic freedom do so less from disinterested motives than from a wish to protect their own turf and avoid reasonable scrutiny', conclude Peter Coaldrake and Laurence Stedman in their recent book on Australian universities *On the Brink* (p. 149). They discuss collegiality entirely as a practice of institutional self-management derived from universities' medieval foundations and so fail to see the centrality of collegiality not only to traditions of university organisation but to the disciplinary organisations within which academics produce knowledge. For collegiality is not just embodied in the traditional powers of the faculty or the professorial board, but in the professional and cooperative aspects of discipline-based academic work— refereeing papers, marking theses, serving on professional bodies, editing journals, organising and attending conferences.

This is a symptomatic oversight. The interest of most of those pushing for university reform is in power and how it operates, rather than knowledge and how it is produced. The men and women in suits who run our universities have long ago left the coal face of the blank page and the laboratory bench; and the men and women in suits from the government were never there. They look at collegiality as an organisational barrier to their reforming intentions and fail to see its role in producing the outcomes they in fact desire—innovative and important research, new knowledge, and checks on the fraud and the glib-tongued fool. And for university managers in the new competitive environment, what else can they do? They are by the nature of their job responsible for the fate of the institution they manage, not the discipline which trained them or even the intellectual culture which nurtured them.

But our identity as academics begins as a disciplinary rather than an institutional one. We begin our training in particular disciplines and generally develop academically within some more or less loosely defined disciplinary boundaries—submitting to disciplinary journals, giving papers to displinary conferences, and so on. This professional disciplinary life is embodied both in formal professional associations and in the informal networks of colleagues which we each build through our working lives. These networks develop on the basis of the shared traditions of disciplinary enquiry and of the personal intellectual affinities we discover among our professional colleagues. They have very little to do with our particular employing institutions, except that in some we may find more conducive colleagues than in others; and they are vital to the productivity of most effective academic researchers.

These professional, collegial relations, however, are being placed under great strain by the increased competition between institutions for students, research money and prestige which has come from recent government reforms. In this competition it is in the interest of the instutitions to boast of the achievements of their staff and students, as if these were entirely an institutional outcome, owing nothing to any other person or instituion (except, at gradution ceremonies, the students' parents). Universities have thus been increasing their grip on the academics who work in them, such that the academics' institutional identity can entirely replace their individual identity, co-opting their achivments as evidence of the institution's worth. Similar claims are made about the achievements of institutions' alumni.

For example, the University of Melbourne under its new vice-chancellor, Professor Alan Gilbert, has been aggresively pushing its claims to positional status in an attempt to lift itself and the other pre-war universities well above the ruck of both the redbrick universities of the 1960s and 1970s and the hordes of post-Dawkins jumped-up techicial colleges and Colleges of Advanced Education. As part of this it produces a glossy alumni magazine, *Gazette*, in which it boasts of the university's achievements and co-opts into this the achievements of anyone who ever went there. But it gives only the Melbourne degrees of the achieving people who were once its students. In the issue for Autumn 1997, for example, it included in its list of the achievements of prominent graduates Dr Tom Griffiths' prize-winning book, *Hunters and Collectors*. The author's qualifications were given as BA Hons 79, MA 91. Omitted was his PhD from Monash, even though it was on this that the prize-winning book is based. Presumably the editor of the *Gazette* did not want to give free advertising to the competition.

I am continually congratulated at La Trobe University (where I work) for having such a high public profile—as are other colleagues like Robert Manne and Dennis Altman. Given the embattled position of La Trobe in the competition for positional status in the city of Melbourne, this is understandable, but it points, I think, to a larger problem. The enhanced emphasis on competition and, in particular, the ruthless exploitation of positional advantage by the pre-Second-World-War universities (such as the University of Melbourne) are straining collegial relations across the campuses. I now would not want the University of Melbourne to claim me as an alumni, not because I am not very grateful for the good teaching I received there in the 1960s and 1970s, but because I do not want to be co-opted into its marketing strategies, particularly when these are directed against the place at which I now work and my colleagues there.

Every time I read yet again the Vice-Chancellor of Melbourne making one of his claims to the universal excellence of his institution I feel a surge of resentment, and a desire to hit back and to point out some of the many ways in which the University of Melbourne is not excellent. I realise, of course, that this is pointless and that in the short term positional status is immune to evidence about quality (Marginson 1997b). As well as exposing me to inevitable accusations of sour grapes, to give in to such temptations would draw me into participating in the very destruction of relations of cooperation and trust on which our collective professional life depends.

PSYCHOLOGICAL CONDITIONS NECESSARY FOR CREATIVE INTELLECTUAL WORK

In the end, the quality of our research as academics depends on the quality of our thought. We begin with thinking—the flash of insight in some accounts, the struggle to bring the half-formed thought into focus in others. Various disciplines develop different skills and methods to control and enhance this thinking, and individuals develop these to different levels. These are important in contributing to new work, but they remain means.

One of my enduring interests is in the institutional and cultural conditions which enable creative intellectual work, which enable people actually to have the flash of insight or to bring the half-formed thought into focus, and then to shape these private experiences into public and convincing forms. Does the increased emphasis on competition enhance or inhibit creative intellectual work?

Advocates of competition will not hesitate to say enhance. They will argue that competition will spur intellectual endeavour, make people work harder, longer, smarter. This is an article of faith for the men and women in suits who advocate competition. I am prepared to accept that competition does have a place in the motivation of academic work. It has, however, a secondary, after-the-fact place. It can indeed be a valuable spur to finishing a paper or a manuscript, to getting work taken seriously, to arguing hard to defend your position. But it is not always of help in the development of that position itself. Working hard to come up with a good idea will not guarantee you will have one. Earnest endeavour generally produces earnest work, rarely anything that sparkles or surprises. I am even prepared to concede that competition might enable some people to be creative; but there are many it will not help at all at the moment of thought; and some it may postively harm.

For many the moment of creative thought needs a quite different emotional and psychological context from anything competition has to offer, quite different conditions of subjectivity. Competition is engaged in by well-formed, bounded selves with clear identities and clear positions. It is these well-formed identities and positions which provide the basis of the competition. By contrast, many theorists of creativity have described the way in which the boundaries of the self blur during creative endeavour. The intense focus of attention on the object of thought leads the rest of the world to fade away, as in the stock figure of the absent-minded professor, or as in the lines of Wallace Stevens' poem, 'The room was quiet and the world was calm/ The reader became the book'.

The psychoanalyst Donald Winnicott (1971) has described the space of cultural activity as a transitional space, a space in which objects are experienced both as part of and separate from the self. This space is bounded and safe, yet charged with possibility. And it has nothing to do with competition. Its features are those of the ideal relationship between mother and child. It is contained and special, a circle of meaning and significance a little separate from the everyday; and inside the circle one finds trust, safety, acceptance, the expectation of being attended to, the expectation of being understood.

When you look at the lives of many creative individuals you find often a special friend, a special group or circle who created the space which made that person's early work psychologically possible. People do not create alone, they are members of groups or circles, they write for particular magazines, they paint for particular patrons or galleries, they share their boldest thoughts with one chosen other. Even when they may seem to be alone and solitary they will be working within particular traditions which involve dialogues with historical figures or long-dead mentors and teachers. Here the expectation of being understood, or at least listened to attentively and sympathetically, is crucial. Many people only discover what they think when they are trying to explain themselves to a sympathetic other. We all know this. Yet to privilege competition as the spur to intellectual work is to assume that the main point of communication is to win the argument.

Heinz Kohut, an American psychoanalyst, has a very interesting essay on Freud's relationship with Wilhelm Fliess in which he explores the vulnerability of the self engaged in deeply creative work (Kohut 1978). Fliess was Freud's confidante during the most creative period of his life, when he was 'discovering' the basic insights of psychoanalysis and writing *The Interpretation of Dreams*. Kohut argues that Freud used Fliess to help him maintain his psychological integrity while he took great intellectual and emotional risks, following the intuitions and trains of thought which led to the creation of psychoanalysis.

It has always been rather hit and miss as to whether universities provided their working academics with the transitional spaces conducive to creative intellectual work. These spaces must to some extent be created by the people who need them, but the possibility of creating them will be enhanced by institutional settings which encourage the development of relations of trust between people, of the friendships and informal networks within which like-minded people can find each other and work together.

The best we can hope for is that the enhancement of competitive market mechanisms in the academic work place will simply miss the target, having nothing at all to offer to the conditions which enable creative work, although perhaps providing some sort of incentive for people to get their work and ideas about, once developed. The best we can hope for is that creative individuals will find or make for themselve the sort of conditions they need in which to work effectively, despite everything university managers do to prevent them. The pessimistic scenario is that the new competitive mechanisms will gradually erode the possibility of the relationships of trust and mutual significance which enable creative work; then universities will indeed have become workshops of the mediocre.

THE GIFT RELATIONSHIP

My last argument I owe to Freya Mathews (1990). It is about the role of the gift relationship in the universities and in the cultural production and transmission of knowledge. Mathews draws on the work of the anthropologist Marcel Mauss on gift exchange (Mauss 1970) in which the obligation to both give and receive binds societies and people together in complex systems of social reciprocity which have both a spatial and temporal dimension. She uses the gift relationship to draw attention to three aspects of the traditional organisation of academic work.

The first is the extent to which it has been embedded in social relations based on trust rather than on contract. The imperatives of bureaucratic rationality have been tidying this up for quite a while now, in relation to such things as academics' leave entitlements or workers' compensation, and they have been eyeing off our working hours and our intellectual property. Such tidying-up, she argues, is likely to be corrosive. As academics are increasingly forced to think of the allocation of their energies in terms of such measures of efficiency as money or contributions to the research quantum, much of what they now do for free will come into question. Why would anyone mark a PhD for example, read a draft for a student you are not supervising and who is therefore not part of your EFTSU load, read papers submitted to journals, talk to the ABC, serve on a government committee, write references, or even organise a conference, if it is not going to generate any money, or a measurable research publication, or a grant application. The answer is twofold. We do some of it, like marking PhDs and writing references, because other people did that for us. It is a gift we received and we now feel an obligation to pass it on; and we do it because we believe in the common enterprise of advancing understanding or knowledge as an end in itself. We do it because we still feel ourselves to be part of a common collegial enterprise, as discussed in my first point.

The second aspect of academic work Mathews discusses is the commitment to knowledge as an intrinsic end embodied in much, though not all, academic teaching and research. Systems of gift exchange differ from systems of market exchange in that the item of exchange, the gift, is understood by both giver and receiver to be of intrinsic value. By contrast, the market is a system of exchange in which the value of the goods derives, to varying degrees, from the system of exchange rather than inhering in the goods themselves. Value is, if you like, created through the exchange. There is thus a close relationship between market mechanisms and instrumental behaviour: one takes a particular activity or course of action, not because it is good in itself but because it will earn money or research points, or advance some other end which has a contingent relationship to the activity being pursued. The use of competitive mechanisms to achieve desired outcomes depends on this sort or relationship. The third is the way gifts are seen to carry something in them of the spirit and identity of the original owner. In the exchange of gifts, societies and individual thus recognise the extent to which they owe their identity and very existence to others, and they contribute to the conditions of possibility for the continuation of their form of life. This aspect of the gift exchange is most fully realised in academic work in our teaching. It is here that we give to our students ideas and knowledge which we hold to be of intrinsic worth, and give them in ways which indelibly carry the marks of ourselves—of the teaching we received, and of what we have made of it. We try to teach well because we were taught well, and were drawn into the shared enterprise of the construction of knowledge by people who in teaching us gave us something of themselves. Again, this is a relationship to which enhanced competitiveness has nothing to contribute. The best we can hope for is that it misses the mark, but the more likely outcome is that it will be destructive of the very gift relations on which the collective enterprise of the creation and transmission of knowledge depends. Once teaching becomes instrumentalised, once students start to feel they are simply dollars, or EFTSUs, on legs, and not part of a generational chain of giving and receiving, once academics see themselves as earning money rather than teaching students, then universities as we have known them are over.

CONCLUSION

The traditional idea of the university saw the university as a place in which the pursuit of knowledge for its own sake had a central if not exclusive place. It was to some extent a place apart, protected by various privileges and traditions from the forces of the market. Freya Mathews argues that the ethos of the traditional university, with its stress on collegiality and on autonomy, 'reflected the requirements of epistemology as much as those of politics' (Mathews 1990: 20). That is, the institutional forms of the traditional university were in good part a response to characteristics inherent in its two core functions: the pursuit of knowledge and the teaching of students. They recognised the essentially collective nature of the production and transmission of knowledge; and they recognised that it is only when knowledge, or truth, or understanding are pursued as intrinsic ends that they are likely to be achieved.

Universities are no longer protected from competitive market forces, and traditional arguments are proving weak in the face of zealous reformers convinced that increased competition will lead to enhanced performance. In this chapter I have focussed on certain aspects of the nature of academic work, to show how they *in fact* depend on relations of cooperation. This is most obvious in academics' collegial and disciplinary life, but it is also the case in relation to academics' research and writing, where many people's creativity is enhanced by relations of trust with a small group of others. And it is central to the reciprocity of the student–teacher relationship.

I have emphasised the words 'in fact'. My arguments are not arguments about abstract value or definition, but about the nature of academic work, and they depend on certain empirical claims about the conditions which enable people to produce the sort of knowledge which universities have traditionally produced, and which they are still expected to produce, at least to some extent. No one, it should be noted, has yet argued that universities should produce *only* applied knowledge, that there is *no* place for curiosity-driven or pure research, that it should provide *only* vocational training. Insofar as universities are still expected to produce people able to value, create and teach knowledge for its own sake, these goals are threatened by the present mania for competitive mechanisms to regulate the activities of academics.

This argument could lead one to profound pessimism, to the conclusion that much of the academy's ability to contribute to the production of knowledge will be destroyed by current 'reforms'. It also contains, however, a ray of hope. This is that the conditions of cooperation, trust and reciprocity which,

I have argued, are necessary for productive academic and intellectual work are indeed necessary and will stubbornly persist and that this stubbornly persisting empirical reality will defeat the reformers.

References

Coaldrake, Peter and Stedman, Lawrence 1998, *On the Brink: Australia's Universities Confronting Their Future*, University of Queensland Press, Brisbane.

Kohut, Heinz 1978, 'Creativeness, Charisma, Group Psychology: Reflections on the Self-Analysis of Freud' in Paul Ornsteic (ed.), *The Search of the Self: The Selected Writings of Heinz Kohut*, International Universities Press, New York, vol. 2, pp. 793–844.

Marginson, Simon 1997a, 'Steering From a Distance: Power Relations in Australian Higher Education', *Higher Education*, 34, pp. 63–80.

——1997b, 'Competition and Contestability in Australian Higher Education, 1987–1997', *Australian Universities' Review*, 40 (1), pp. 5–14.

Mathews, Freya 1990, 'Destroying the Gift: Rationalising Research in the Humanities', *Australian Universities' Review*, 1&2, pp. 19–22.

Mauss, Marcel 1970, *The Gift: Forms and Functions of Exchange in Archaic Societies*, Cohen & West, London.

Winnicott, Donald 1971, *Playing and Reality*, Tavistock Publications, London.

Part III

Looking Ahead

· 10 ·

Funding universities

PETER KARMEL

Most issues that presently confront higher education, whether in relation to the system as a whole or to individual universities or to academics working within the institutions, stem from funding problems. Likewise the Commonwealth government's concerns are largely connected with funding.

This chapter is about reforming the way in which universities are funded for their teaching activities so that the most pressing problems facing them can be ameliorated.[1] The question of funding research is a separate one, to which brief reference will be made at the end of the chapter.

SYSTEMIC ISSUES
At the system level the main issues relate to the scale of higher education, the volume of government funding, diversity, quality assurance, priority setting.

Scale of higher education
The scale of higher education depends on the rate at which people access it and the length of time they spend enrolled. At present some 45 per cent of a cohort of Australians make

an initial enrolment in higher education either within several years of leaving secondary school or somewhat later during their lifetimes. (On a gender-specific basis the proportions are approximately 38 per cent for males and 51 per cent for females.) This represents a high level by world standards and is probably close to the United States experience in relation to universities and four-year colleges.

Total enrolments depend not only on the rate of access, that is, the rate at which people enrol in universities for the first time, but also on the length of courses, the success rates of students and the extent to which people enrol for second undergraduate qualifications and for postgraduate degrees. Over the decade 1987–97 the total enrolments in higher education in Australia increased by 67 per cent to 659,000; undergraduate enrolments increased by 58 per cent to 521,000 and post-graduate enrolments by 116 per cent to 138,000.

The remarkable increase in enrolments over the past decade has been driven by three factors.

Student demand

Retention rates to the completion of secondary school rose from 49 per cent in 1986 to 71 per cent in 1996 (having peaked at 77 per cent in 1992). This had some impact on the number of Australian students enrolling in universities for the first time, rather more than offsetting declining numbers in the relevant age groups. However, of much greater significance have been enrolments of people seeking to upgrade qualifications they already held (from diploma to degree), enrolments for second undergraduate degrees (including double degrees), enrolments in postgraduate courses and research training and enrolments of overseas students.

Government encouragement

Expansion of university places was government policy over the period from 1988 to 1995. Dawkins' Green Paper of 1987 suggested an indicative target of 125,000 graduates by 2001 (against an actual number of 78,000 in 1986).

Institutional ambition

Growth became an objective of institutional planning at all universities, both because enlarging institutions was being encouraged by government policy and because growth was seen as the means of attracting additional funds.

The extent of access to higher education is reflected in entry standards. In general, the greater the access, the lower must be minimum entry standards. Universities do not appear to lay down formal minimum entry standards as they once did. Rather, the minimum entry standard is determined by filling quotas of enrolments. Minimum entry standards vary from institution to institution and from course to course. In some courses in some institutions students need to be in the top one or two per cent of the order of merit list in order to be admitted; however, some institutions are admitting students with results even below the 70th percentile from the top. Mature students are admitted on the basis of judgements about their equivalence to school entry students. An issue which needs to be confronted is whether standards should be merely a refection of the scale of higher education or the scale determined from adherence to fixed minimum standards.

Government funding

For a given scale of higher education, the level of government funding required depends on the standards of service to be provided to students by the institutions, the institutions' efficiency and the extent to which students carry the costs themselves. At present students cover some 35 to 40 per cent of operating costs through the Higher Education Contribution Scheme (HECS). By world standards this is a relatively high proportion for people attending publicly supported institutions.

Scale, the level of government funding, the services provided to students and their financial contribution are interrelated. For example, the quality of universities' services to students could be raised, other things being equal, by increasing government expenditure or reducing student numbers or increasing the students' share of costs or by some combination of these.

As far as quality and efficiency are concerned, it should be noted that over the period 1988 to 1996, while student load increased by 49 per cent, academic and general staff numbers increased by only 26 per cent, giving an increase in productivity of 18.5 per cent, a significant improvement, assuming, of course, that the quality of services offered did not decline. Some decline in quality seems to have been likely, given the increase in class sizes and the elimination of tutorials in some areas. While on the subject of productivity, an even more marked increase can be demonstrated in relation to the number of courses completed: course completions increased in an eight-year period by 75 per cent to 141,000 in 1995 (as against Dawkins' 1987 target of 125,000 for 2001), an improvement in productivity of almost 40 per cent even before taking into account the current cuts in staffing. The magnitude of this improvement seems not to have been appreciated.

As one would expect, given the growth in student numbers, total government expenditure has risen over recent years. The increase has, however, been moderated by the assumption by students of a significant fraction of costs through HECS. As a proportion of gross domestic product, government outlays on higher education rose from 1.0 per cent in 1987–88 to 1.2 per cent in 1994–95. The recent cuts in higher education expenditure and increases in HECS will bring this figure back toward 1.0 per cent. It is worth noting that this proportion was at its maximum, 1.5 per cent, in 1975–76: there has been a significant long-term decline in the government's commitment to funding higher education in relation to the scale of the Australian economy.

Diversity

When the Unified National System (UNS) of higher education was established in 1988 emphasis was placed on the desirability of encouraging diversity. Diversity in and among universities is important in order to meet the differing needs of students, both in terms of the courses offered and styles of learning. As participation in higher education has risen to the point where close to half of the population may be expected to become involved at some stage of their lives, the student body has become increasingly diverse and a responsive diversity in the system has become important.

The development of the UNS has brought with it increasing competition among universities for students. This has produced tendencies towards both convergence and differentiation. There is little doubt that the institutions themselves have become more diverse in the courses they offer, the functions they undertake and their styles of teaching. On the other hand, the newer universities have tended to mimic many of the activities of the older ones in an attempt to lay claim to the prestige that they enjoy. The rapid spread of MBA programs and the remarkable increase in the number of law schools are examples, as is the importance attached to involvement in research.

The way in which the universities established post-1987 have fallen into line with the older institutions is illustrated by the following:

- Teaching-only staff constituted 28 per cent of all higher education staff in 1988; by 1996 this had fallen to four per cent;
- Enrolments in undergraduate diploma courses were seventeen per cent of all higher education enrolments in 1988; by 1997 they had fallen to two per cent;
- PhD enrolments in the post-1987 universities were about 100 in 1988; by 1997 they had risen to 5,800.

Thus, while diversity within institutions has undoubtedly been effectively promoted, there is arguably less diversity between institutions than existed under the pre-1987 binary arrangements. The case for seeking diversity between institutions rests quite simply on the benefits of specialisation and the division of labour: institutions with a clearly focussed set of goals are likely to be more efficient than institutions attempting to be all things to all students. This point also gives rise to the question as to whether research and research training ought not to be concentrated in fewer than the 36 public universities.

Quality assurance

The rapid growth of enrolments in higher education, much of it in the former Colleges of Advanced Education, triggered concerns about quality. Questions about the quality of courses offered to students and of the teaching involved, and the standards of the myriad degrees awarded by the universities, began to be raised as the number of students entering universities approached 50 per cent of the age cohort. The Commonwealth government also wished to ensure that it was getting a worthwhile return for its very substantial investment in higher education. These concerns led to the quality exercises conducted over the three years 1993 to 1995.

In many respects these exercises were flawed. There was no clear conceptualisation of what was meant by quality in the university context and many of the performance indicators used were of dubious validity. There was a tendency to encourage universities to comply with the values expressed by those conducting the evaluation. The ranking of whole institutions was itself a serious weakness. The offering of prizes to those ranked highly caused institutions to exaggerate their strengths and minimise their weaknesses, and undercut arguments for the better resourcing of university activities.

Accordingly, the quality exercises of 1993 to 1995 do not provide a firm foundation for the future consideration of quality. There is still the question of whether quality should be certified by auditors external to the institutions or whether quality assurance and enhancement should be internalised and become an integral element in the institutions' operations or, again, whether there should be a combination of these two approaches. Whatever its shortcomings, the Committee for Quality Assurance in Higher Education placed quality firmly on the agenda and raised questions of process and outcomes in the consciousness of the institutions.

Priority-setting

Over the past four decades or so, the Commonwealth government has given increasing emphasis to the view that, since universities are largely funded by it, the Commonwealth should set 'national priorities' to which universities should conform. However, this view is challengeable. In its *Sixth Report* (May 1975), the Universities Commission expressed its views on the decentralised *versus* centralised setting of priorities in the following terms:

> The Commission's commitment to university autonomy . . . stems from a conviction that universities will in general better achieve their purposes by self-government than by detailed intervention on the part of the public authorities. The purposes for which universities are founded and for which society continues to maintain them include the preservation, transmission and extension of knowledge, the training of highly skilled manpower and the critical evaluation of the society in which we live. No university performs its functions perfectly; and it is not difficult to criticise aspects of university teaching and administration. Nevertheless the Commission is convinced that society is better served if the universities are allowed a wide freedom to determine the manner in which they should develop their activities and carry out their tasks.
>
> In a free society, universities are not expected to bend all their energies towards meeting so-called national objectives which, if not those of a monolithic society, are usually themselves ill-defined or subject to controversy and change. One of the roles of a university in a free society is to be the conscience and critic of that society; such a role cannot be fulfilled if the university is expected to be an arm of government policy. Moreover, universities must prepare their students for life in a world the characteristics of which are necessarily imperfectly foreseen. An institution which geared its activities to *known* requirements could hardly provide an education appropriate to meet as yet unknown problems.
>
> None of the above implies that universities would make their full contribution to social life if they were unresponsive to community needs . . . (4.22–4.25)

An implication of this statement is that institutions following a plurality of priorities are more likely to promote a creative and innovative atmosphere for higher education than the articulation of a single set of national priorities determined by central government fiat. The national interest may best be served by such a plurality in the same way as an individualistic market economy is likely to be more effective in producing a strong and prosperous economy than one controlled by a central command structure.

INSTITUTIONAL ISSUES

There are implications for institutional management in the system level issues that have just been discussed. In addition there are three areas of particular concern within institutions which relate to institutional–government relations, resources and their management, and enterprise bargaining.

Institutional–government relations

Until the end of 1987, the Commonwealth's relations with institutions of higher education were managed through statutory authorities created for that purpose. With the abolition of the Commonwealth Tertiary Education Commission in 1987 this ceased to be the case. The minister and his or her department became considerations and assumed a much greater role. The desirability of re-establishing a statutory body is discussed in the final pages of this chapter.

On the whole, the Commonwealth has avoided interfering with the internal management of institutions. Indeed, since 1988 it has reduced the controls that used to be exercised in relation to new developments, equipment and capital projects. It has also dropped the accreditation of courses that applied in the advanced education sector. On the other hand it has emphasised that much of the universities' activities are an expression of government policy and that the universities are policy instruments.

The Commonwealth has exercised quite strict control over student numbers and the fees that may be charged to various classes of students. Significant planning and administrative problems have been created by the changing rules that the Commonwealth has laid down in relation to student numbers and by the growing complexity of the permissible fee structure.

The Commonwealth has also placed considerable demands on institutions for the provision of data relating to students, staff and finance. It has expected rapid response to a stream of reports and policy documents emanating from Commonwealth agencies. It has pressed current management methodologies on the institutions (for example, strategic planning, research management plans, performance indicators, total quality management). It has become increasingly involved in quality issues.

Resources

The most pressing problems that face universities today relate to the volume of resources at their disposal and their management. Over the period from 1997 to 2000 the Commonwealth government is cutting higher education funding by a total of six per cent. When the impact of the current round of salary increases is added to this the universities are facing gaps in their budgets of around thirteen to fifteen per cent. This is equivalent to a cut in their real resources of that amount. They have little control over that part of their revenue relating to undergraduate teaching and no effective influence on student numbers which are set at levels agreed with the Department of Education Training and Youth Affairs. Consequently most of the impact of the funding gap is falling on staff numbers which are being significantly reduced.

As far as the internal allocation of resources is concerned, universities are allowing themselves to be influenced by externally determined funding relativities. In particular, the Relativities Funding Model tends to be used as a means of distributing funds internally, although it was never intended for that purpose. The use of funding formulae is a convenience and a way of avoiding internal conflict, but it introduces a kind of tyranny within institutions that inhibits flexible management.

Within institutions resources also tend to be absorbed by the modern management techniques that universities have been encouraged to adopt; for example, strategic planning, the development of research management plans and equity programs all involve significant managerial effort.

Enterprise bargaining

As pointed out above, the current round of salary increases has had or will have the effect of cutting the institutions' command over real resources by some seven to nine per cent. By the year 2000 there will almost certainly have been another round of salary increases.

It is difficult to see how the institutions can cope with enterprise bargaining without a greater degree of control over their revenues from undergraduates. In theory, they have a measure of control because they can admit a proportion of full fee-paying Australian students and they can over-enrol HECS-liable students; but the availability of significant numbers of full fee-paying Australian students is very doubtful and the recompense for over-enrolment is below long-run marginal costs.

There is no question but that the universities need to adjust salary scales from time to time in order to be able to retain and attract high quality staff nationally and internationally. The institutions are coping with the present round by economies involving, for the most part, reductions of staff numbers. No doubt there is room for some economies but they cannot be contemplated on the current scale as a recurring phenomenon. Measures to cope with the enterprise bargaining issue are of the greatest urgency. Yet in its submission to the Review of Higher Education Financing and Policy, the Australian Vice-Chancellors' Committee (AVCC) did not raise the funding salaries issue—an extraordinary omission.[2]

FUNDING REFORMS

Are there any reforms in the way in which institutions of higher education are funded which would ameliorate all or some of the problems that have been discussed? Seven possible models of funding arrangements are discussed below. The model involving a comprehensive program of national scholarships is set out in detail as it is the direction in which I believe we should be heading.

Retention of present arrangements

In its submission to the Review of Higher Education Financing and Policy the AVCC proposed that enrolments should be kept as a constant percentage of the population aged fifteen to 64, and that this percentage should be no less than the current figure and no less than those for comparable OECD countries. This implies that student numbers should grow roughly in proportion to population. The AVCC also recommended increases in funding in relation to student numbers (nineteen out of 43 separate recommendations related to funding). In effect, it suggested a continuation of the present arrangements with more liberal funding.

Clearly this has two defects. It takes no account of the impact of enterprise bargaining and it assumes the highly improbable result of more generous Commonwealth funding. In fact, from 1997 onwards the situation has been that both funding and funded student numbers are being reduced somewhat below planned levels. In addition, the institutions are being forced to absorb most of the salary increases that have been or are being negotiated.

Alternatively, student numbers might be reduced without cuts in funding. This would allow for greater resources per student. However, it seems unlikely that the Commonwealth would agree to move sufficiently far in this direction to effect real reform.

Another possibility within the present arrangements would be to modify HECS in various ways. The Industry Commission, for example, has suggested, among other things, that HECS charges should be based on a uniform proportion of standard costs, that there might be provision for some fee flexibility among universities and that HECS might be made available to full fee paying Australian students.

Performance-based funding

Universities are presently funded in relation to an agreed level of enrolments. This constitutes a kind of performance-based funding, the performance involved being the enrolment of students. However, suggestions for performance-based funding usually relate to the performance of desirable outcomes, for example, the number of graduates or the number of graduates obtaining employment after graduation (Anderson et al. 1996). The purpose of such performance-based funding is to make institutions more efficient in producing desired outcomes and to encourage them to behave in conformity with the values of the funding government. Thus, performance-based funding implies the imposition of a centrally determined value system on the institutions. The wisdom of this is clearly challengeable.

Performance-based funding may produce unintended, but quite predictable, consequences. For example, if funding relates to graduations, there is an incentive to lower standards. It is certainly the case that the use of performance outcomes in the allocation of research funds (for example, the publication of papers) has produced at least some undesirable consequences (for example, emphasising quantity at the expense of quality, diverting effort from teaching to research).

There are also conceptual difficulties in specifying performance indicators to which funds are tied. Performance indicators almost inevitably place emphasis on quantity rather than quality. Moreover, the value of a university degree occurs not at the point of graduation but accrues gradually over many years. It is impossible to take this into account in designing performance-based funding arrangements.

Competitive tendering

In 1992 the National Board of Employment, Education and Training suggested that the Commonwealth might seek tenders for increased enrolments in certain courses (1997). More recently it has been proposed by the Industry Commission as a possible reform to funding arrangements, to be applied either to all university enrolments or to marginal increases. The object of competitive tendering is clear: it aims to achieve economies in the provision of services.

Competitive tendering may be a sensible approach in particular cases but there are strong objections against it as a general policy both in principle and in practice. The notion of competitive tendering is based on the purchaser–provider principle; it enshrines the Commonwealth as the purchaser and the universities as the providers.

In the context of higher education, the purchaser–provider principle rests most uneasily in a democratic market-based society. In the first place, it is the very opposite of a competitive arrangement since the Commonwealth as the sole purchaser would be in a monopsonistic situation. Secondly, it assumes that the Commonwealth knows better than the students what they want—it would produce a highly centralised arrangement much more in keeping with a centrally planned economy than with one relying on the decentralised decision-making of the market, as does Australia. Moreover, there are serious practical difficulties in the idea. The Commonwealth would face enormous problems in writing specifications in sufficient detail to enable proper responses from institutions and adequate monitoring. How could the Commonwealth possibly have the skills to do this? The monitoring would present huge problems. It would require significant additional bureaucratic resources at a time when the Commonwealth government is contracting the public service.

Comprehensive program of national scholarship

A comprehensive program of national scholarships would involve the universities in receiving government funds through the funding of students rather than through direct government grants.[3] The program might work in the following way.

Scholarships

Scholarships would be available to students commencing higher education for the first time. The number of scholarships could be related to the proportion of a cohort that is deemed appropriate for entry to higher education. For example, the number of Australian students enrolling for the first time has in recent years been about 120,000. This number constitutes about 45 per cent of a cohort: that is, at current levels of access, 45 per cent of people enrol in higher education either shortly after leaving school or at some time later in their lives—of the 45 per cent about seven-tenths enrol within several years of completing school.

Alternatively, the number of scholarships might be determined in relation to students' tertiary entry (TE) scores. For example, scholarships could be provided for all those wishing to enter higher education with TE scores at or above, say, the 50th percentile, with an appropriate provision for mature-age students.

Access to higher education is reflected in the number of students enrolling in higher education for the first time. Thus access could be maintained, expanded or reduced by modifying appropriately the number of scholarships. The accompanying expansion or contraction of individual institutions would reflect student demand.

How might scholarships be awarded? About 70 per cent of new students enrol shortly after, or within several years of, leaving school on the basis of their tertiary entrance results. Tertiary entrance is currently administered on a state basis, but from 1997 there has been a capacity to convert state and Territory rankings to a national standard which could be used to allocate national scholarships. Thus some 70 per cent of the scholarships could be allocated to students who wish to enrol in a university course in accordance with the national rank order of their TE results. The remaining scholarships would be available for mature-age or special entries. A portion of these could be allocated nationally on the basis of candidates' results in the Special Tertiary Admissions Test. (The STAT is a test, administered by the Australian Council for Educational Research, which is already widely used for admitting mature-age entrants.) The rest might be allocated direct to universities for award to special cases or to meet regional needs.

The scholarships would be for a limited tenure, say, for a maximum of five years of successful full-time university study or the equivalent of part-time study. Beyond these, students would be expected to pay for their studies. The value of scholarships could be related to a schedule of standard costs for different categories of courses (perhaps four or five categories). At present the average proportion of subsidy provided by the Commonwealth is between 60 and 65 per cent. Thus the scholarship might cover some 60 to 65 per cent of costs, the remainder being paid by the students under HECS arrangements.

In an arrangement of the kind outlined above, the individual universities should be free to determine tuition fees to be charged for their various courses (against which the scholarships would be an offset). They should also be able to admit full fee-paying local students who had not received scholarships; these should be eligible to receive a later year scholarship on the basis of successful university performance.

Fees might be expected to reflect relative costs of courses, as do the values of the scholarships, although cross-subsidisation of less popular or more expensive courses would be for individual universities to determine. The current HECS arrangements (which do not prejudice access and are equitable in their impact) would need to continue to stand. Ideally, HECS arrangements should be available to cover all fees payable by students. However, the government might insist on some limitation on HECS-liable fees. In this case, if an institution charged fees beyond this limit, the excess would need to be the student's responsibility, either to pay up-front or by way of a loan.

Students would apply for admission to institutions in exactly the same way as at present. Universities would decide which students would receive an offer of a place and how many students to enrol.

Advantages

Considerable advantages would flow from such arrangements. Higher education would be largely deregulated. Political and bureaucratic intervention would be reduced as would bilateral dealing between institutions and government officials. The grant assessment and profile-negotiation functions of the Department of Education, Training and Youth Affairs (DETYA) would be removed; the number of enrolments would be a matter for each institution to determine. The universities would become patently responsible for their affairs; they would not be underwritten by the government. There would be economies in public administration.

At the same time, the Commonwealth would be in a position to control its expenditure on higher education teaching through the three dimensions of the quantum, value and length of tenure of scholarships and through the conditions under which HECS operates. The Commonwealth could still influence the development of higher education through the quantum of scholarships and their value, and through the provision of capital to establish and foster new institutions. the quantum of scholarships and entry standards would be clearly linked. Governments could also influence access for special groups by the quantum and distribution of special scholarship schemes. It would remain open to the Commonwealth to provide funding to particular institutions for specific purposes under contractual arrangements. Moreover, the allocation of the scholarships in accordance with a national rank order would eliminate political pressures directed toward increasing enrolments in particular states; state enrolments would be determined by the demand from students in relation to their performance on a nationally calibrated scale.

Accountability would be assured through the statutory reporting requirements of the institutions and the periodic reports of the higher education authority as well as through the market mechanisms provided by the scholarships program. The emphasis would be on quality assurance and enhancement as internal responsibilities of the individual institutions.

A comprehensive scholarship program of this kind would enable universities to set their own priorities rather than be required to conform to national priorities laid down centrally. Universities are involved in preparing students for a lifetime's activities in a future which is unknown and uncertain. As already pointed out, there is a powerful argument that the pluralist approach of institutions' determining priorities in relation to their particular strengths and their perceptions of the future is more in the long-term interests of society than forcing conformity to a single set of priorities laid down by the central government. It is a case of decentralised decision making versus central planning.

Higher education would become market oriented. Effective market orientation of the provision of higher education services would be introduced by empowering institutions to offer services at prices and in quantities determined by them having regard to costs, and by allowing students to weigh services offered against fees charged: a shift from a producer-dominated system to a consumer-sensitive market. The power of students as consumers would almost certainly lead to some reorientation of university priorities towards teaching and would impose a discipline that would promote the quality of the courses offered. The relative costs of courses would probably reduce the relative weight of higher degree enrolments which have increased markedly since 1987.

The proposed arrangements would also have positive results from the point of view of equity. The cost of higher education would be shared explicitly between the two beneficiaries: society and the individual student. The student would be able to balance the benefit received from enrolment against the cost incurred, including the cost of enrolling in institutions charging higher fees.

Diversity in universities would be promoted as each strove to find a market for its services. Product differentiation would occur in the nature of courses, the levels at which they are pitched, the size of the institutions, the facilities available, the emphasis and ethos of the institution.

All courses would be treated similarly with respect to fees: different categories of courses would be unnecessary. Invidious distinctions between full fee-paying overseas students and other students would be eliminated. Public and private universities could be treated on an equal footing. Full fee-paying (non-scholarship) domestic students could be catered for.

Institutional efficiency and effectiveness would be improved by avoiding the rigidities imposed on university management through the present publicly known, and thus unavoidably influential, relative funding formula. Institutions would have greater control over budgets through fee structures and enrolment numbers.

Universities in this scheme of things would be able to balance costs against revenues. Having greater control over their budgets through the level of fees, they would be able to adjust the educational services they provide to the revenues they are able to earn. Financial responsibility would be promoted. Universities would be free to reorganise themselves in any way they chose. There might be some splitting of institutions and some combining.

The greater control over revenues would enable institutions to respond to labour market conditions in employing staff. It would make possible a realistic approach to enterprise bargaining in the determination of salaries and conditions—indeed, it is difficult to conceive of successful enterprise bargaining in universities without their having greater control over their revenues. The present dilemma of how to fund salary increases would be ameliorated. From time to time there would need to be negotiation between the Commonwealth and the universities on the value of the scholarships.

Finally, the establishment of a market in higher education services would accord with the emphasis currently being given to a competitive market orientation of the Australian economy. The equal treatment of public and private institutions would be in line with competition policy.

Objections

Proposals for a comprehensive national scholarship program are not popular. Much of the opposition is because of misunderstandings involving wrongly based assumptions that such a scheme would involve the imposition of up-front fees or the imposition of greater costs on students, or both. In fact the scheme offers no specific support for up-front fees, although full fee-paying Australian students could be included within its scope. If government funding remains at present levels, students would on average incur about the same costs as at present which they would be able to pay up-front or through HECS, again as at present; costs might be higher in some cases, but a significant fraction of students would enjoy lower costs.

Some objections that have been raised against the scheme require consideration.

Metropolitan institutions will drain students from regional institutions and may force them to close. If this were to happen in a particular case and if the Commonwealth desired to ensure the viability of a regional institution it could provide it with a lump sum subsidy. A better solution might be to provide an annual endowment of, say, $10 million to all public institutions, offset by a reduction in the value of scholarships. This would have the advantage of treating all institutions equally and thus avoid the seeking and giving of special favours;

Students are not well enough informed to make the right choices. Students already make choices by expressing preferences in their applications to admission centres—the situation under the national scholarship proposal would be no different;

Some of the stronger institutions may be tempted to expand to the point of destroying weaker ones. If such expansion were threatened it would be possible to impose limits on the growth of predatory institutions, for example, by capping the number of scholarship-holders able to enrol at particular institutions;

A deregulated system would produce more uncertainty which would be difficult to manage, given current staff tenure arrangements. While the existence of tenure does inhibit flexibility, it is not as total as is sometimes claimed: in 1996 for example, 44 per cent of academic staff and 36 per cent of general staff were not tenured. In any case, universities are able to terminate the employment of redundant staff. Universities are currently demonstrating that they have mechanisms for coping with the need to reduce resources in certain areas;

The allocation of scholarships could not be made on a national basis because it is difficult to achieve an acceptable national rank order list. While it is true there might be some difficulties in using a national rank order, students are admitted into universities in states other than the one in which they completed their schooling and these admissions are based on comparability of rank orders among states. A national rank order can be established, although there may be some debate about precise equivalences;

Disciplines with low enrolments may have their viability threatened. Viability of disciplines with low enrolments would be threatened if those with large enrolments were able to claim the full value of the revenue they had 'earned'. The fees of students should, in general, cover teaching costs and contribute to university overheads. However, the maintenance of teaching in relatively low enrolment disciplines would almost certainly require cross-subsidisation. Some disciplines, judged to be essential elements in a university (for example, philosophy), may not attract large enrolments; these would require cross-subsidisation from university revenues derived from disciplines with large enrolments.

Implicit vouchers

Paul Miller and Jonathan Pincus have suggested a funding scheme in which universities should be permitted to enrol students as they wish and charge them fees (1997). The Commonwealth would pay the universities directly 50 per cent of the costs of teaching the number of students enrolled (based on a schedule of standard costs). The students would pay the balance as fees. They would do this up-front or, more commonly, through HECS. In the latter case they would be liable for a surcharge of 33⅓ per cent on their HECS liabilities to the Commonwealth for the implied interest subsidy, administration costs and risks of default involved; the university would receive the balance as an advance from the Commonwealth. It should be noted that the full Miller–Pincus proposal includes the capitalisation of fees paid and their amortisation against taxable income over, say, a twenty-year period.

The advantage of the implicit voucher scheme over national scholarships is that the Commonwealth would not have to administer the award of scholarships. The disadvantages are that the Commonwealth would be liable to fund whatever number of students the universities enrolled and there would still be funding relationships between the Commonwealth and the institutions. The national scholarship arrangement, on the other hand, would eliminate direct Commonwealth funding of the institutions and would emphasise the client relationship between students and universities.

HECS Premium

As indicated earlier, the Industry Commission has suggested that, in the absence of more radical changes, modifications might be made to HECS. Bruce Chapman has proposed a specific reform to allow universities to exercise some price flexibility and give them increased financial autonomy (1997).

The present HECS arrangements would remain as a cost-recovery mechanism for the Commonwealth. These would constitute 'base level HECS'. Institutions would be permitted to charge a 'HECS premium' of up to 25 per cent above the base level. This could be paid up-front by the student or collected through the HECS mechanism. In the latter case, the HECS liability would be increased by, say, one-third (equivalent to a 25 per cent discount) to compensate the Commonwealth for the implied interest subsidy, administrative costs and risk of default.

Institutions should also be permitted to charge less than base level HECS. In this case the Commonwealth's subsidy to the institutions would be reduced, thus maintaining base level HECS as a mechanism for recovering costs from students.

The merit of this proposal is that the universities would gain a measure of control over their revenue and would have some capacity to deal with enterprise bargaining and associated salary issues. They could also introduce an element of price competition into their recruiting of students to undergraduate courses.

The advantages of the HECS premium scheme over national scholarships or implicit vouchers is that much less radical changes are involved, and the Commonwealth's liability can be capped. The disadvantages are that it leaves the determination of student numbers in the hands of the Commonwealth, and retains a high level of centralised control over the institutions with their continued direct funding by the Commonwealth. However, it is a first step towards a market approach.

Post-school education right

It has already been pointed out that, at current rates of enrolment, some 45 per cent of an age cohort enrol in universities sooner or later. There are also large numbers enrolling in vocational education and training (VET) award courses, mainly in TAFE institutions. The proportion of a cohort enrolling in a recognised post-school award course is probably close to 70 per cent. This raises the question as to whether it might be possible to give all individuals an entitlement to up to a given number of years of formal post-school education. Such entitlement or right was suggested in a paper by the Hon. Peter Baldwin (1997).

Such a right, when combined with the freedom of institutions to determine enrolment numbers and course fees, as in the national scholarships scheme, and with HECS arrangements of the kind proposed by Miller/Pincus and Chapman, would yield great educational benefits. Moreover, it would be relatively simple to administer because it would not involve making decisions as to who should receive awards: the entitlement would be universal.

However, there are problems that need to be confronted. If participation in post-school award education is not close to saturation, a universal entitlement would involve substantial additional expenditure. There would also be the possibility (even likelihood) that the VET sector might gradually lose its special characteristics and become more like the higher education sector, thus creating a gap in the range of post-school educational opportunities. Further, the funding arrangements as between Commonwealth and states would need to be sorted out—a difficult but by no means insuperable problem. Nevertheless, we may be sufficiently close to saturation in post-school award education to make a universal entitlement scheme a realistic target for the relatively near future.

The West Report

In January 1997 the Commonwealth Minister for Employment, Education, Training and Youth Affairs appointed a committee to review higher education financing and policy, under the chairmanship of Roderick West. The committee issued its final report in April 1998. It strongly advocated student-centred funding for higher education, arguing that student choice should drive funding and there should be price competition among universities.

The West Report proposed four options which might be implemented as separate options or in order (1998: 24–8; rec. 12, 36). The options were to apply to all students other than those undertaking research training. The options were designated as follows:

Stage 1: Continue to fund on negotiated targets, allow institutions to set fees, provide some support for private providers and strengthen consumer protection arrangements in the higher education system.
Stage 2: Government funding moves when shares of enrolments change.
Stage 3: Government funding is directly driven by student choice and public and private providers are treated equally.
Stage 4: A lifelong learning entitlement to post-secondary education and training.

The report recommended moving to Stage 1 or Stage 2 as soon as possible and the immediate examination of the implementation of Stage 3. Stage 4 was recommended as a somewhat longer-term proposition.

Stage 1 and Stage 2 are close to the 'HECS premium' model above. Stage 3 is somewhat similar to the 'comprehensive program of national scholarships' above, although the Commonwealth is to continue to allocate and fund places. The proposal has none of the simplicity of a national scholarship scheme and leaves the Commonwealth involved in funding places in individual universities rather than determining the aggregate number of funded places and funding them through students. Stage 4 corresponds closely to the 'post-school education right' set out above.

In brief, the West Report did not advance the debate significantly beyond the questions covered by the seven models discussed above.

CONCLUSIONS

Of the seven models discussed above (and the four stages proposed in the West Report), the universal entitlement is unquestionably the most attractive, even if some time away. Apart from this, my clear preference is for a national scholarship scheme, although the implicit voucher scheme of Miller and

Pincus would be a reasonable alternative. Chapman's HECS premium scheme, in my view, constitutes a fall-back position, and would be significantly better than doing nothing. Leaving things as they are, or as they are with minor modifications, is not a helpful option, while funding on the basis of performance indicators or through competitive tendering would be even worse alternatives.

Three additional points need to be made. First, the above discussion relates to the funding of teaching. The funding of research is a separate issue. Since scholarly activity, including research, is an essential element in the teaching of university courses, the funding of teaching provides, and should continue to provide, some resources for these activities. However, much university scholarship and research is funded separately, either through block grants, such as the research quantum, or through the funding of specific projects. At present the research quantum equals about five per cent of the recurrent funding of the institutions. The balance between the funding of research and the funding of teaching can be modified by altering the proportion that the research quantum bears to the total. Thus, if it were judged desirable, the Commonwealth could put rather more into the research quantum (say ten to fifteen per cent) with a corresponding reduction in its support for teaching. The manner in which research block grants are distributed to individual institutions needs to be considered apart from the funding of teaching, and options are not canvassed in this chapter.

Second, my support for a national scholarship scheme is not based on the argument that the establishment of a market for the universities' teaching services is a panacea for all present troubles. In the real world, markets do not work perfectly and are by no means unproblematic. However, the funding of the universities' teaching activities through the students rather than directly from the Commonwealth government will, to a large extent, free the institutions from political and bureaucratic restrictions and from government decisions made on political grounds. It is in this respect that I believe a national scholarship scheme would be superior to implicit vouchers.

Finally, whatever arrangements are made for funding the

institutions, the Commonwealth government will need to have dealings with the universities and will no doubt want to be in a position to influence at least some of the directions they are taking. The argument that the government's relations with the universities should be through a statutory authority is in my view a very powerful one.

Over the 30 years from 1959 to 1987 dealings between the Commonwealth government and the institutions of higher education were conducted through statutory commissions. The commissions, comprising a mix of senior experienced and well-respected academics and leaders from business and the professions, were served by small but well-informed secretariats. They developed relatively stable policies which were well understood by higher education institutions. They published reports of their evaluations of the state of higher education and their advice and recommendations to the Commonwealth were included as public information.

The abolition of the Commonwealth Tertiary Education Commission in 1987 resulted in a loss of memory of the development of tertiary education in Australia; a loss of bureaucratic expertise in institutional–government relations; frequent personnel changes; direct ministerial and bureaucratic involvement in detailed decision-making with resultant political lobbying; delays in decision-making and less transparent processes.

The existence of a statutory body as a buffer between the institutions and the Commonwealth government is of the first importance, whatever the nature of any funding reform. A statutory body can be a protection against political interference, some guarantee of institutional autonomy and a force for maintaining a plurality of priorities among institutions in contrast to a régime of central direction. Such a statutory body should be made up of two or three senior academics and a greater number of leaders from business and the professions (it certainly should not be a representative body); be chaired by a person of high status; have a small, knowledgeable and stable secretariat; administer the programs with which it is directly involved (any other arrangement is a recipe for its increasing irrelevance) and make public its reports and recommendations to the Commonwealth.

Finally, such a statutory body should advise the Commonwealth on higher education matters, report (say triennially) on the state of higher education in Australia and be the authority to deal with the institutions on behalf of the Commonwealth.

Notes

1. The sections on systemic and institutional issues are based on my submission to the Review of Higher Education Financing and Policy. This can be found at http://www.deetya.gov.au/divisions/hed/hereview/submissions/K/karmel.htm.

2. 'Shaping Australia's Future—Investing in Higher Education', Australian Vice-Chancellors' Committee Submission to the Review of Higher Education Financing and Policy (http://www.avcc.edu.au/avcc/other/hereview.htm).

3. This section is based on my paper 'A Comprehensive Program of National Scholarships' in *Policy Perspectives on Higher Education Funding*, Centre for Economic Policy Research, Discussion Paper No. 360, Australian National University, Canberra, February 1997.

References

Anderson, Don, Johnson, Richard and Milligan, Bruce 1996, *Performance-Based Funding of Universities*, Higher Education Council, Commissioned Report No. 51, AGPS, Canberra.

Baldwin, Peter 1997, *The Lighthouse: Towards a Labor Vision for the Learning Society*, April, http://education.labor.net.au/.

Chapman, Bruce 1997, 'Some Financing Issues for Australian Higher Education Teaching', paper prepared for the Review of Higher Education Financing and Policy, August 1997, http://www.deetya.gov.au/divisions/hed/hereview/submissions/commissioned/chapman1.htm

Higher Education Financing and Policy Review Committee (Australia) 1998, 'Learning for Life', *Review of Higher Education Financing and Policy*, Final Report, Department of Employment, Education, Training and Youth Affairs, Canberra.

Industry Commission Submission to the Review of Higher Education Financing and Policy, July 1997, http://www.deetya.gov.au/divisions/hed/hereview/submissions/I/ic_cont.htm.

Miller, Paul W. and Pincus, Jonathan J. 1997, 'SuperHECS: A Proposal for Funding Higher Education', paper prepared for conference

'Funding Higher Education: Performance and Diversity', Adelaide, 21–22 July.

National Board of Employment, Education and Training 1992, *Post-compulsory Education and Training: Fitting the Need*, AGPS, Canberra.

Universities Commission 1975, *Sixth Report*, AGPS, Canberra, May.

· 11 ·

Research as a managed economy: the costs

SIMON MARGINSON

University research has now become modelled as an economic performance system in which the objectives are to maximise research-related income and competitive position and, to a lesser extent, to maximise research output. In this process research organisation and researcher identity are being substantially reworked, or actually transformed. These transformations in the research process, which are creating serious anomalies and tensions, are explored in this chapter in some detail, with reference to data gathered in a recent study of management practices in Australian universities.

THE WILL TO MANAGE

Success in research, which is now generally equated with success in the competition for research funding, is central to the claims of excellence that universities make. Yet in the era of the managed university, for those who regard research and scholarship as worth pursuing in themselves, this apparent centrality of research carries danger. For research in this context is a means rather than an end. The 'higher' end is not truth-telling for its own sake, or for what it might teach us. Nor is it the closer engagement of truth-telling with the world. It is the glory of the university, and the augmentation of its balance sheet.

One sign of this is the tales different Australian universities recount about their performance in research, in their quality prospectuses, annual reports and marketing campaigns. Each older university reworks the comparative data on research performance so as to demonstrate its superiority over all others. Each new university compels the reader with its carefully designed upward trajectory. Taken together, it is apparent that research is flourishing: mere budget cuts cannot dampen the spirit of inquiry. Or so it seems.

Thus the University of New South Wales (UNSW) focusses on the total level of Australian Research Council (ARC) large grants and of ARC collaborative grants with industry, where in both cases it leads the nation. It complains because the Commonwealth research quantum does not incorporate commercial income, where again it is number one. The University of Melbourne adds to its ARC income its National Health and Medical Research Council (NHMRC) income, where it outstrips the rest, to demonstrate its overall superiority in the competitive grants supporting discipline-based academic research. The smaller universities cannot compete in these aggregate terms and resort to per capita measures. At different times the Universities of Western Australia (UWA) and Adelaide have been first in national competitive grant funds per head. Adelaide finds in 1993 that it is number one in ARC large grants per member of the research and teaching staff—providing medicine staff are omitted. In 1995 Adelaide published a newspaper advertisement with selective research data ranking itself highest in the state on all criteria and on some criteria ranking the University of South Australia, which is less than a decade old, ahead of its rival, Flinders University. Yet taking size into account Flinders finds that it is second in the land in NHMRC funding. The University of Queensland points to its success in bidding for the Cooperative Research Centres (CRCs) with industry. James Cook University and the University of Tasmania look good when CRC funding per staff member is calculated, and so on.

The importance of research 'performance' has become so obvious as to be taken for granted. It is readily measured, or so it seems. It is a primary source of income. It touches both the academic and the corporate status of institutions. In their study of commercialisation in American and Australian universities Sheila Slaughter and Larry Leslie (1997) remark that universities are both prestige maximisers and profit maximisers. Monetary income is one but not the only source of prestige. The more traditional goal of high academic standing remains an end in itself. It appears that measured research performance, resting on indices of competitive income for research combined with indices of publications and other outputs of research, neatly satisfies both kinds of objective at the same time.

The compulsion to manage research as an economic system, so as to drive the continuous improvement of measured performance, has its roots in quasi-economic pressures that are external to the university: the growing stringency in public funds, the reorganisation of the higher education sector as a national system-competition (Marginson 1997a, 1997b), and the methods of output measurement employed by the Commonwealth government's ARC and Department of Education, Training and Youth Affairs (DETYA) when calculating and allocating research support. As corporate institutions the universities have a strong incentive to treat research in economic terms. Direct Commonwealth research funding is close to one billion dollars a year, with over $600 million from DETYA in targeted programs and the research quantum of operating grants, $153 million in the operating costs of the Australian National University (ANU) Institute of Advanced Studies, and about $200 million in other Commonwealth portfolios, including over $80 million in NHMRC grants (Table 1). Then there is commercial research income. In 1995 'other research grants and contracts' totalled $290.1 million (3.8 per cent) of the income of Australian higher education institutions (Williams 1997: 28, 32; Gallagher 1997: 8).

When all research dollars are included in the calculation, in 1995 Australian universities received over $1.3 billion per

Table 1 Commonwealth university research funding via
DETYA, 1997*

Nature of funding	$ million	%
Research quantum of operating grants	222.0	35.6
Research infrastructure (block grant)	85.2	13.7
Research infrastructure (equipment, facilities)	19.3	3.1
ARC grants	126.0	20.2
Centres, collaborative grants	44.5	7.1
Assistance to research students	83.3	13.4
Research fellowships (ARC fellows etc.)	43.2	6.9
Total	**623.5**	**100.0**

* In addition institutions receive research funding under the NHMRC program ($80.2 million in 1996), approximately $120 million more from other Commonwealth portfolios (1997), and $153 million for the ANU Institute of Advanced Studies (1997).
Sources: DEETYA (1996: Table 6.1); Williams (1997: 20, 32); Gallagher (1997: 8).

annum for research purposes, and research sustained almost twenty per cent of their total incomes.

The external pressures are a given, but the response of researchers is not. In this context the role of university managers is crucial. They interpret the requirements placed on the university, rechannelling the external economic compulsion into a structured systems of internal measures and pressures. These internal systems of research performance management, whose logic is utilitarian and whose standard is monetary value, come to stand for university research as a whole. It is as if academics would not gather, interpret and publish and thus expand the truths of their various intellectual disciplines, unless such incentives were present (Gaita 1997).

In the reconfiguration of external pressures as internal sanctions and incentives, a decisive role is played—in both the mechanics and the politics of university research—by competition. For example the UNSW *Corporate Plan 1994–99* states:

UNSW operates in a highly competitive local, national and
international market for higher education. We have responded
positively to changes in government policy on higher
education that have opened up the competition for funding, to
the broadening array of higher education options and the
public's awareness of them, to the growing demand for quality

and to an increasingly international environment. Planning is directed towards achieving and maintaining a competitive edge in the intense competition for high performing students, high quality staff, scarce funds and eminent standing. (UNSW 1995a: 5).

Instead of protecting research from the negative effects of competitive pressures, such as the weakening of collaboration, and the tendency to ever-shortening project times, the role of management becomes one of amplifying those pressures, turning them into both a driver of the research operation and a means to internal control. Thus the Griffith University *Research Management Plan* states that 'the University has a policy of pursuing research excellence through competitive funding mechanisms which emphasise the quality of the project' (Griffith 1995: 3). Flinders boasts that its internal research grants have been allocated competitively since 1967. The privileging of competition legitimates research scarcity, and managerial control via scarcity. It provides a meritocratic gloss to allocations that are often determined by the policy and management-controlled criteria used in the competition for funds, and it helps to sustain the drive to measured performance at every level.

The will to research management is expressed in both the imposition of new controls on previously existing activities and the spread of performance-oriented research management to new areas and new personnel. The pressure to raise more research monies and conduct more research projects becomes relentless. It is striking how even at the strongest research universities the terrain of measured research is continually being extended and reinvented. For its size, Flinders was always very successful in raising funds for peer-reviewed academic projects administered by the ARC and NHMRC. When the CRCs became a principal source, a new focus on collaboration with industry quickly developed. The UNSW is by any measure a successful research university, yet its Research Management Plan. talks about 'fostering a research culture'. Though three-quarters of academic staff are already actively engaged in research, UNSW would like to push the level closer to 90 per cent, that of some US universities. School and faculty administrators whose 'benchmarked performance' falls below that of their disciplinary competitors at other Australian universities are expected to improve their performance indicators by ten per cent per annum (UNSW 1995b: 3). It seems that the quantity of research and research funding can *always* be increased.

Nevertheless, these systems of research management often collide with actual research practices, and especially with those practices originating in a time before modern corporate management was introduced. Research that is auto-driven by the desires to know and to make—with rhythms of work sustained by disciplinary traditions rather than money and management, with loosely defined work programs and power relations often opaque, and with research findings that are freely exchanged— has little in common with corporate organisation and the protection of legally codified intellectual property. Prior to corporate management there was an identifiable economy of research. It was subject to competition and scarcity, but its system of exchange was largely non monetary in kind, and it varied markedly in its character from discipline to discipline. This older academic economy of research is *not* readily evolved, fast-forward mode, into a money economy.

And management cannot afford to subsume the older kind of research economy altogether. Research is about innovation: research management (among other things) is about seizing on 'strategic' breakthroughs that can be translated into commercially viable products, and such innovations cannot be altogether programmed. They emerge from that mysterious space, the object of research management, in which researchers must move. In the second half of 1995, the research team on the Australian Research Council-financed project 'Management Practices in Higher Education' visited a pre-1987 university of small-to-medium size with a good research reputation in certain fields. The first interview was with the leading non-academic administrator. He talked fluently and at length about the strategic issues before the university, about its decision-making and financial systems, and relations between academic and administrative wings. This was straight forward. But when

he began talking about research, the matter-of-fact tone gave
way to the richer voice timbres of the patron and connoisseur
of the arts. There was a respectful distancing; the world of
research with its different secrets was a world that he as an
executive could never grasp completely. Yet research and researchers posed difficulties. How could all that creative energy
be harnessed so as to maximise the university's position?
The problem, as he put it, was 'to make the butterflies fly in
formation'.

'Flying the butterflies in formation' is the dilemma of the
management of research, a dilemma that management imposes on
itself in the struggle for competitive advantage. By externalising
a university's research it can be imagined as a single system. By
imagining it this way it becomes possible to count it and control
it. Everyone knows that in their natural state academics have a
notorious tendency to dither. Would research not benefit from
more focus and accountability? If research could be channelled
more efficiently into the fulfilment of institutional goals, then
could not more research be achieved, and more research of a more
useful kind? Would that not benefit the nation's research effort,
not to mention the university's income?

This is the temptation of research management. The price is
that in driving the corporate production of more research of
certain kinds, there is less research of other kinds. This lessening
can even undermine the aims of management. The systems used
in research management do not understand the classical economy
of knowledges in its own terms, and cannot systematically
manipulate its workings so as to enhance the conditions in which
knowledges are created, except in that one, crucial, respect: the
use of economic necessity as the driver of knowledge production.
Yet even commercial research draws on more than market
impulses, being fed also by curiosity-driven research, research
that in its own right is always of dubious economic potential.
The drivers of basic research, that continuing desire to question
and transform, are part of the mystery that confronts managers.
Though research management introduces one kind of reflexivity
in the form of a continual self-questioning about the level of
measured research performance, this reflexivity extends only to

research as it is modelled by management, research as an input–output system. It does not extend to the evolution of knowledge, or even to the achievement of a closer synthesis of the knowledge and money economies. For their part, traditional researchers engage in their own continuous self-questioning about their research fields, but in spaces removed from management and, at worst, hostile to it.

If creative research is an 'other' to the corporate university, and maintenance of the flow of its mysterious benefits depends on respect for its otherness, then it is also an other that the managed university must constantly transform into something more like itself.

HOW RESEARCH IS MANAGED

The move to the management of research is a double move, in which each aspect becomes implicated in the other. First, research is reconstructed as an economic system with inputs and outputs. Second, management colonises the identities of researchers themselves. Their autonomous behaviours are subtly reworked. Their freedom is made subject to management—*without* abolishing that freedom altogether—using systems and mechanisms based on 'steering from a distance' that are drawn from the corporate textbook.

Research as an economic system

Research in a money economy must become research that happens in recognisable chunks that are capable of sale and calculation, like pieces of meat. In research administration and funding, the project format becomes dominant, and this has implications for the character of the research. Projects require precise objectives that are forecast and limited in advance. This in turn lends the research process more readily to all kinds of utilitarian purposes, including the structured competitions for research funding itself. By the same token, speculative and open-ended research programs become hard to sustain. They are rarely funded. Funding—its amount, its method of allocation, the terms and conditions attached to it—becomes the overwhelming driver of research activity. It is not simply that the particular funding schemes tend to determine the directions that research may take. The effects of the money economy are more profound. Research management depends on a system that is common and across the university. Money becomes the common language of this system *and the common index of measurement of value in research.*

In this respect, the most important move in Australian universities was the Commonwealth's decision—when establishing the research quantum of operating grants—to define research activity largely in terms of income for research. In one stroke this installed money as the uniform measure of value in research, while at the same time providing institutions with an incentive to maximise money income *rather than* the research activity which the quantum was meant to represent and augment. Exchange value subsumed use value. The mysterious otherness of research was displaced by an all-too-concrete, visible and familiar presence. Research management was made easy. The financial bottom line separated success from unsuccess and, in the minds of managers, this was the line between good research and bad. At the same time, funds controlled activity. With part of institutions' operating grants for research having been redistributed to the ARC, and the remaining operating funds squeezed more and more tightly, there could be little research without specific research income. Because research activity and research income were equated, the former gave way to the latter.

The research quantum is notionally designed to provide infrastructural support for existing research. However, there is no mechanism that requires institutions to allocate the quantum to specific projects, and the quantum simply operates as a performance-driven supplement to total operating funds. Under the quantum arrangement, the Commonwealth makes available a constant proportion of total operating grants—in 1997 this proportion was 4.9 per cent—for distribution between institutions on the basis of their measured research 'activity'. It calculates the quantity of each institution's 'research activity' by using standard formula, and then distributes each institution's

Table 2   Components of the Commonwealth research quantum, 1997

Item	Description	%
Research income	Academically competitive grants—ARC, NHMRC and other recognised programs, but not commercial research—calculated by the National Competitive Grants Index (NCGI)	82.5
Publications	Books, book chapters, journal articles, other publications—using a weighted index	12.5
Higher degree research completions	Number of graduating research students	5.0
Total		**100.0**

share of the research quantum on the basis of proportion of this total research activity. In 1997 the research quantum allocated to individual universities varied from less than one per cent to 10.4 per cent of their total operating funds (Williams 1997: 20).

In the all-important formula for the quantum index, the largest single element (82.5 per cent) is the income from nationally competitive research grants. These include ARC, NHMRC and other recognised national schemes. Success in the large-grant ARC program has strong flow-through effects on funding. These grants are notoriously scarce (the current success rate is 21 per cent), but the large grants program influences three-quarters of the funding for other competitive grants, and affects the allocation of postgraduate awards, as well as directly feeding into the quantum (Gallagher 1997: 9). The other elements in the index are research publications (12.5 per cent) and research higher degree completions (5.0 per cent). Because these elements play a minor role, institutions have a much stronger incentive to focus on the research income aspect.

It is by creating the direct economic relationship between research activity and future income that the quantum formula drives a continual expansion in the volume of measured research. In the jargon this is often equated with continual 'improvement' in research performance.

The quantum mechanism also provides a handy device for

institutional managers in creating their own internal research economy. They can distribute part or all of the quantum funding—and if they wish, a further proportion of operating grants—to faculties, departments and centres according to the contribution of each unit to total research activity, whether measured by the strict quantum formula, or by a formula of their own devising which modifies the pattern of incentives. For example, a research manager might change the balance between the different elements of the Commonwealth index, or might introduce new elements, such as income from commercial projects, which are consistent with the research priorities and strategies of the institution, or reflect an institution-specific power balance between disciplines. When institutional research managers refer to 'creating a performance-based culture' in research, this usually includes reform of the internal research funding systems so as to distribute some or all research monies in this manner. At the Curtin University of Technology quantum funding is distributed not just to the academic unit but to the individual. This is seen as the ultimate performance driver.

Though every Australian university has unique funding arrangements, all exhibit the tendencies towards performance-based research funding. After establishing performance-based funding distribution from the centre to the faculties, the next step is to cajole faculty managers into themselves distributing research monies on a performance basis, often using the central data on research income and outputs—and to encourage faculties and departments to take a more proactive approach to project creation, behaving like entrepreneurial local firms within a larger conglomerate.

The modelling of research as a money economy leads to predictable and well established effects. First, there is the tendency to the *homogenisation* of research activity within and across disciplines. The language of research, the structure of work and the format of outcomes start to merge everywhere. The effect is reinforced by the central research offices in each institution whose job it is to massage each application for funding so as to fit it to the common rules (formal and informal) as well as possible.

Second, the focus on research incomes as the principal measure of activity pulls management support and institutional activity away from low income-generating areas in research and towards the high income-generating areas, whatever the academic discipline concerned or the respective academic merits. The quantum formula doubles this effect.

Third, the overwhelming drive to quantitative growth in measured research activity creates an inevitable trade-off between quantity and quality. At any given time—even while the capacity to execute projects is finite—the more research projects and the more large projects, the better. Similarly, while it is important to maximise the number of publications there is no motive (within the funding system) to maximise the quality. Again, researcher time is finite and at a certain point each increase in quantity leads to a fall in average quality. Yet the projects that secure the most competitive grants, or earn the most income, are not necessarily the same as the projects that generate the major breakthroughs or produce works of lasting importance and beauty—or even those that generate the most economic value.

It is widely assumed that because research-granting programs are competitive then grant income is a de facto measure of research quality; and the more intense the competition for grants, the higher the quality of successful applications will tend to be. But research funding is a competition for rankings, not for quality. Whether the projects are better or worse, the same total monies are distributed. The quality of proposals is not consistently referenced against a standard external to those proposals themselves. Further, the very quality of the terms and conditions of the competition shape the nature of the projects that are supported. For example, using the ARC and NHMRC formats, projects with limited life and imaginable outcomes are more readily funded than open-ended fundamental inquiry—though the latter might be qualitatively superior by criteria such as the potential long-term contribution to knowledge.

Fourth, in the shift to a performance-based system, an increasing proportion of research support tends to go to areas and projects that are already active and successful. Track record, always important in peer decisions about research, becomes overwhelmingly decisive. This creates a barrier to support for innovations, especially in new or emerging fields.

In the outcome, management strategies in which research is modelled as a money economy are not only inhibiting of research with low measured economic value, they inhibit research of high economic value in certain crucial respects. That is, they contain their own self-limiting contradictions. The imperative towards quantity (research activity in every corner of every university) conflicts with the imperative to concentration and critical mass. Policies of forming larger groups of researchers in order to secure critical mass can force people into less productive collaborations at the price of more desired and more potentially fruitful lines of inquiry. The focus on grant income neglects efficiency in research work. 'What ought to be prized are the people who travel vast distances on the smell of an oily rag', stated one researcher in science to the project team. 'The people that are prized are the people who get large amounts of money and blow it away in expensive programs that may well be quite unproductive'. Ironically, a culture which places a greater emphasis on major research projects is less concerned with research content. Because research funding is an end in itself, universities as institutions must have less interest in what is achieved. Yet it is strength in the specifics of knowledge which creates long-term research capacity.

Another set of problems is created by the focus on track record. Even where special funds are created to assist new researchers and new programs, these schemes are working against the whole system dynamic of funding. This is not to say established researchers are incapable of innovations. Nevertheless, all else being equal, a system that is overwhelmingly focussed on reinforcing existing strengths must be slower to essay major new approaches. Because of resource concentration it is difficult for new areas of strength to even begin to develop, while within established fields, tried and tested ways are retained at the expense of new ones, and new researchers are dependent on the sponsorship of chief investigators to an unhealthy extent—chief investigators good at raising grants but often so caught in the tasks of management that their best work is done. Though ARC post-doctoral fellowships and senior research fellowships are meant to provide full-time research opportunities at both junior and senior levels, the number of fellowships is too small to overcome the difficulties, and this factor is compounded by the demands of growing teaching loads and the lack of jobs and job security.

The identities of researchers

The contemporary changes to research cannot be understood simply as the imposition of management power from above. Research work is executed by autonomous individuals, and in all but the most rudimentary functions it must be so. Although research is embedded in university organisation and shaped by the changing character of management, the changes in research cannot occur unless they are self-managed, self-regulated and self-imposed. The new systems of management encourage devolution, albeit a devolution different from the older collegial forms, and it is in the colonisation of researcher identity that management secures its subtlety and power. 'There is no subjugation so complete as that which preserves the forms of freedom', remarked Rousseau. 'It is thus the will itself is taken captive.'

Research autonomy is maintained, and transformed. In the transition from collegial departments and free-standing individuals subject to the norms of traditional academic life, to productive work groups/business units and entrepreneurial individuals who are focussed on the strategic plan, there are important continuities. Competition and the language of competition are pervasive in both modes, though competition intensifies in the corporate mode (where the capacity to manipulate its intensity becomes a key organisational tool). The ubiquitous discourse of selectivity and concentration resonates with older notions of academic excellence. Similarly, 'innovation' is a key term in the modernist management lexicon. Its frequency of use appears to offer a generous shelter to research. As with all such universals the offer can be deceptive. In management language 'innovation' refers to strategies of continuous organisational change that are led by the managerial general staff. Specific forms of intellectual creativity are collapsed into the talk about re-engineering and responsiveness, in which inventing new knowledges or creating a new research application are equated with changing a funding formula or creating a new layer of management. Thus management uses the universalist cast of its own discourse to establish equivalences between old autonomy and new autonomy, and to ease the transition from the one zone to the other.

In the new zone management remakes research and researchers while holding them at arm's length. Academic freedom is retained even while subjected to standardised descriptors of research activity, the systems of performance indicators and targets, and money incentives that are managed from the centre and common to the university as a whole. Increasingly, too, that academic freedom is shaped by market forces originating from the commercial world, with the encouragement of management. Again, in client-based research the mode is that of steering from a distance.

Research managers know that if they move too close there is the danger of swallowing research and its practitioners altogether. People who manage their own work are more likely to take the initiatives necessary to secure institutional objectives, and less likely to resist. Self-regulation seems consistent with the traditional forms of academic research, arcane norms that continue to be compelling. Self-regulation also means that it is the researchers themselves that overlay the matrix of knowledge with the matrix of money, and manage the uneven and uneasy junctions between the two. Researcher identity, always multiple, becomes more complex than before. All the fine shadings between self-employed entrepreneur and disinterested scholar appear, shifting and changing even within a single individual's work. At the same time, with the spread of commercial projects and of intellectual property arrangements in place of free publication and exchange there is a shift in the balance, towards market economic incentives and market economic forms of behaviour (Marginson 1997a: 257–77).

Managed devolution takes collective as well as individual

forms. In the corporate university, the paradigmatic work group is the research unit, approximating as it does the local business firm. Though in terms of size, legal arrangements, financial character, commercial role and academic boundaries (inter-disciplinary or discipline-based) the research centre form is so eclectic that it is difficult to generalise, all centres have one element in common: they are the product of governmental or managerial intervention in the organisation of research. The centre form has proven to be a flexible and malleable policy mechanism. By selecting and funding centres governments can secure control of the larger research priorities and establish protected zones of activity. Centres with core government funding tend also to attract extra resources from the universities concerned. Internally-generated centres are similar. Compared to corporate managers in other fields, university managers can rarely intervene directly in the normal research activities of faculties and departments. Scarcity of resources and competition for funds provide institutional managers with leverage. By concentrating resources in selected areas called centres, they can shape research priorities and sponsor favoured individuals. At the opposite extreme, the aims of management are also served by closing down research centres. Annual reports make a virtue of the periodic spring-cleanings in which centres are dis-established, because this signifies focus, efficiency and the corporate hard-headedness.

When a centre is created it is usually hoped it will attract outside funding. This is one of the core arguments for centres, which are seen (without clear evidence) as inherently more responsive to outside agents and market forces than are the traditional structures of departments and faculties. Inevitably it is specified that core funding is temporary and the centre is expected to become self-sustaining over time. Mostly these hopes are disappointed: even those centres producing saleable intellectual property and significant consultancy work are rarely able to finance all of their salaries and overheads from these sources, and the centres with the best long-term prospects are those with significant numbers of postgraduates. Despite the fact that few centres are commercially viable, the forms of behaviour that they encourage are those of the entrepreneur. Centre directors often have greater scope to keep the money they raise and spend it how they like, greater scope to shape their work programs and try something new, than conventional departmental heads who are bound by academic tradition and more detailed regulation. In discussing the enhanced freedom which centres bring, centre heads rarely distinguish between academic and economic freedom. Yet the new freedoms are the market economic freedoms.

Again, it is this loose equation between the old form of autonomy and the new form of autonomy that smooths the slippage between them.

The shaping of researcher identity from a distance makes possible the economisation of research. The reorganisation of research as an economic system tends to be strongly resisted when it is imposed directly, but whereas open managerial dictates appear as moves in a conventional game of power and therefore are vulnerable to political resistance, external market forces—once introduced into research—are soon naturalised. It seems that while other forms of power are open to debate, economic power is a 'reality' that must be accepted as part of the ordinary business of life. Similarly, the modelling of internal research organisation as an economic system where, again, control is exercised from a distance, confers on internal research funding and management the same sense of taken-for-grantedness.

Although devolution is necessary to the economic model, the economic model is not in itself necessary to devolution in research, which has a longer history. However, once established as the method of organisation, economisation colours research identity to an increasing degree.

TENSIONS

This reconstruction of research is complex and problematic. It is fraught with tensions, which contribute to the larger set of tensions characterising academic life in the late 1990s. The tensions characteristic of research are both overt and covert.

The overt tensions are twofold: conflicts between the imperatives of commercial and non-commercial forms of research activity, and problems of managed homogenisation in discipline-specific settings. The returns from commercial research tend to be less lucrative than expected. In Australia, more so than the United States, the level of industry demand for research and development is less than hoped. Intellectual property is expensive to protect and while all institutional research managers dream about great commercial applications, few patents generate significant returns. Despite this, once research is reformed, and competitive market forces have been installed in their twin role of ideological goal and practical method of organisation, the commercial ethos exercises an influence that is out of proportion to the income generated.

This in turn brings it into conflict with established collegial practices. One area where there are increasing tensions is that of postgraduate research pursued in industry, for example under the Australian Postgraduate Award (Industry) scheme. Companies often insist on retaining control of the intellectual property so generated, inhibiting or preventing students from publishing their findings, or disclosing them at all, with negative effects on their early career development. It is a stark illustration of the more general tension between intellectual property and unpaid research exchange. In her study of Commonwealth postgraduate scholarships in industry, Margaret Powles (1994) surveyed three groups: the postgraduate students working in industry, their academic supervisors, and their industry supervisors. Whereas 40 per cent of academic staff and 36 per cent of students felt that 'the academic institution should maintain control over publication rights or refuse to do the research in an academic setting', only nine per cent of industry representatives agreed. A high 70 per cent of students believed 'industry's commercial in-confidence requirements are in conflict with academics' desire to communicate research results'. Some 53 per cent of the students believed that intellectual property restrictions hampered the acknowledgement that they believed their research should receive, though only 26 per cent of academic supervisors and 24 per cent of industry representatives agreed.

Sam Ricketson draws attention to tension between the commercial dynamic in research and the democratic-political obligations of universities and academics. 'Intellectual property rights can be used to suppress free speech and access to information . . . [and] block the sources of knowledge that are so vital to democratic decision making and informed expression of political opinion' (1991: 17, 24). Commercial research is also associated with some tensions inside management, between university consulting companies and the research office, or between the company and individual academics. Some researchers active in commercial research tend to avoid the company if it taxes income or commits errors or creates delays.

More broadly felt are the collisions between the homogenising systems used to measure and manage research, and the specifics of different fields of knowledge. In tabulating research income and output in a fixed manner that is consistent across different fields, the systems of management based on the quantum and its variations must apply arbitrary weightings, common to all fields, that approximate more closely the practices of some fields than others. Further, there is more potential for commercial research in some fields than in others, so that systems of funding which reward commercial income tend to produce a gradual shift in favour of potentially commercial research. At worst, research systems create perverse incentives and disincentives which over time tend to distort research and scholarship in some fields. These problems are rarely acknowledged by research managers, who have vested interests in avoiding any line of argument which might lead to troublesome claims for an internal redistribution of research resources.

As noted, in the measurement of research activity the largest weight is given to grants, an approach fitting best with medicine, engineering and the applied sciences. It is inappropriate for the humanities, the theoretical sciences and parts of the social sciences, including education and law, where publications constitute a more useful summary of activity; and where the main resource need is researcher time, rather than research assistance or equipment. (If ARC grants could be used to pay part or all the researcher's salary then they would probably be a more useful measure of research in the latter group of disciplines.) A rare official recognition of these tensions was the 1992 report of a Monash University Research Review Committee that was created to review research policy and management. The committee argued that 'all fields of knowledge represented within the University are entitled to parity of esteem'. It expressed concern that orthodox systems of recording outputs and distributing funds tended to favour some fields over others.

> In the submissions received, there is a clear divergence of view between those, primarily but not exclusively, from the laboratory faculties who perceived a direct relationship between the monetary value of grants and the level of research performance, and those, mainly from the humanities and social sciences, who saw little or no such relationship. It is important, in our judgement, to distinguish between two features of grants as an index of research performance. Insofar as the obtaining of a grant is a sign of the recipient's success in the process of peer review, we support the view that recipients of grants are especially deserving of the resources of time, library resources and equipment to enable them to prosecute their inquiries. But grants are by no means the only such indications of research activity. There is no unique relationship between the money value of the grant and the recipient's need for additional resources. While the use of the publications index may moderate any consequent maldistribution of resources, the committee notes that the degree of variability between faculties in the monetary value of the grants is much greater than for the index of publications. We also note that the pools of funds for which the various disciplines compete under the ARC vary greatly. So do the proportions of applications which receive funding. Any formula that rewards faculties according to success in ARC funding will therefore reflect not only their comparative standing in the process of peer review but also the priorities which the ARC at that time gives to the various research fields.
>
> Under these circumstances, there is a danger, we believe,

that the use of the monetary value of grants as the sole index of research performance, while providing a strong stimulus to maximise clawback funds, will have deleterious longer-term consequences upon the morale and performance of researchers, especially in those fields where large-dollar grant-based research is not the norm . . . At a time of steadily rising staff–student ratios, we are concerned that the use of a grant-based index of performance as the sole determinant of the magnitude of a research quantum available to a faculty will erode even that basic quantum of time upon which all academics rely for research. (Monash University 1992: 18–19)

Further, the different disciplines vary in their publications practices. In science-based disciplines the major breakthroughs are published in journal articles and refereed conference papers. Books are of lesser importance, mostly taking the form of textbooks summarising what is already known. While academics working in the humanities and the social sciences also publish textbooks, in these fields some books contain original and pathbreaking work. The other such medium is journal articles: conference papers are mostly not refereed, being less significant than in the sciences. The balance between number and quality of publications can vary. In some disciplines the norm is to publish a large number of papers, so that such disciplines must benefit from quantitative measures of output which, over time, will tend to distribute resources in their favour. In other disciplines the norm is to publish a smaller number of more selected and high quality papers.

A striking example of the problems caused by homogenisation is that of law. Arguably, for academics working in law the most important form of research and scholarship—the main manner in which academics create legal knowledge—lies in the production of case books. Producing these books does not fit the conventional definition of a research project because it requires scholarship rather than empirical research, and depends on researcher time more than on research assistance. Like other academics, law academics are under pressure to raise ARC money and thereby boost departmental income, both directly and through the quantum. It is actually easier for a law academic to gain an ARC grant for a sociological or historical project about law—that is, a project conducted outside law itself—than to gain a grant for creating legal knowledge in the form of a major case book (McInnis and Marginson 1993). In this manner the operations of the orthodox systems of research funding and management actually tend to diminish the field.

Another example lies in the visual and plastic arts. There the processes of reflection on the field, teaching-reflective synergy, and work at the cutting edge, take place not in laboratory research as in the science-based disciplines, or scholarship as in the humanities, but the production of works of art. And if the humanities can be difficult to fit with conventional definitions of research, it is near impossible to stretch the definitions to include works of art. During the fieldwork phase of the research on 'Management practices in higher education', the research team interviewed one deputy director in a school of art whose task was 'to establish some sort of research culture'. The difficulty was to create a culture which met the conventional requirements for research, *and* contributed to the fields. He noted that one device was to include in a project certain aspects that 'follow more traditional research modes' and could be used as a basis for applications for research funding, using 'any funding you might get as a spin-off to actually do the production'. For example, two staff had received a small ARC grant in ceramics:

> They produce moulds and they can pump out the plates and cups and so forth according to a certain design. Then they have them painted by various artists, so they become unique contributions, but they wouldn't get any funding for that. So what they did was take all the preparatory work that was involved in analysing the most appropriate types of clay, the glazes, fire temperatures, shapes and so forth and they built up a systematic way of actually evaluating those components that then go together to make a finished product. So they were able to get funding for that. That was declared research.
> (Deputy Director responsible for research management, university art college, 1995)

The problem could not always be solved circuitously. Many visual artists 'just don't relate to paper work'. At the above school of art some 'have difficulty stringing four words together in written form', and were reluctant to undertake scholarship in a very different medium, but nevertheless they were 'absolutely brilliant' as visual artists. The only way to adequately encompass the specificity of these disciplines would be to enable their creative work to be treated as equivalent to research and scholarship.

Other tensions within managed research are implicit, running through the multiple research programs and the different roles that academics play, becoming so endemic as to be scarcely remarked. The impact of the changes in research organisation tends to be hidden in the mysterious otherness of research and the self-regulating character of its activities. For example, it is likely that many academics have turned away from—and been turned away from—research that they might otherwise have done out of preference, because the contemporary mix of financial sanctions and incentives has pushed them in certain other more institutionally strategic directions. Yet this outcome is more likely to take the form of self-censorship than overt managerial direction, and it is still possible to enjoy working on research projects of second or third choice, even projects of someone else's choice. Whether such second or third choice research projects constitute the most desirable use of their capacities—and in the longer term, the most desirable direction for the development of those capacities—is another question. The imperatives of day-to-day survival tend to suppress from view the processes of self-censorship, the slippage in project control and definition, and the declining capacity to sustain long-term programs in areas determined by the researcher. Behind the maintenance of researcher *autonomy* there is concealed a partial decline in researcher *independence*, though the decline varies by field of study and the age and seniority of the researcher.

The evidence gathered in the 1995–97 field research on 'Management practices in higher education' suggests a higher education system in which management's priority setting and resource-driven systems prestructure the boundaries and the nature of innovation; and they may even prescribe the detailed inquiry itself. The resulting pattern of research activities may be better in some respects, worse in others, but it is different to what it otherwise would have been, though the alternatives cannot be formulated with precision. The system has clear biases with predictable consequences, such as the individualistic reading of research output and the conditions for research performance, the tendency to growth in measurable and measured outputs, the quantity-quality trade-offs, the favouring of large project research in the sciences, the growing dependence on management to be the engine of research activity (witness the stagnation of research in institutions where research management falters), and the privileging of competition.

The ubiquitous use of competition as an organising device is also one of the means whereby the underlying tensions are kept implicit. The competition for research funds becomes a marketing-based contest in which all institutions always tend to perform 'better than ever'—at least in terms of *measured* activity —if only because they must keep improving merely to hold their previous share of the quantum in what is a zero-sum game. This conceals the very real problems of inadequate operating resources, due to the relative decline in the government funding of universities as a proportion of total university income. At the same time this ever-increasing 'output' also conceals the effect of the competition for research dollars on the character of research and the balances between different kinds of research.

The result is that increasingly, any quantitative expansion of research must come from the expansion and intensification of research work by the researchers themselves, by an increase in the rate of exploitation', as Marx described it. At the same time researchers are required to spend an increasing amount of effort on chasing funds and satisfying commercial clients. Researchers generate an increasing proportion of research funds by their own efforts. In the outcome, as I observed earlier, university research is being transformed from a set of practices that were self-controlled and other-financed, to practices that are self-financed and increasingly other-controlled. Disturbingly, and with few exceptions, there is little reflection on these trends except in the most universal terms where analysis has a limited role and the claims are underpinned only by further anti-managerialist polemic. Yet what is at stake are quite fundamental questions: the differing effects of different kinds of financing and accountability in research; how the results of research are understood; whether academics control their own programs of research.

Academic work is not defined as a set of targets, a job description, a range of tasks or any other listable set. It is defined by its underpinning quality: its intellectualism and its scholarship. What effect does performance management have in such a system? (Hort 1996: 5).

Within the orthodox framework, debate becomes debate about one or another indicator, and disciplinary interests are expressed in efforts to re-work the weightings to improve the position of the particular discipline. It might be better to look at the more general effects of the technologies of research performance management. A reflexivity centred on the finer details means that a reflexivity centred on research management is being evaded.

RECOVERING RESEARCH

Universities will continue to be managed. To this point, the dominant models of corporate management have been drawn largely from outside the university sector. The foregoing argument suggests that the recovery of research depends on two elements. First, the fostering of a more independent research culture in the different disciplines, one that draws its identity separately from university management. Second, work in the strategic middle ground between research and management, so as to effect the management of research (and perhaps to affect the formation of a more university-specific model of university management). The two elements are interdependent. The formation of a stronger independent culture enables the 'personality' of research to be sustained on that strategic middle ground. Work in the middle ground ensures that management does not monopolise questions of general institutional organisation, and enables independent research to become more strategically competent than before.

In that strategic middle ground, researchers in all disciplines have a common interest in moving away from a system in which their claims become the standard ploys of a zero-sum game. Here the key move is to develop indicators of activity, and formulae for the distribution of funds, that are discipline-specific rather than universal. Enlightened managements can agree, because more sensitive indicators are also more inclusive and enable a more subtle and effective management. A second move is to measure research activity by measures of research outputs rather than measures of grant income. This again enables a more discipline-specific approach, and a focus on the intellectual and social value of research, rather than a focus on financial values derived from the artificial economic model. This would remove the perverse incentive in the current system, in which the actual research is irrelevant, and the main objective is money itself. A third move is to respond to the bias in favour of track record by allocating more of research support to new researchers and innovatory projects.

On their own, such strategies have their limits. Even when pursuing discipline specificity and grants for young researchers, there is a gravitational pull back to convention and homogenisation. To fund innovations in a system which prestructures innovation in narrow terms is not to fund the range of research potential. The deeper conservatism of a performance-based system, in which the potential outputs are pre-ordained, is not overcome. The more basic problem to address is the loss of researcher control over the research agenda: the question of identity, the self-as-researcher. Here the crucial issue is not autonomy (which as the foregoing suggests, is readily turned to one or another power structure) but independence. The strategic need is to broaden the spaces for independent work, in which the system of funding or project definition does *not* pre-set the outcomes of research.

This suggests the need for research funding systems that provide time-relief for principal researchers, and not just grants for infrastructure, travel, materials and research assistants. It also suggests more funding for the two kinds of research program which enable self-determined work free of the project format or client control: postgraduate research, and research fellowships of the ARC post-doctoral and senior fellow type, where the full salaries of researchers are paid. The cause of independent research is better served by an expansion of fellowships than of ARC large grants.

Another mechanism could be the structuring of academic careers so as to enable a mid-career break of two to four years of concentrated full-time, or largely full-time, research work. In the present context, in which rising teaching loads impact heavily on the capacity for ongoing research, the creation of a midterm research period seems a more practical strategy than trying to lift average weekly research hours. The relevance of the teaching–research nexus as a norm of academic life must now be questioned. The creation of a mid-term research 'window' would replicate the research potential provided by the doctorate, while providing that opportunity at a time of greater personal and intellectual maturity.

References

Department of Employment, Education, Training and Youth Affairs (DEETYA) 1996, *Higher Education Funding Report for the 1997–99 Triennium*, DEETYA, Canberra.

Gaita, Raimond 1997, 'Truth and the Idea of a University', *Australian Universities Review*, 40 (2), pp. 13–18.

Gallagher, Michael 1997, (First Assistant Secretary, Higher Education Division, DEETYA) *Current Approaches and Challenges in Higher Education*, paper to a conference on 'Funding our future', Southern Cross University, 28 August.

Griffith University 1995, *Research Management Plan*, Griffith University, Brisbane.

Hort, Linda 1996, 'Managing Academics' Work: Future Performance in Higher Education', *Australian Universities Review*, 39(2).

McInnis, Craig and Marginson, Simon 1993, *Australian Law Schools After the 1987 Pearce Report*, Commonwealth Department of Employment, Education and Training, AGPS, Canberra.

Marginson, Simon 1997a, *Markets in Education*, Allen & Unwin, Sydney.

——1997b, 'Competition and Contestability in Australian Higher Education', *Australian Universities Review*, 40(1), pp. 5–14.

Monash University 1992, *Report of the Research Review Committee*, Academic Board papers, April, Monash University, Melbourne.

Powles, Margaret 1994, *Postgraduates as Partners in University–Industry Liaisons*, AGPS, Canberra.

Ricketson, Sam 1991, *New Wine in Old Bottles: Technological Change and Intellectual Property Rights*, Centre for International Research on Communications and Information Technologies (CIRCIT) Working Paper 1991.5, CIRCIT, Melbourne.

Slaughter, Sheila and Leslie, Larry 1997, *Academic Capitalism*, The Johns Hopkins University Press, Baltimore.

University of New South Wales (UNSW) 1995a, *UNSW Corporate Plan 1994–99*, UNSW, Sydney.

——1995b, *Quality Portfolio 1995*, UNSW, Sydney.

Williams, Ross (Department of Economics, University of Melbourne) 1997, *Funding Higher Education in Australia*, paper prepared for the Commonwealth Review of Higher Education Financing and Policy (West Committee), August.

· 12 ·

Australian universities:
a contestable future

JANE MARCEAU

What are universities for? The trite phrase, so often used to answer this question, is 'the generation and transmission of knowledge' or some variant thereof. People giving that answer usually take it no further. And yet all the terms—generation, knowledge, transmission and many others—are contestable and should be contested if universities are to flourish in the twenty-first century.

Modern Western societies have developed their economies and social institutions in what might be called a series of currents or strands. Some of these are intimately connected, each changing as the others change. Some have less direct interrelationships but are nonetheless linked so that changes in one strand sooner or later generate changes in others. These changes might occur for different reasons—they may be politically or policy driven, market driven, driven by national or international forces or by some combination of these.

Thus, for example, in the nineteenth century universities grew in Western countries during an explicitly nation-building era. Universities grew as other elements of their societies grew—cities, wealth, scientific discoveries. But they grew differently in different countries. In France, for example, for several decades in the nineteenth century they became little more than places for polite public discussion. In their place the *Grandes Ecoles*, elite technical teaching institutions, were created to take the state's aims forward. The importance of that distinction still colours the higher education landscape in France today.

In the 1960s, very roughly speaking, a mixture of notions of 'career open to talent' (meritocracy) and the view that education was a driver of economic growth led to the expansion of university-level education in most OECD countries. In more recent years, similar motivations encouraged further expansion of university student numbers, from a few tens of thousands to the approximately 600,000 students in the present Australian higher education system.

To think sensibly about the future of universities a comparative perspective is necessary, to get rid of preconceptions. Macintyre and Marginson (in chapter 3 of this book) show the tensions apparent in the history of Australian universities about the means and ends of the institutions. Looking further afield we see the particular and unusually contingent nature of Australian universities, modelled on the Scottish system mixed with some elements of that of the US as they are. European universities are built on quite different models. Since in Europe students who complete secondary education are guaranteed a place by law and are supported by a series of social measures as long as they are students, universities are flooded with young people who mostly drop in and out and in again over many years. A senior professor at the University of Rome once told me that 100,000 students were enrolled, but 'thank God only a small proportion ever turn up'. In the 1970s, I taught at the University of Paris X, the Nanterre of 1960s' revolutionary fame: no chalk for teachers to use in the lecture rooms, let alone offices in which to work; one *Salle des Professeurs* for staff was engaged to teach 5,000 students in Economics alone; no staff expected to do research.

These illustrations are simply to emphasise that knowledge generation and transmission can take many forms. We need to recognise that there is no one best way. Everything can and should be rethought as the social context and role of universities change. The essential thing is to rethink broadly enough.

This chapter is more about knowledge generation than transmission but the nature of the organisation that transmits is also touched upon.

The chapter is in two parts. The first sketches out important elements of the context in which universities will operate in Australia in the future. The section points to the central role of knowledge in the economies to come and the role in the economy that universities now play in this country because of the low-technology industrial structure inherited from the past which discourages business investment in research and development (R&D). It places the discussion in the framework of international work on innovation economics. The point of that is simply to indicate that just as there are paradigm shifts in the technologies used for productive purposes so there are organisational paradigm shifts which require complete institutional rethinking. It is my contention here that higher education in this country faces such an organisational paradigm shift. The section provides the framework in which to do the rethinking necessary for the new organisational forms devised to meet needs. To make the shift and move forward successfully universities need to refocus the lenses which they use to view themselves, to find a sophisticated answer to the question 'What are universities for?' Part two of the chapter suggests a way in which the lenses could usefully be refocussed.

UNIVERSITIES IN THE KNOWLEDGE ECONOMY

Over the last decade or so there has been increasing international attention paid to the drivers of economic growth, both now and in the future. Since 1990 especially, the OECD has been in the forefront of work bringing together and refining approaches to the question developed in specialist institutes in member countries. An increasing concern with the question as to where are jobs to come from focussed OECD countries' attention on technological change and its links to employment generation. It soon became clear that stable high-paying jobs were disproportionately generated in industries using advanced technologies.

The reasons for the perceived link between job creation and high technology industries, it also became clear, were the underlying links between technological advance and innovation. Innovation is now recognised as *the* driver of growth in the twenty-first century.

Work by the OECD suggests that countries (and companies and regions within them) now have a critical choice to make. This choice concerns the basis on which they will compete in the future. The choice they have to make is between reliance on competition via investment in high technology and innovation and reliance on competition on the basis of exchange and wage rates. Innovation and high levels of technology are more important as competitive weapons in knowledge-intensive industries but are increasingly important to the success of all industries. Competition via wages and exchange rates is more important in industries producing standardised, lower technology goods and services.

The new work suggests that taking the route implied by acceptance of competition via innovation and technological advance maximises higher-skilled, higher-paid employment and improved living standards.

In contrast, there is great danger in selecting the second path: the route of forcing down the price of labour and hoping for a cheap Australian dollar. The danger arises in part because a country the size of Australia cannot hope to control the exchange rate (our dollar is the fifth or sixth most traded currency in the world). This leaves reliance on wage rates. The problem here is that reliance on wage rates involves an endless race to the bottom and fuels a retreat from welfare and other social measures (including investment in higher education and skill training) judged 'too expensive'. If we take that route there is increasing international evidence of consequences which would be ultimately highly dangerous for Australia's social fabric and long-term economic welfare.

One critical element in the argument is the discovery that markets alone will not help a country shift from the 'low road' to the 'high road'. This means that there must be some active policy intervention to encourage business investment in the knowledge-intensive sectors and to upgrade the technologies innovation strategies used by firms. This policy push onto a different track is especially important because it seems that once a path has been selected the advantages and disadvantages of the choice are cumulative, making a later shift between roads much harder.

Australia thus has a critically important choice to make and must make it soon. We know that technological change can also cause fundamental shifts in the rules of the competitive game. Technologies, it seems, develop along a specific trajectory, gradually creating a situation where one becomes dominant for a while. In the background, however, new technologies are also developing. When the first reaches a phase of 'maturity' where no further gains in productivity or other competitive gains can be made, a second takes over. This rise of an often radically different technology creates a technological paradigm shift.

Technologies usually need specific new organisational arrangements to work to best advantage. One well-known example of this can be seen in the rise of the Japanese or Toyotist model of automotive production that in the 1980s greatly threatened the dominance of older American and European models. Organisational arrangements can thus also face paradigm shifts and the move to a new model and trajectory. Combined, the physical and organisational technologies create the new bases for competition and action.

The importance of such organisational and physical technology changes, which have been occurring gradually over a long period now, means that whole economies are shifting competitive tack. This is seen in the creation of the knowledge- or innovation-intensive economies now emerging in most OECD countries.

Over the long run, it is now clear that a country's competitive advantage will be in those areas where its rates of learning are higher than those of other countries. These areas concern firms, industries, regional and national structures and institutions.

The building of learning capability and the generation of the knowledge underpinning innovation are thus critical to our national development as we too begin the shift to a learning economy.

What, then, is a learning economy? In summary, it is flexible and adaptable, reliant on high levels of knowledge, trust and networking, concerned to invest in high levels of education, skills and training in all fields (nation, industry, firm) so as to generate, spread and absorb new knowledge and transform it quickly into new products and processes. It is an economy where firms seek linkages to access complementary resources. Most important of all, it is an economy where organisations collaborate at least as much as they compete.

The new theories thus place knowledge generation and its diffusion at the heart of the development of the new economy. In Australia this puts the universities and the CSIRO centre-stage. The generally low level of both technological and organisational innovation in the firms comprising our industrial structure constitutes a major threat to our future development. Although business R&D increased in Australia from the mid-1980s to the mid-1990s, it is now dropping; innovation is also shown by the latest ABS Innovation Survey to have dropped from the early 1990s, as is training investment. More than half our research and development will continue to be performed in the public sector for the foreseeable future.

What happens to the funding and organisation of research conducted by CSIRO and the universities is thus critical. In some countries, such as Japan and the UK, certain firms undertake more basic research than do medium-sized universities. This is certainly not the case in Australia. While Australia's science base is still remarkably strong for a country our size (the famous two per cent of world research performed by a country with less than one per cent of the world's population) this will not survive under present conditions. In Japan, even though its firms spend a lot on R&D, the government is spending more on basic research. In Canada, too, the minister has just announced an extra $1.5 billion Canadian dollars over three years to boost the research budget. This is not happening here on the scale needed.

In Australia, in terms of infrastructure alone there is a problem. The UK has decided, in conjunction with the Wellcome Foundation, to spend almost one and a half billion pounds over the next three years on research infrastructure to bring their labs up to world best practice and remain ahead. The equivalent in Australia would be the same figure in dollars ($1.4 billion). In sharp contrast, even the most optimistic forecast of what our universities may possibly get over the same period is $90 million. Perhaps even more important in Australia than the paucity of funding, although that should certainly not be underestimated, is the fact that not enough thought has been given to maximising the potential of a small country operating in a world knowledge-generation system.

The current paradigm of the organisation of the knowledge-generation and transmission system is failing Australia precisely at the time when the country has a critical choice to make. Current proposals as to how to 'solve' the crisis seem grossly inadequate to meet the need. This is in part, as the next section of this chapter suggests, because innovations proposed have not been based on proper analysis of the key terms of the debate. As a consequence, the shifts in the organisation of research funding (to block grants, etc) coming forward from the West Committee of review and from other key players, including the Department of Education, Training and Youth Affairs, entirely miss the point. The radical shifts proposed by such bodies would push Australia in exactly the opposite direction from the one that international work (by the OECD and others) tells us is necessary. More not less knowledge is needed. More flexible, not more rigid, knowledge-generation and transmission mechanisms are required and must be properly funded and managed. One possible way forward is proposed at the end of this chapter.

RETHINKING THE ORGANISATION OF RESEARCH

Australian universities and researchers need to start thinking about their situation by being both proud and modest. They need to look again at the whole system of knowledge generation in modern Australian society. The first thing they will see, of course, is that most new knowledge is generated *outside* universities. This has always been the case and is indisputably even more the case now. When we talk of universities 'generating knowledge' (research) we usually have in mind knowledge based on recognised discipline categories. It is there that we see the 'two per cent'. The knowledge produced by university staff (which, importantly, is *not* the same thing as 'universities') in Australia is relatively specialised, overall is disparate and, except in patches, not very cumulative, even inside our own knowledge-generation arena. Refocussing analytical lenses will also show Australian universities holding an even more modest place in the generation of new knowledge in the international arena.

A serious attempt to work out where we sit in the broader schema of knowledge generation and what is happening there is thus the first step to rethinking sensibly the policies that regulate that part of university staff activity.

The second thing that needs to be done is for universities to figure out how and where what they recognise as 'research' is actually carried out and where it is located. Answering this question is not a simple matter, as recent investigations have shown (see, for example, Marceau 1998 and other papers collected in the August 1998 issue of *Industry and Higher Education*). The how and the where questions come together in a new look at where research is currently located. This is a highly relevant question in the context of current Australian debates about the 'Big 8' and their alleged superiority as research institutions, which is taken to justify more automatic access to specific research funding. Once we start asking where research is presently located, using location in a broad sense, this debate loses all sense.

There are two closely related issues which need to be considered here. The first is that the institutional location of staff conducting research is assumed to be the same as that of staff teaching, that is to say that teaching and research are done by the same staff whose affiliation is an organisation called the University of Wherever. This institutional 'ownership' of staff in both their teaching and research capacities by something called a university is a contingent, not a necessary, result of a series of past and present administrative decisions about what constitutes organisational boundaries. These decisions are really about convenience of funding and systems of recruitment of both staff and students, not about the organisation of research. Such institutional 'ownership' therefore needs to be examined and its appropriateness questioned in relation to research.

There is no necessary knowledge-generation reason for such decisions about boundaries. Indeed, there could be many counter-indications to these boundaries were a *research* perspective to be paramount. At present, much research is funded by the use of the notional 30 per cent of staff time left after teaching and administrative obligations have been met. This assumption about *when* research is done means that it is organisationally more convenient to have a single payment control unit. But such boundaries often bear little relationship as to *how* university research is actually carried out and *where* it is located, let alone to how more general knowledge-generation functions are organised in modern Western societies. Let us see how research actually proceeds in practice and whether such organisational and physical proximity to other staff in the 'same' field ('same' also being a highly contestable term in this context) matters.

The second issue concerns the question 'what constitutes a research community?' In many of our major research universities the different parts of the campus barely interact. Relevant communities for many are found not among colleagues in the same institution or even among colleagues in other Australian universities. Rather they are found in Princeton, Stanford, the Max Planck Institute or one of the Cambridges. In many staff common rooms the talk is of children, dogs and bushwalking, seldom of new growth theories, the median voter or postmodern interpretations of gender. Yet, once staff return to their offices across their emails come national and international exchanges of the latest papers and information on the progress and results of cutting-edge projects. Perfect strangers participate in animated debates on matters of research technique or project findings on web sites focussing on anything from particle physics to innovation management or the writing of biography. In these conditions where *is* research located? We can see immediately that we need to separate what we see as the location of research itself from the institutional ownership of the staff who conduct research. Recognising this is a major step forward in meeting the challenge of the paradigm shift needed in the organisation of research in a country the size of Australia.

Further, the difficulty found in answering the apparently simple question about the real location of research is considerable even in relation to the established disciplines with long traditions. How much harder is it, then, in relation to multidisciplinary or emerging areas. In these cases, not only do relevant collaborations cross traditional intellectual boundaries but they may take a completely different organisational form. Not only must universities come to grips with mechatronics, astrobiology, urban or cultural studies and innovation theory but they must often do so with an in-house (that is, inside a given university) staff 'owned' by organisational units with different intellectual justifications and resource control powers. The walls created by this lack of fit are serious impediments to the emergence of sensible arrangements for the conduct of research in emerging areas.

Much publicly-funded research in OECD countries is now multidisciplinary. Indeed, the new European Framework supports *exclusively* research proposals which are interdisciplinary, in areas ranging from the environment to the social.

The increasing importance of such interdisciplinarity is central to the significant trend identified by Gibbons and his colleagues and reported in a book entitled *The New Production of Knowledge* (1994). These observers describe a shift to 'Mode Two' knowledge generation. Mode Two involves the development of multidisciplinary research carried out in the context of application by teams specifically put together for the purpose and funded by the client or commissioner of the project.

Discussion of Mode Two brings us back to my earlier question about the place of the university in the context of the total knowledge-generation process. In Mode Two research endeavours many of the researchers are not university staff at all but are members of government departments, community groups, private companies or public sector laboratories. As Gibbons and his colleagues say, universities have produced far more research-trained people than they can employ so university staff by no means have a monopoly on even formally imparted research skills. The growth of research consultancies and R&D-only enterprises, both wholly within the private sphere and as joint university–private sector endeavours, indicates the trend. The teams thus created work with groups located well beyond the university world. Many partners in common projects operate according to different rules, use different payment systems and produce their work in ways quite different from that common in the single-discipline hierarchies of universities. This is, of course, not to say that single-discipline research does not have a central place in a nation's research endeavour. It *is* to say that sensible and productive research policies must recognise the new diversity and give it appropriate weight.

So what are the relevant boundaries involved in the present organisation of university research? Perhaps they are not wholly matters of institutional or indeed geographic proximity. The academic enterprise is riven and always has been by divisions of many kinds—discipline, status, 'purity', degree of linkage to professional career specialisations and so on. On most of these dimensions most universities find that they have centres and peripheries determined on a complex mix of elements. If geographical proximity were essential to university endeavours, Adelaide would link with Flinders and the University of South Australia, not Western Australia, and Universitas 21 would be an organisational joke.

So let's refocus our lenses again and try a different mental image: one which sees all universities as part of the same knowledge-production system and recognises that all knowledge-generation groups and individuals reach out to other groups and individuals. This, of course, is not unique to universities; we know that even in companies which present themselves as legal entities with 'walls' around them, research scientists maintain close links with colleagues in other entities—including not only governments, universities and hospitals but also other firms, often their competitors. They could not do their jobs any other way.

If this extra-boundary networking happens with companies, how much more an essential part of the academic world are such networks? The academic endeavour by tradition, indeed almost by definition, is one where formal organisational boundaries have meant least. In the mediaeval Europe of warring fiefdoms, the clerks of the time spoke Latin and travelled freely. The free exchange of ideas and the notion of 'peers', wherever those peers may be, as the true community of scholars have continued to be central to the concept of academic life. In this fundamental sense the whole of academic life is organised as one vast multi-campus operation. It never has been and cannot be otherwise.

These links, of course, are well recognised by researchers. Halfway between market and hierarchy, these networks are an essential living element of the formal boundaried organisations in which individual network members 'live' and to which they are supposed to be loyal. The present problem is that they have no salience at all in the organisation of research; instead they remain largely 'invisible' and individual-centred, receiving little formal organisational recognition and support.

In contrast, if it is clear that researchers always link to other researchers it is also equally clear that faculties seldom link to faculties. Yet most university organisation hinges on its faculties. Thus another one of our central problems is that our two principal current forms of organisation no longer go well with each other. Scholars link with other scholars, and find distance only a relatively small problem even when measured in thousands of kilometres. And yet faculties fight faculties, departments within faculties fight other departments, campuses fight campuses (in this sense competition in the academic world is certainly not new). In the past the academic endeavour has often had only loose forms of organisation structure and broad 'colleges'. Faculties were roughly grouped clusters of disciplines and departments. These forms of organisation were only there for limited purposes—student enrolment and progression, curriculum approval, staff recruitment. While departments ran meetings where staff were often extremely vociferous, these generated a good deal more noise than light but it didn't matter because staff largely ran their individual lives within a broad consensus about time spent on teaching, research and administration.

In the past, then, faculties had very few tasks, basically those of support for individual activities; now they have been given new jobs and hence new meanings and their heads have new formal powers. In the new competition for resources (described by Marginson in chapter 11 of this volume and part of the daily experience of all academics), the organisation forms traditional to the universities have had to begin to deal with tasks such as strategic planning, downsizing, responding fast to market signals (student demand), choosing between areas to which to allocate exceedingly scarce resources. This means that we are trying to run highly complex and expensive multipurpose institutions using essentially mediaeval categories and organisational arrangements designed for a different purpose and in a different age. In particular, universities are by and large trying to run both teaching and research using the same organisational structures. No wonder there is a crisis.

The critical reasons for the shift to new control roles for faculties are shortage of resources and an environment in which universities have lost a sense of their distinctiveness and purpose, especially their national purpose. As institutions they have been required to behave quite differently. But differently in relation to what task? The answer to my initial question 'what are universities for?' has not received the attention it deserves. Until adequate and informed attention is directed to that question the crisis can only worsen and very damaging policy decisions, both at national and institutional levels, will inevitably continue to be made.

One reason for the intensity of such resource competition is that universities are still behaving as though all the resources to which they have access or could have access are those that they directly *own* and hence control. The emphasis on competition to *own* resources is as damaging to universities as it is to knowledge-based firms. The present government's focus on competition alone, whether for firms or universities, means that universities are being asked to behave not just like 'firms' but like *old-fashioned firms*, just exactly the kind most likely to go out of business. In the new knowledge economy *access* to resources rather than 'ownership' of them is what counts. It is *networks* not *entities* that matter.

Existing rigid structures are as ill-adapted to research as they are to the other tasks of university life. We know, as I suggested earlier, that the critical activity of research does not follow current organisational boundaries. Quite the reverse; these boundaries inhibit research connections, which tend to be made *despite* rather than *because* of the organisational arrangements which dominate academic life. We know, from Tim Turpin's work, for example, that research groups do not coincide with departmental, let alone faculty, boundaries; they are normally smaller and often cross such divides (Turpin 1996). Nor, increasingly, do disciplines coincide with even broad academic administrative boundaries. In the *Australian Higher Education Supplement* not long ago there was an article on the emergence of new disciplines, seventeen or so as I recall, within the last few years. Where do these fit into our ancient categories?

Very important parts of the academic endeavour, when seen from the point of view of the staff, totally fail to coincide with the administrative boundaries within which their daily lives are structured and to which they are required to devote increasing amounts of time and attention. Competition for ownership of research inputs and outputs is now not only between institutions but also between faculties because their income depends on it. The 'walls' around faculties are often getting higher. In contrast, the effective conduct of research, especially at the cutting edge, demands both freedom and capacity (power) to make extra-organisational links. Particular links may change as research develops and they may be latent for periods, but they have a recognisable pattern.

What, then, is the solution to the lack of fit between critical parts of the organisation of our academic endeavour? Marginson correctly points out that universities have been reduced to abandoning their nation-building role and to competing for clients via customer service in ways which are quite unacceptable.

His recipe for solving this is for universities to work more effectively with government and business in a more equal and consensual manner designed to put universities back into their older role (1998).

I believe that we may need to go further and examine what each of these terms—government, industry, universities—actually means. The future indeed does depend on the creation of strong academic networks and a more fruitful functioning of the relationships encapsulated in Leydesdorf and Etzkovitz's notion of the 'Triple Helix' of government, industry and universities. However, as they correctly point out, universities are now increasingly hybrid creatures. The implications of their analysis now need to be drawn out.

The problem with the analysis is that it is whole universities rather than their constituent elements which are seen as the academic strand of the Triple Helix. Similarly, little recognition is given to the fact that government and business have many shapes and different roles even in relation to research, being stimulators, regulators, funders and clients. Each strand of the Helix needs to be analysed in terms of its constituent parts if we are to improve relevant relationships. In practice, no whole institutions can develop the necessary interrelationships using present organisational forms. The organisational form of the future in business will be dynamic and ever-changing networks. Universities need to figure out how to go down the same road. The challenge for all concerned, especially for university managers and government but also for teachers and researchers, is how to create, nurture, develop and reshape the flexible networks that should take the place of faculties, departments, campuses and even whole institutions. On the government side, policies rely too heavily on crude concepts of market and competition; on the academic side, university staff too often rely on the romantic notions of a lost collegiality as the way to run academic affairs. Creating a new set of policies and practice to replace those derived from the blinkered views of both sides is perhaps the major challenge facing academics for the coming decades.

CONCLUSIONS

In order to tackle the task of creatively rethinking the organisation of both knowledge generation and transmission we need to take seriously the arguments presented in the first part of this chapter. These suggest that the driving factor in economic growth in the twenty-first century will be innovation. Innovation includes both technological and organisational innovation and existing organisations may need to make paradigm shifts as well as gentler changes. Many high-tech firms have been experimenting in recent years with hybrid, sometimes 'cellular', forms of organisation which represent an attempt to come to terms with the value systems and peer interlinkages which drive scientific research in the universities and mix these in new ways to meet the needs of the production system.

It is time for universities to rethink their internal organisation and their external relationships. If universities can be thought of as loose and flexible collections of staff united in the aim of teaching students and furthering knowledge creation *for different parts of their time* we may move one step ahead. We need to return again to the fact that most research does not take place *inside* particular institutions, except when the focus is on provision of resources (laboratories etc.) and the administrative location of staff. Why then do we assume that the 70 per cent of staff time for teaching and the 30 per cent for research need to be used in the *same* organisational environment? Why do staff look to carve out careers within a *particular* formal organisation? Why can they not teach in one place and research in another, more specialist, arena where the small, flexible groups with which they actually work are more relevant? Why could they not spend part of their time working in a university department and part in another section of the knowledge-generation world, remembering that universities are only one among many such arenas?

Especially important, why do particular institutions think that they 'own' all the professional time of their staff? In part this is because current contracts are usually with one organisation full time; staff particularly seek such contracts because they are seen as more secure. It is normal for that organisation to expect staff to fulfil what they are contracted to do on a full-time basis. The problem arises because such an attitude equally obliges universities to provide appropriate facilities for all staff who wish to undertake research even though the institutions find that provision next to impossible in straitened academic circumstances. It also obliges universities to accept being judged on the research performance of 'their' staff alone when the relevant unit of analysis of research success may be a quite different one. Why does anyone continue to think in this nonsensical way at all?

The answer, of course, is that that is the way the government thinks. And, in the ways of governments, they do so because it is convenient—in the short term. In the long term, however, this blinkered vision can only lead to staff disillusionment and to a division of the system into the more or less successful institutions as judged on a series of criteria which only the long-established can meet because they thought up the criteria and designed the parameters. Present proposals to reduce the competition for funding for projects and to increase the amount of money for research going into block grants and hence to *institutions* go in precisely the wrong direction. This approach will increase both boundary impermeability and fixation on the ownership of all 'their' staff activities by administrators keen to show success in the new game. The game, however, is the problem. The rules of the game as it is now being set up are based on particularly crude conceptions of the 'market' and no knowledge or recognition at all about how research is actually carried out.

One possible way out, therefore, involves deliberately separating the research function from the teaching functions in which staff engage. This does not mean the separation of teaching and research in the intellectual sense. It could mean devising new organisational forms whereby staff are recruited and paid in different ways for the different ways in which they spend their time. They could thus choose different organisational environments for the different segments of their activities. They may choose to teach in smaller universities where care for students is paramount, where innovative mechanisms for teaching are being developed or where the special missions or focus of the institutions concerned allow them to develop specific expertise and particular interests in the courses they teach. They may decide to teach only 40 per cent of their time, or 90 per cent. They may change the percentage from year to year or agreed period to period. They may even be tenured in several institutions for different amounts of their time. Or be tenured in the university system as a whole rather than in any one institution. Equally, they may also opt to conduct their research in organisations which have chosen to fund research in their fields as a special area of interest.

The organisations where staff do their research need not be 'universities' as such at all. They could be units which, as it were, 'rent' space within universities. Physical inclusion inside university spaces where that is appropriate should in no sense imply organisational 'ownership' but simply a decision about the location of management which has been outsourced, just as the running and management of the new court in Victoria has been outsourced to a private firm without in any way at all implying that the managing firm owns the court. The particular research activities should be open to staff and graduate students of all other universities on a competitive basis. Expensive scientific research could thus be concentrated in a geographical sense but the arrangement would remove the link between such facilities and the basically irrelevant organisational boundaries that presently fuel so much competition for resources and prevent the most effective use of what is provided.

Funding for these flexible research organisations could be on a competitive basis over a given period. Proposals would have to show that the research teams were indeed open to the best staff regardless of the organisations in which they chose to teach. Each research team's 'centre' would be a node in a network and would have to operate as a network structure. The nodes could be run on a collegial basis by the staff concerned on the strict working understanding that the staff 'owned' the organisation, not the other way round. Equally, if the network did not reach the standards agreed with the funding body or bodies, all would have to accept that the formal part of its activity would be closed after the regular reviews and the money reallocated elsewhere in the system. Specific incentives in the funding allocation system would ensure that smaller players had the chance to bid for new networks or new nodes in existing ones so as to bid for the 30 per cent of staff salaries which went with the proposed research.

Some staff may also make the choice to work part (the research 30 per cent or whatever) of their time in governments, community organisations or businesses. At present such choices are administratively difficult; the Triple Helix will work better if they are made easier. At present, universities are encouraging the commercialisation of research by getting into business themselves (spin-off firms, etc); it may be better, less risky and less expensive when capital is scarce, for universities to let their staff transfer the technology themselves by transferring in person to existing firms in partnership with universities and for part of their time. Many observers now recognise that research and teaching, and indeed other activities, can be conducted serially over time as well as within the same academic year. It is now time to recognise that they can usefully be conducted in a variety of institutions and organisational forms.

Some of these changes are not nearly so radical as they may seem at first glance. In practice university organisations are already moving towards such divisions of function and the creation of special arrangements for different disciplines. In the professional faculties of Medicine and Law, staff often have dual appointments, partly, for instance, within the medical school for teaching and part with hospitals for research and professional practice. The Cooperative Research Centres (CRCs) are another variant on the same theme; there university staff teach within one framework and conduct at least part of their research in another. Consulting to outside organisations by staff is another and very longstanding variant. The American system of nine-month contracts is another.

In exchange for the (carefully planned and phased in) changes to be made to the organisation of research and teaching, the bodies charged with funding research across the spectrum from the humanities to astrobiology would have to be professionally run. Supporting research on a national scale should not be the domain of the present amateurism, however well-intentioned. The bodies would have to be both reactive and proactive, specifically encouraging new activities and foci for investigation, specifically preferring collaborative projects and those linked internationally. They would need to be outward-looking, well informed on international trends and practices and able to link Australian directions to those of the rest of the world. Above all, they would need to call all present forms of the organisation of research into question.

This is just one proposal and a considerable break with present practice. It is understandable that readers will immediately find much to disagree with and plead all sorts of impossibilities and impracticalities. Some of these will certainly bear further scrutiny. The proposal does, however, have one clear advantage. It overcomes a problem bedevilling the present system. This is the problem of uneven status and power as between the institutions of the allegedly National Unified System of higher education. Many problems have been diagnosed in relation to the present system. No one is prepared, however, to face the critical problem of differences of status and power within the system which are constantly presented as issues of capacity and capability as though these were not the product of particular past strategies and positioning before the new rules of the game were even thought of. Such attitudes are now more than ever both irrelevant and dangerous to Australia's future. As Marginson again has said, no universities in Australia can realistically claim to be in the top 50 in the world (1998). We have to stop even trying to compete with present organisational arrangements. We need to rethink both goals and strategies. We need to recognise that the organisations of the innovation-intensive economy will be different. We cannot expect businesses to improve their collaboration and innovation record if we as university staff are not willing to do so ourselves.

What needs to change now is the 'lens' that universities and 'their' staff use to view the functioning of the knowledge-generation system and their place within it. We need to radically reorient our conceptions and expectations about possibilities, re-view and rethink our operations and organisations. We should not be led by outdated ideas about organisational forms or crude conceptions of competitive markets. Research conducted by university staff both inside and outside their universities is critical to Australia's future. It needs to be treated in a way which reflects that importance and emerging needs. We must stop looking to the past as the basis for moving forwards. We need more knowledge generation, not less. We need to liberate and fulfil the potential of all researchers, not find funding and other excuses for limiting opportunities to a few.

We are a small nation with particular needs and challenges, including that of geographical distance both internally and externally. We do not need to add pretension to these problems; we do need to recognise that there are many ways of skinning the cat. Australians are renowned for their inventiveness when in a tight corner. Now is the time for academic staff to shake off the shackles of the thinking which is currently dominating the debate about the future of universities. We need to exercise our creative talents and devise organisational forms which are more academically satisfactory and which go beyond current paradigms, forms which are able to meet the challenges of the knowledge economy so that Australia may maintain its standard of living into the next century, let alone improve it.

References

Gibbons, M., Limoges, C., Nowotny, H., Schwartzman, S., Scott, P. and Trow, M. 1994, *The New Production of Knowledge*, Sage, London.

Leydesdorf, L. and Etzkovitz, H. 1998, 'The Triple Helix as a Model for Innovation Studies', *Science and Public Policy*, Special Issue, June.

Marceau, J. 1998, 'Triple Helix Relationships in a National Context: The Location of Research in the Australian Biomedical Industry', *Industry and Higher Education*, August, pp. 251–8.

Marginson, S. 1998, 'Harvards of the Antipodes? Nation-building in a Global Environment', Winter Lecture Series, University of Auckland, 21 July.

Turpin, T. et al. 1996, *Knowledge-based Cooperation: University–Industry Linkages in Australia*, AGPS, Canberra.

• AFTERWORD •

The body in question

MORAG FRASER

The English novelist P. D. James set one of her more trenchant mysteries in a grand English publishing house called Peverell Press. James has a keen eye for the rich mise-en-scène.

Her press had a past—call it tradition—and a vexed present, which involved reputation, prestige, intrigues over selection and rejection of manuscripts, financial expediencies and a straining of loyalties within and without the institution. And of course it all led to a clutch of corpses—sufficient to persuade even George Orwell that English murder is no longer in decline.

In our present case the body in question is not a publisher with a guilty secret, nor even an aggrieved author. It is a book—a book and the institution about which the book concerns itself: the university. It is a book that was rejected by the publishing house, Melbourne University Press (MUP), which carries the name and prestige of one of the institutions under the book's microscope. It is a book written by academics who are themselves in many ways connected with the University of Melbourne. Some of them are its graduates, some have had (or still enjoy) long and distinguished careers within the institution itself, and have been published by its Press. Their essays, taken together, constitute a critical and broad-ranging conversation about the current and future state of one of Australia's most crucial public institutions. Yet by the judgement of the board of Melbourne University Press, that conversation did not make the grade as a work fit, or appropriate, to appear under its imprint.

The intriguing publishing history of *Why Universities Matter* is in itself a pocket instantiation of some of the fundamental and unresolved conflicts that lie behind the high gloss public relations face of Australian universities in the late 1990s. And because university matters are also matters of general public interest, for the many reasons cogently discussed in the preceding pages, this book's rejection by MUP became an issue of broad public interest. This was not just a storm in an ivy-patterned teacup.

The story begins in May 1998, with a publishing proposal that would make anyone versed in the trade sit up and listen. It was for a book with the provisional title *Why Universities Matter*. MUP's commissioning editor, Teresa Pitt, opened her initial recommendation-in-principle to the MUP Publications Committee with a quotation from her proposed author/editor, Tony Coady, a former journalist, whose straight speaking has not been blunted by his subsequent career as an academic philosopher.

> It is an understatement to say that university education in Australia is in turmoil. The pressures put upon universities by 'the Dawkins revolution' have had far-reaching effects, a few of them good, some ambiguous, and many bad. The progressive withdrawal of the federal government from the funding of universities has created a financial crisis with disturbing consequences for teaching loads, quality of teaching and research, academic tenure and job security and much else.
>
> But accompanying these changes has been something much less discussed, namely, the impact the 'revolution' has had upon the university's understanding of itself. The question of what a university should stand for, what central values it ought to embody, is seldom addressed directly and in depth, although it is really the most fundamental question in the present crisis. It is gestured at in 'mission statements', 'strategic

plans', and in other attempts to mimic the corporate world, but few can find the time or the inclination to address the challenge.

Pitt's proposal detailed the original provenance of the material in question: a workshop conducted, as part of its academic research brief, by the University of Melbourne's Centre for Philosophy and Public Issues. It also made a point of noting that the book had 'grown' out of that workshop, and for publication purposes was to be expanded, appropriately edited, and augmented with other essays specially commissioned for the purpose. She listed the proposed contributors and made a brief comment on the proposal's intrinsic merit—its detailed examination of fundamental ethical and value problems 'made more urgent by the present plight of Australian universities'—and its likely success in the general marketplace for books of ideas.

Something must have alarmed certain members of the publications committee because they asked that the proposal be resubmitted. Professor Coady's forthright phrasing did not find universal favour with his fellow academics on the committee.

It is instructive at this point to take a brief look at the rhetoric of the web site of the University of Melbourne. Let me quote from its opening page:

The University of Melbourne
Operational Plan 1999

The Melbourne Agenda

The Strategic Plan of the University of Melbourne reflects a vision of Melbourne as one of the great universities of the world. Realising the vision will create in Melbourne a University committed to the highest values of international scholarship, competitively resourced in international terms, able to transcend the limits of national funding and regulatory constraints, and with the confidence to re-think its role and destiny in ambitious global terms.

The 'Melbourne Agenda' describes a complex set of strategies and priorities through which the University is seeking, over a 15–25 year period, to give substance and meaning to its ambitious vision.

Pursuing the 'Melbourne Agenda' in 1999 will involve the same fundamental strategic challenges that shaped the operational management of the University in 1998.
1. Internationalisation
2. Enhancing research performance
3. Transforming teaching and learning
4. Diversifying the funding base
Securing a strategic vision in the end comes down to efficient, effective, tenacious operational management. Until we realise the vision of Melbourne as one of the great universities in the world, these long-term strategic imperatives will continue, year-in-year-out, to provide the essential focus of operational management.

The Operational Plan is in itself remarkable enough. Would Harvard, one might ask, present itself like this? And in an academic context, does 'securing a strategic vision' really come down, in the end, to 'efficient, effective, tenacious operational management'?

Teresa Pitt's more self-conscious or wry version of 'tenacious operational management' saw to it that the publishing proposal for *Why Universities Matter* was resubmitted to the MUP Publications Committee in July 1998, minus Tony Coady's rousing paragraphs, but with an added outline of the contents of each contributor's chapter, plus an analysis of the proposed book's distinctiveness and market viability compared with its most recent publishing competition, namely Coaldrake and Stedman's *On the Brink: Australia's Universities Confronting Their Future* (University of Queensland Press, 1998).

It is at this point the story starts to become complicated. The complications involve the disposition and actions of the *dramatis personae*, onstage and offstage.

The book's commissioning editor, Teresa Pitt, was not able to attend the MUP Publications Committee of the Board of Management meeting on 13 July. Sir Andrew Grimwade also tendered his apologies. Present were MUP's director, John Meckan, Ms Susan Holmes, Professors Barry Sheehan, J. R. V. Prescott and Kwong Lee Dow and Mr Andrew Watson.

A set of minutes emerged from this meeting. The copy in my possession, headed 'MUP PUBLICATIONS COMMITTEE, MINUTES, Meeting no. 3, 1998', records an endorsement in principle to publish eleven books, with various provisos relating to confirmation of subsidies and further investigation of market potential and so on. The Coady book was endorsed in the following terms:

> Coady (ed): *Why Universities Matter* (resubmission).
> Members noted that the content was drawn from papers submitted to a conference and were not necessarily the result of new research and expressed the view that it might not be well balanced in the range of opinions. The Director reported that sales of a similar book by UQP had not met expectations. *After discussion, the Committee endorsed in principle the proposal to publish this work* [my emphasis], subject to a lower print run and confirmation of a bigger subsidy. The Director undertook to discuss this with the editor.

A handwritten marginal note reads 'author informed by phone 15/7'. Professor Coady confirms that he was so informed, though not by the director.

The next scheduled meeting was set for 14 September.

In early August I received a phone call. A wellknown literary figure wanted to know whether I had heard about the rejection of Tony Coady's anthology of essays about the university. It was a one-sided conversation because I had not heard and he was wrought into the kind of grandiloquent rage that is the gift of powerful word-spinners under fire. It was rage fuelled more by offended loyalty than anything else: he was a University of Melbourne graduate, as I was, and had been published by MUP. What did they think they were doing, he wanted to know. These were writers with track records. What on earth was going on?

Very soon it was a question being asked all around Melbourne. It even stirred some interstate interrogations. What *had* happened between the Publications Committee Meeting of 13 July when the minutes recorded an in-principle endorsement to publish *Why Universities Matter*, and the beginning of August, when news of the book's rejection began to fuel a wildfire of speculation and a series of press articles and questions?

On Monday 27 July, the Board of Management of MUP had met again. On the instructions of that meeting a letter of rejection to Professor Coady was drafted by the director, John Meckan (the task was further delegated by Mr Meckan to the commissioning editor, Teresa Pitt), and submitted to the chairman, Professor Barry Sheehan, for vetting before being sent. The letter, dated 30 July, and following Professor Sheehan's redrafting of several paragraphs, reads as follows:

Dear Professor Coady

Coady (ed) *Why Universities Matter*

The Board of Management of MUP has asked me to inform you that, at its meeting of Monday 27 July 1998, the Board decided not to approve this project for publication.
The Board had a number of reasons for its decision.

Discussion at the Board indicated a common view among Board members that the book, as proposed, promoted a 'traditional' (and important and laudable) view of universities, without clear or sufficient representations from the proponents of countervailing views.

Neither does the book appear to the Board to add much that is new to an already substantial literature on this topic, or to provide a systematic view of how universities should operate in their social, cultural and economic context in the future. The proposed book is essentially a collection of conference papers with little of the content based on new or recent research.

Whether we like it or not, MUP must pay attention to its market. The Board noted the content of Coaldrake and Stedman's recent publication *On the Brink: Australia's Universities Confronting Their Future* (UQP, 1998) and assessed 'intelligence' on its sales performance. The Board took the view that—regardless of quality of content—there is no room in the very limited market for such works for another book on the same subject at the same time.

After lengthy consideration, the Board decided against acceptance for publication.

The remaining paragraphs express regret, good wishes and anticipation of a continuation of 'our excellent working relationship' in future. (Coady, as editor of the 'Ethics in Public Life' series, had already published one volume and another was in press.) It is signed by John Meckan, with copies noted to Barry Sheehan, Chairman, and Teresa Pitt, Commissioning Editor.

Some anomalies begin to draw attention to themselves at this stage. By 30 July, the date of the rejection letter, no member of the MUP board had read the manuscript of the book, or the manuscripts of individual contributors. Yet the letter indicates that the 'common view' of the board was that the book, as proposed, 'promoted' a traditional view of universities. It is deduction based on scant evidence. Some of the information available to the board through the publishing proposal in fact indicates the contrary: the views were too various to be subsumed under 'traditional'.

One of the chapter synopses provided by Teresa Pitt in the resubmission contained the following outline of Peter Karmel's contribution:

> Professor Karmel examines the economic problems facing
> Australian Universities in the context of their history and their
> central animating values. He provides a comparative assessment
> of funding options available and assesses them against criteria
> of equity, efficiency, and personal and institutional autonomy.

I suppose 'central animating values' might be read as code for a traditional view, but the rest of Professor Karmel's focus is clearly on issues that are not too far from some of the desiderata of the 'Melbourne Agenda' of the university's web site: efficiency, institutional autonomy.

Another synopsis, this time from physicist, Professor Tony Klein, argues, in brief, that: 'present indications are that pure scientific enquiry within Australian Universities is under threat'. This is hardly a 'traditional' view. But it is a view endorsed daily in the metropolitan press by distinguished Australian researchers, some of them still working in this country, others—most recently

Dr Bryan Gaensler, 1999 Young Australian of the Year, currently on a NASA Hubble Fellowship to the Massachusetts Institute of Technology—lamenting a future in which prevailing conditions and the squeeze on funding will mean that they cannot continue their research careers in this country. They will no longer be able to maintain the enviable reputation for outstanding work that has marked Australia out as a disproportionately successful science environment for so long.

Given the information provided by the resubmitted publishing proposal it is difficult to understand how the board could have arrived at its rationale for rejection. The reasons given do not fit the proposal outlined. And then there is the very odd claim that the proposed book does not give 'clear or sufficient representation from the proponents of countervailing views'. It has not been MUP's practice to insist on 'clear or sufficient representation' of countervailing views in the books it has published throughout its distinguished history. This is not to say that it does not insist on integrity of argument and scholarly rigour. But the books which have helped make the name of the Press have often been argued, and vigorously, from a particular point of view. Was Manning Clark constrained into 'balance'? Gareth Evans is a former MUP author. It is stretching credibility to expect that his account of Australia's foreign affairs policy would give 'countervailing' weight to the views of his then Opposition; or that John Cain's account of his premiership, also published by MUP (1995), should include a section representing the views of his opponents. Should John Quiggin and John Langmore (MUP 1994) have given the Institute of Public Affairs equal time when they made their case against prevailing economic regimes? Coherence and honesty one can legitimately expect in the publications of a distinguished house, but 'countervailing balance' sounds suspiciously like a cousin to the artificial formula of 'equal time' upon which the ABC is bound. What profit to the public in such exercises? And what does one make of an academic publishing house which has such a limited expectation of its readers' capacity to project 'a countervailing view'? One begins to smell a rat.

It took two weeks for the media to pick up the story of

the book's rejection. The critic and one-time *Scripsi* editor, Peter Craven, 'broke' the story, in an *Age* column headlined 'How Melbourne Uni muzzled mild dissent'. The sub-editor, responsible for the headline, also rammed home the publicity point in the breakout quote: 'This is precisely the kind of book we need from our great university presses and there is little doubt it would sell'.

The praise ('great university press') and the promotion-in-advance ('little doubt it would sell') failed to endear Craven or the cause of Coady's book to the University of Melbourne or to the management board of its Press. The Chancellor (and member of MUP's board), Sir Edward Woodward, responded immediately with a letter to the editor. Craven's sources had misled him on some factual details (for example, his claim that the Vice-Chancellor had been present at the Board meeting). But among other criticisms, Sir Edward's letter included this curious sentence: 'The committee's reservations centred on the likelihood that the book would not sell well because there are already a substantial number of publications on the subject and the collection of papers did not attempt to present a balance of current ideas in higher education management'.

'Higher education management' was only incidentally the proposed book's focus and was unlikely ever to have been an integral part of its rhetoric. About the book's central concern Professor Coady (and Teresa Pitt after him) could not have been clearer: 'This is a book about the values of universities'. It was never intended as a forum for discussion of competing management techniques. It entailed a much more fundamental inquiry.

The University of Melbourne's Operational Plan itself indicates that those in charge of the institution are not unaware of the push for fundamental re-examination of university values. The web site document, as early as the page one from which I quoted above, acknowledges that the university is currently in an 'unstable political, policy and regulatory environment', in which 'interest group lobbying' and 'short-term perturbations' may do long-term damage to quality and morale in the university. 'Unless', as it says, such perturbations are 'well-managed'.

At the time, if one listened, as a citizen, to the gathering protests upon campuses around Australia, it became all too clear that academics and students and their concerned parents were not focussed simply upon 'a balance of current ideas in higher education management'. Their 'perturbations' went much deeper.

Some of those perturbations came to a head about the same time as the MUP decision, when Professor David Robinson, the Vice-Chancellor of Melbourne's second-oldest campus, attempted to 'manage' disquiet and dissent at Monash University by locking staff and students out of a campus lecture theatre in which there was a scheduled protest meeting about funding cuts. I was one of the invited speakers at that protest meeting (which did go ahead, but only at the last minute). It felt like a very seemly and serious affair to one who has a memory of on-campus anti-Vietnam War protests and all their Maoist offshoots. The administration certainly took it seriously enough to try to prevent its taking place, and to threaten staff involved. Because I came from outside academe, no sanctions could be employed against me. Not so for another speaker, former Dean of the Monash Faculty of Arts, Professor John Legge. He was threatened with the loss of his room on campus. It was not a 'well managed' incident. But the perturbation was real.

Meanwhile, at the University of Melbourne, the decision about the book was causing a stir in both academic and publishing quarters. Sir Edward Woodward's letter to the *Australian* generated an angry response from one member of the editorial staff at MUP. The acting Dean of Arts at Melbourne, Professor Patricia Grimshaw, wrote to Barry Sheehan asking for clarification of the board's process in relation to the book's rejection.

Sheehan's response is interesting. What it suggests is that a mistake had been made between cup and lip. The minutes of 13 July had somehow got the intention of the meeting wrong, at least in so far as it related to the endorsement of the Coady book. Professor Sheehan provided another version of the minutes of 13 July. The crucial section reads as follows:

> Members noted that the content of this book was drawn
> from papers submitted to a conference and not necessarily the

result of new research. They expressed the view the book might not be well balanced in the range of opinions as to the way universities might successfully operate in the future. The Director reported that sales of a similar book recently published by UQP had not met expectations. *After discussion, the Committee was reluctant to endorse this publication* [my emphasis], even with a lower print run and/or a bigger subsidy. The Director undertook to discuss this with the Editor of the work.

There was, he indicated, an earlier draft of these minutes which had been 'leaked' (this is the draft of which I possess a copy) but that draft 'had no status'. From Professor Sheehan's account it also appears that, if the drafter of the earlier set of minutes had got the details of the decision wrong, then so had the director of MUP. 'Regrettably, as sometimes happens,' Professor Sheehan continued, 'the request from the Committee to the Director might have been clearer'.

But now the position was clear, and the board's decision was definite. There was some disquiet about the way in which the decision might be interpreted. Professor Prescott acknowledged 'the Committee's concern about a perception of the possibility of "censorship" '. In view of the sensitivity of the issue the board agreed that 'the Chairman should "vet" a draft of the letter'.

At this point a budding publisher might ask what was the function of the professional committees—editorial and finance— and the director of MUP, and what standing had they in the decision-making process, regarding this or any other book? Past practice at MUP has set much greater store by the professional judgement and recommendations of Press staff. This case represented a departure from usual procedures. The Publications Committee had recommended the book. The full board's role had previously been to refine, not overturn, the recommendation of its own professional committee. What effect, one can only wonder, will this particular board directive have on MUP's reputation as an independent academic publisher of standing?

In his reply to Professor Grimshaw, Professor Sheehan argues that 'the processes of MUP were as they have been for quite some time'. If that is the case, one can only speculate about whether the board of management of MUP will undertake the additional task of reading the manuscripts about which it makes decisions, or scrutinising more carefully the detailed publishing proposals which currently provide the grounds upon which its publishing decisions are made. One of the more curious, and frankly disturbing, aspects of the list of reasons given by the board for rejecting *Why Universities Matter* was not just its lack of fit with the details of the book as proposed but its revision of the facts of MUP's established publishing practice.

Most members of the University of Melbourne learned of the book's rejection through media reports, as Stuart Macintyre and Simon Marginson note in their chapter on the university and its public (chapter 3). Peter Craven was followed by Guy Healy, education reporter for the *Australian*'s Higher Education Supplement. One of Healy's reports quoted the University of Melbourne Vice-Chancellor, Alan Gilbert, as reassuring his staff that academic freedom would not be compromised by the university's push into privatisation. Professor Barry Sheehan denied that there was any conflict of interest between his dual roles as chief executive of the new Melbourne University Private venture and chair of Melbourne University Press. The matter of the book's rejection went before the Academic Board of the University of Melbourne where the decision was staunchly defended by the Vice-Chancellor. Other presses, riding the wave of valuable and unforeseen publicity, expressed keen interest in publishing the book.

Academic perturbation continued into 1999. In May, the Victoria University of Technology temporarily suspended the access of one of its academics to the university's email: Professor Allen Patience had used the system to circulate to his colleagues criticism of the University's decision to allocate $100,000 for rental of a corporate box at Victoria's Docklands Stadium. In June, a University of New South Wales law lecturer, Cathy Sherry, went public in the *Age* with a story about the kind of reaction academics could expect if they penned public criticisms of government policy. Sherry had a letter about native title published in the *Sydney Morning Herald*. Federal Liberal MP

Wilson Tuckey responded by contacting her vice-chancellor. Also in June, a coalition of Melbourne academics formed the Association for the Public University, and used the media to publish their strong protest against the accelerating corporatisation of Australian universities.

Against this background of academic disquiet, what do we conclude about this particular case? By now you have the advantage over the MUP board in that you have read the book and can make an informed judgement about the exact nature and interplay of its contributions to the debate about the university and values—'the question of values and the conflict between types of values', as Professor Tony Klein puts it in his chapter.

Tony Klein is a physicist. One of the more gratifying aspects of his and other contributions to the conversation that this book sustains is its collegial and its civic reach. Klein discusses the problems facing fundamental inquiry—often referred to as 'pure' research—in Australian universities (not just one particular university) in a context that includes the relevance, broadly and narrowly conceived, of scientific research in Australian society generally, indeed in any society. In other words, his conception of it is neither self-validating nor nostalgic. He has his eye very much on realistic limits to growth in fundamental scientific research, but also on the solutions being adopted to solve the same problem in other places, notably Japan, the USA and Europe. He looks forward to their intelligent adaptation to Australia's circumstances (without being too optimistic).

Contrast Klein's broad sweep with the competitive, single-institution focus enshrined in the 'Melbourne Agenda' web site documents. As part of its 1999 targets, the University of Melbourne specifies a ten per cent increase in postgraduate scholarships, in the event that such awards should be allocated to individuals not institutions. Accountability for this and other percentage increases is devolved to Deputy Vice-Chancellor Frank Larkins.

What happens then if, in a particular research case, with a funded postgraduate attached to it, the University of Melbourne turns out not to be the best place for postgraduate study? Does the Deputy Vice-Chancellor's 'accountability' constrain his capacity to make a disinterested decision to that effect? What price his academic freedom or his academic integrity? What place within such a competitive schema is there for the essentially disinterested speculations and suggestions of a Tony Klein? What room would there be for his suggested 'cross-subsidisation' of fundamental disciplines, or his notion that individual departments, not whole institutions might be the more appropriate (and equitable) focus for the highest level research?

And what could possibly have happened to the University of Melbourne if its Press had published a set of essays that followed in the venerable, though never comfortable, academic tradition of free-speaking, no-holds-barred, critical self-scrutiny? The venture would hardly have undermined the financial viability of its Press, which has chanced its arm on riskier projects. It would have reassured not just the university but its alumni, friends, critics, enemies and the public at large that the oldest university in the State of Victoria is an institution which esteems independent intellectual enquiry more than it values corporate loyalty.

This is a difficult time for universities. Government disenchantment with higher education ('training' they find less problematic) and distrust of academics had become a feature of Australian political life even before Susan Ryan, as Education Minister in the Hawke Labor Government, had to fight her often losing battles with the cost-cutting Minister for Finance Senator Peter Walsh in the mid-eighties. The situation since then has deteriorated considerably, and no full-colour, multimedia institutional promotions can paper over the cracks that every student and every teacher and researcher in Australian universities must negotiate daily.

There is residual goodwill—and a deal of anxiety—in the public's understanding of the plight of universities. Polls regularly demonstrate that Australians support increased investment, public and private, in tertiary education. The public has also grown reliant—for good reason—on academics as a source of disinterested public commentary on issues as diverse as the safety of water supplies and the equity of food's inclusion in a GST.

The University of Melbourne, through Melbourne University Press, had an opportunity to bolster that public understanding of the current condition of our universities. It also had a chance to engender and sustain the kind of trust that the public will vest in institutions that are open to criticism, institutions that listen to voices from within and below as well as to voices from the top. It chose not to take the opportunity.

The book, of course, has been published. The controversy has made it a phenomenon of a different order, and the public is left to savour the quince tang of irony about the circumstances. There are better tastes to leave in the mouth.

Index